UNITED STATES GOVERNMENT
How and Why It Works

UNITED STATES GOVERNMENT
How and Why It Works

By

Jane W. Smith

and

Carol Sullivan

AUTHORS

Jane Wilcox Smith, M.A.
Reading Specialist
Forsyth County High School
Cumming, Georgia

Carol Sullivan, B.S.
Special Education Teacher
Forsyth County High School
Cumming, Georgia

CONSULTANTS

John L. Napp, M.S.
Social Studies Teacher
Talmudical Academy
Pikesville, Maryland

Wayne King, M.S.
Academic Department Head
Baltimore School for the Arts
Baltimore, Maryland

Howard Berkowitz, M.A.
Senior Social Studies Teacher
Glenelg Country High School
Glenelg, Maryland

Editors: Barbara Pokrinchak, Ed.D.
Beryl D. Little, B.A.
Art: Gregory Broadnax

Photo credits: pp. 28, 36, 109, 140, 147, 149, 198, 201, 219, 253 — The Library of Congress

Copyright ©1987 by Media Materials, Inc., 1821 Portal Street, Baltimore, Maryland 21224. All rights reserved. No part of the material protected by this copyright notice may be reproduced or utilized in any form or by any means, electronic or mechanical, including photocopying, recording, or by any information storage or retrieval system, without written permission from the copyright owner.

ISBN: 0-86601-615-5   Printed in the U.S.A.

06 90 VG/ATB 7.5

Contents

Preface ix

1 **Development of American Government** 1
    1.1 All Groups of People Need Rules 1
    1.2 What Is Government? How Did It Develop? ... 2
    1.3 Influence of Ancient Governments
         on Modern Government 4
    1.4 Forms of Government 8
    1.5 The Influence of English History
         on American Government 9
    1.6 Political Ideas Also Came from the
         Thirteen Original Colonies 15
    1.7 American Colonies Join Together
         to End English Rule 19
    Summary of Chapter 1 22
    Chapter Review Activity 24

2 **Creation of American Government** 25
    2.1 Joining the Colonies Together
         as a Country 26
    2.2 The Constitutional Convention
         in Philadelphia 27
    2.3 Compromises Made at the
         Constitutional Convention 31
    2.4 Guiding Principles of the Constitution 33
    2.5 The Struggle for Approval 37
    2.6 The New Nation Begins under the
         Constitution 38
    Summary of Chapter 2 39
    Chapter Review Activity 41

3 A Look at the Constitution **42**
    3.1 The Preamble and the First Three Articles ... 45
    3.2 Article IV (Four): How the States
          Should Treat Each Other 47
    3.3 Article V (Five): Making Amendments
          to the Constitution 48
    3.4 Articles VI (Six) and VII (Seven) 49
    3.5 In 1791, the Bill of Rights Was Added 50
    3.6 Amendments Eleven through Fifteen 60
    3.7 Amendments Sixteen through Twenty-Six 63
    Summary of Chapter 3 65
    Chapter Review Activity 67

4 The Legislative Branch **68**
    4.1 The Three Branches of Government 68
    4.2 The Legislative Branch 69
    4.3 How Congress Is Organized 71
    4.4 Who Can Be a Member of Congress? 74
    4.5 How Congress Carries On Its Work 75
    4.6 How a Bill Becomes Law 80
    4.7 Powers of Congress 84
    Summary of Chapter 4 88
    Chapter Review Activity 90

5 The Executive Branch **91**
    5.1 What Is the Executive Branch? 91
    5.2 The President Is the Leader
          of the Executive Branch 92
    5.3 The Process We Use to Elect a President 95
    5.4 The Duties of the President 98
    5.5 The Office of the President May
          Become Vacant 101
    5.6 People Who Advise the President 103
    Summary of Chapter 5 107
    Chapter Review Activity 108

6 Departments of the Executive Branch **109**
    6.1 The First Departments 109
    6.2 How the Departments Changed
          and Increased 110

6.3　Duties of the Departments................. 112
　　　Summary of Chapter 6.......................... 122
　　　Chapter Review Activity........................ 123

7　**The Independent Agencies** **124**
　　　7.1　The First Independent Agency.............. 124
　　　7.2　How the Independent Agencies Work....... 125
　　　7.3　Some Regulatory Agencies................. 126
　　　7.4　Some Service Agencies 130
　　　7.5　The Federal Bureaucracy: Where
　　　　　Agencies Fit 136
　　　Summary of Chapter 7.......................... 138
　　　Chapter Review Activity........................ 139

8　**The Judicial Branch** **140**
　　　8.1　Laws Are Intended to Protect the
　　　　　Rights of All Citizens....................... 141
　　　8.2　Federal Courts Hear Certain Cases 142
　　　8.3　District Courts 143
　　　8.4　United States Courts of Appeals............ 145
　　　8.5　The Supreme Court 147
　　　Summary of Chapter 8.......................... 155
　　　Chapter Review Activity........................ 157

9　**State Government** **158**
　　　9.1　The Country Grows from Thirteen
　　　　　to Fifty States 159
　　　9.2　Each State Has Its Own Constitution 162
　　　9.3　State Governments Need Money........... 168
　　　9.4　States Spend Money 170
　　　9.5　Organization of State Government 172
　　　Summary of Chapter 9.......................... 182
　　　Chapter Review Activity........................ 184

10　**Local Government** **185**
　　　10.1　County Governments 186
　　　10.2　City Governments........................ 189
　　　10.3　Other Types of Local Government......... 191
　　　Summary of Chapter 10......................... 194
　　　Chapter Review Activity........................ 194

11 Politics and Voting ... 195
- 11.1 Political Parties ... 195
- 11.2 How Political Parties Developed ... 196
- 11.3 Two Major Political Parties ... 199
- 11.4 Minor Parties ... 203
- 11.5 The Parties in Action ... 205
- 11.6 State Primary Elections ... 208
- 11.7 National Political Conventions ... 210
- 11.8 Political Campaigns ... 213
- 11.9 The Right to Vote ... 216
- 11.10 How People Can Have a Part in Making Laws ... 223
- Summary of Chapter 11 ... 225
- Chapter Review Activity ... 227

12 A Look at Other Governments ... 228
- 12.1 Governments Differ ... 228
- 12.2 The United States Government Is a Democracy ... 229
- 12.3 Democratic Forms of Government ... 230
- 12.4 Comparing the Governments of Great Britain and the United States ... 233
- 12.5 Some Governments Are Not Democracies ... 239
- 12.6 Communist Government of the Soviet Union ... 239
- Summary of Chapter 12 ... 248
- Chapter Review Activity ... 250

13 Citizenship ... 251
- 13.1 United States Citizens ... 251
- 13.2 Many People Have Settled in the United States ... 252
- 13.3 Types of Citizenship ... 256
- 13.4 Rights of Citizenship ... 260
- 13.5 Duties of Citizens ... 266
- Summary of Chapter 13 ... 269
- Chapter Review Activity ... 270

Appendix: The Declaration of Independence ... 271
The Constitution of the United States ... 275

Index ... 297

Preface

United States Government: How and Why It Works is a textbook for students who need a simplified presentation of our system of government. This book grew from the authors' quest over the years for instructional material that could be comprehended and managed comfortably by their students.

Chapters 1 through 3 include a concise look at the influences on the government of the thirteen colonies, the significance of the Declaration of Independence, and the writing of the United States Constitution.

Chapters 4 through 8 discuss the three branches of the federal government, along with the executive departments and the independent agencies. State and local governments are analyzed in chapters 9 and 10.

Chapter 11 presents political parties and the election process. Chapter 12 examines the governments in two other countries, Great Britain and the Soviet Union. This chapter is designed to give students a broader world view of government and an appreciation for the American system. The final chapter helps students to understand the responsibilities and privileges of citizenship. They are encouraged to take an active part in their community's political life, especially by voting.

This book has a number of special features:

★ The content is clearly organized. Major sections of each chapter are numbered. There are generous numbers of subheadings. Each chapter ends with a summary and a review activity.

★ Large type and controlled vocabulary help make the book easy to read. Many chapter sections begin with a list of *Words to Know*, so that students can become familiar with certain terms before they meet those words in the text.

★ Photographs, drawings, and charts enhance understanding.

★ Practice activities throughout each chapter encourage students to get involved with learning about our country's government.

★ The *Teacher's Guide and Answer Key* that accompanies this book contains learning objectives, teaching procedures, and complete answers. It also includes reproducible chapter check-ups and supplementary activities.

★ The accompanying student workbook provides additional practice activities that review and reinforce the topics presented in the textbook.

Chapter 1

Development of American Government

1.1 ALL GROUPS OF PEOPLE NEED RULES

Many people live in large cities that are crowded and busy. Others make their homes far out in the country, where they can go for days without seeing another person. In between these two extremes are the people who live in towns and small communities. All of these people living in large or small groups share a common need—the need for rules and laws to help them live peaceful and safe lives.

Every nation has some type of government, which is a plan of action for running that country. Families have rules for their children; schools have rules for their students; and governments have rules for their citizens.

1.2 WHAT IS GOVERNMENT? HOW DID IT DEVELOP?

Words to Know:

Combination — A grouping of people, things, or ideas that are joined together for a special reason.

Custom — A common practice observed by many people.

Community — The people living in an area; a group of people living together with a common interest.

Complicated — Made up of difficult parts; hard to understand.

Consider — To think over carefully.

Ancient — Of times long past; belonging to early history.

Political — Having to do with government or the actions of the government.

A government is a combination of laws and customs that people live by. Governments developed as the needs of people grew. Early tribes of people lived simply, and simple rules were all they needed. They shared food, punished people who did wrong, and joined together for protection. As these tribes grew into larger communities, life became more complicated. Governments grew in size and power in order to meet the needs of the new communities. As land and property became more important to people, rules were needed to protect these possessions.

Workers Cutting Grain, about 5000 B.C.

How Did American Government Develop?

The government of America was formed because the early settlers, or colonists, did not like the way they were treated by England. The young American colonies belonged to England and were ruled by English law. Many things happened under these laws that upset the colonists. They were taxed unfairly and could not choose their own leaders. Soon the colonists decided to form their own government. They broke away from England.

The American colonists were careful to make rules and laws that were fair. The rights of people were also considered and written into the law. The colonists borrowed ideas from the past. All political ideas used by the colonists had their roots in older forms of government. Ancient civilizations such as Greece and Rome had an influence. The greatest influence, however, came from the governments in England and Europe at that time.

★*Activity 1.* Complete each sentence below. Use the words in the box. Copy the sentences on your paper.

```
combination    political    complicated
considered                  community
```

1. Many _____ ideas used by the colonists had their roots in ancient governments.
2. A government is a _____ of laws and customs.
3. People in a _____ need rules and laws to live peaceful lives.
4. Governments grew in size and power when life became more _____.
5. The colonists _____ the rights of the people when they made rules and laws.

4 — What Is Government?

★ **Activity 2.** Number your paper from 1 to 5. Match each term in Column A with its description in Column B. Write the correct letter next to each number.

Column A	Column B
1. England and Europe	a. Combination of laws and customs people live by.
2. ancient	b. Belonging to very early times.
3. government	
4. colonists	c. Early settlers in America.
5. custom	d. Greatest influence on colonial government.
	e. A common practice popular with many people.

1.3 INFLUENCE OF ANCIENT GOVERNMENTS ON MODERN GOVERNMENT

Words to Know:

Dictator — A person ruling with full control, power, and authority.

Revolt — To go against a government or a cause.

Democratic — A form of government in which citizens take part; a way of life that treats people of all classes equally.

Appoint — To name or choose a person for an office, but not by election.

Ancient Greece

The word *democracy*, which comes from the Greek language, means "rule by the people." The idea of a democratic government began in Greece in 600 B.C., about twenty-five hundred years ago. Greece was made up of city-states. These were cities with large amounts of land around them. In the beginning these city-states were ruled by kings, and then they were ruled by landowners. Some were even ruled by dictators. Dictators can rule any way that they please, no matter what the people want. Some dictators became unpopular with the people. The people revolted against them. The people wanted to govern themselves, so they formed democracies.

This "rule by the people," or democratic rule, did not mean that all people could take part in running the city-states. The people were divided into groups. There were free men, women, young males, and slaves. Only free men were members of the ruling body, called an Assembly. All the free males ran the government and took turns holding office. The Greek city-state, Athens, had the best-run government.

A Greek leader speaks to the people.

The city-states of Greece were always at war with one another, and they became weak. Rome, another great power to the west, soon took over the weakened Greek city-states.

Ancient Rome Had a Representative Form of Government

Because Rome had such a large population, all of the free males could not take part in running the government. The citizens elected people to speak and act for them. The people they chose were their representatives. This representative type of government was called a *republic*. Rome was a republic.

Rome, like Greece, did not give slaves, women, or young males a part in running the government. The free men who ran the government were divided into two groups. The wealthy, or rich, males had greater power and were called *patricians*. The common people, or workers, were called the *plebeians*. From the patricians, two *consuls*, or leaders, were chosen. These

The Roman Senate

consuls in turn appointed *senators*, also from the wealthy class. Senators were appointed for life, and the Senate was the most powerful part of the government. The Senate made rules and laws, which could be *vetoed (veto* means "I forbid") by the common people, or plebeians. Rome's government changed several times during its history, but remained a republic for quite a while. When the Roman Empire came to an end, it was being ruled by dictators and emperors, who were like kings.

You can see that our country borrowed many ideas from these ancient civilizations. We have a representative form of government, with elected representatives, who make laws and rules. We even use such words as *Senate, veto, republic, representative,* and *democracy.*

★ *Activity 3.* Number your paper from 1 to 10. Decide if each statement below tells about the Roman government or the Greek government. Write *Greece* or *Rome* after each number.

1. Its representative form of government was known as a republic.
2. The common people were called plebeians.
3. The country was made up of city-states.
4. The ruling body was called an Assembly.
5. All free males took turns holding office.
6. Senators were appointed for life.
7. Consuls, or leaders, were chosen from the wealthy class.
8. The wealthy, or rich, citizens were called patricians.
9. The city-states of this country were always at war.
10. Democracy, or "rule by the people," began with this government.

1.4 FORMS OF GOVERNMENT

Word to Know:

Generation — All people born at about the same time; one step in the line of the family; about thirty years.

Some early forms of government did not have "rule by the people." They were far from being democracies. The power was in the hands of a very few. Three common forms of government were the monarchy, the dictatorship, and the oligarchy.

The Monarchy

In a monarchy the country is ruled by one family, generation after generation. The leadership is passed down to the eldest son or daughter. The rulers have titles like King, Queen, Empress, or Emperor. England was a monarchy when the settlers came to America.

The Dictatorship

A dictator rules alone. The needs and wants of the people may or may not be considered. A dictatorship is different from a monarchy, because a dictator does not have to pass the rule down to the next generation.

The Oligarchy

In an oligarchy, the rule is in the hands of a few. These rulers may be from a military group or from a group given special training by their government. In Greece and Rome there were oligarchies from the class of landowners. They usually took care of their own interests first, and then those of the common people. In modern times, several countries in South America have had rule by a military oligarchy.

1.5 THE INFLUENCE OF ENGLISH HISTORY ON AMERICAN GOVERNMENT

Words to Know:

Decision — Act of making up one's mind; judgment.

Lawsuit — A question or case that is decided in a court of law.

Jury — Group of citizens chosen in a court of law to listen to both sides in a case and to make a decision about it.

Consent — To agree; approval.

Legislature — Lawmaking group of a country or state.

Petition — A formal written request to an official person or group.

Similar — Alike without being the same.

The Rule of Henry II

During the late 1000's and early 1100's, the government of England changed forms many times. The constant changing of power had kept the country in a state of confusion. The rights of the common person had not been considered. In 1154, Henry II became king. He was a strong monarch who made changes in the government that did consider the rights of the common person.

Henry II appointed judges and gave them authority. These judges traveled throughout the country to hold court. They decided how to punish people who disobeyed the law. Soon all these decisions about offenses and their punishments became rules and were followed as law. These laws were divided into two types. The first type, criminal law, included rules that everyone must obey. The second type, private law, had to do with rights and duties between individuals. For instance, if a person had borrowed money and did not pay it back, he could be faced with a lawsuit.

Words such as *plaintiff* (the person offended) and *defendant* (the person who is accused of committing the offense) are words we use today that came from the English private system of law.

Our jury system was also influenced by this law under Henry II. As the judges traveled from place to place, they were told of all the crimes committed in an area. Henry II had appointed special people to inform the judges. Today we have a grand jury system with duties similar to this. They tell our officials if there has been a crime committed and if it should come to trial. If a person, in our system, is accused of a crime, he comes before the grand jury first.

Our trial-by-jury system is also similar to the system Henry II used. Twelve local citizens were asked by the traveling judges to swear under oath whether or not they thought the plaintiff's statements were true. The decision of these twelve citizens helped the judge decide on the punishment for the crime. Today we use a jury system. The jury decides if a person is guilty or not guilty. The judge then decides on the punishment, in most cases.

The Magna Carta (The Great Charter)

The king of England in 1199 was King John. This king was unfair and made many enemies. For one thing, he taxed the people very heavily. The people did not want to pay all the taxes. They believed that the king was spending the money on himself.

The nobles (rich people of the country) decided that something must be done to check the king. They planned very carefully. Together with town leaders and church officials, they presented King John with a petition known as the Magna Carta. In June 1215, King John finally agreed to the demands, and put his seal on the paper.

King John puts his seal on the Magna Carta.

This charter gave certain rights to the English people and limited the king's power. It stated that the king must ask advice of the nobles in important matters. It also said that no special taxes could be raised without the nobles' consent. No free man could be put in prison except after being judged by his peers (equals). Judges and other officials were to be appointed to serve the kingdom.

The important ideas written in the Magna Carta were then used by many people for hundreds of years. For example, one complaint the American colonists had against England was that they were being taxed without their consent and that they had "taxation without representation." The practice of trial by jury developed from the Magna Carta. This charter helped rulers recognize the wants, needs, and rights of the common people.

12 — Influence of England

★Activity 4. Number your paper from 1 to 11. Match each term in Column A with its description in Column B. Write the correct letter next to each number.

Column A

1. Private law
2. Oligarchy
3. Henry II
4. Criminal law
5. Grand jury
6. Magna Carta
7. Plaintiff
8. Defendant
9. Dictatorship
10. Jury
11. Monarchy

Column B

a. A group of people who listen to evidence and decide if a person is guilty or not.

b. Person who is accused of committing an offense.

c. A type of government with one ruler who does not pass the rule to the next generation.

d. Monarch in England who appointed judges.

e. Law that has to do with rights and duties.

f. A form of government that is ruled by a few people.

g. Laws concerning rules that all must obey.

h. Person offended in a lawsuit.

i. The government is ruled by the head of the royal family.

j. Group of people who decide if a case should be tried.

k. A charter that recognized the rights of the people.

The Parliament

Parliament is the name of the law-making body in England. In very early times, only the king and his lords could make laws. Then in the 1200's, common people were allowed to elect representatives to take part in the meetings. The common people were merchants or property owners. By 1400, Parliament had two parts: the House of Lords, which included nobles and church leaders, and the House of Commons, which included knights and common people.

Parliament was used by some rulers and ignored by others. Finally, the Parliament was allowed to make laws on its own. The system that Parliament used to make laws worked very well. The colonists followed the same system. It is the idea behind our Congress and state legislatures.

The Petition of Right and the English Bill of Rights

The "Petition of Right" was drawn up by the English Parliament in 1628 to put a limit on the power a king could have. The kings, or monarchs, always claimed they were given their power by God. This idea was known as the "divine right of kings." By 1628, the members of Parliament felt that the power of the kings had become too strong. In the Petition of Right they listed the things that a king could not do. It said, among other things, that a king could not force rich people to make loans or put people in prison without a jury trial.

Parliament did not always remain strong. Some kings ignored Parliament. During the reign of William and Mary, in 1689, Parliament again gained power and passed the English Bill of Rights. This gave many rights back to the people. It stated the powers that a king or queen had. Under this Bill of Rights, Parliament had to approve all taxes. The king was not allowed to suspend, or stop, the work of Parliament. The people could ask the government for help, and a person accused of a crime had the right to a jury trial.

The settlers who came to America knew about the rights that were included in the English Bill of Rights. When these settlers saw that England was trying to take away some of their rights, they revolted, and a war was fought. The settlers declared their independence from English rule, and a new country was born. When the citizens of this new country wrote a plan for their own government, they also added a Bill of Rights, using what they knew from the English Bill of Rights and the Petition of Right. In chapter 3 you will study the freedoms listed in our Bill of Rights.

★*Activity 5.* Number your paper from 1 to 6. Choose words from the box to complete the paragraph. Write the correct word next to each number.

Parliament was formed to help the 1)_____ run the country. Parliament was made up of the House of 2)_____, which were the knights and the common people, and the House of 3)_____, which were the nobles and church leaders. Common people in the House of Commons were 4)_____ by their own people. Parliament was not used much by some rulers for a while, but finally Parliament was allowed to make 5)_____. Many ideas behind our elected 6)_____, with its two houses, were taken from the English Parliament.

Commons	Congress	elected
Lords	king	laws

1.6 POLITICAL IDEAS ALSO CAME FROM THE THIRTEEN ORIGINAL COLONIES

Words to Know:

Contract — An agreement made by two or more persons.

Loyal — Faithful; true to a country or an ideal.

National — Having to do with the whole country or nation.

Strict — Stern; not changing.

Press — Newspapers, magazines, and the people who work for them.

Criticize — To find fault with.

Publication — Printed or published work, such as a newspaper, magazine, or book.

The early settlers in America had ideas about forming a new government. One group of settlers, the Pilgrims, had left England because they did not want to belong to the Church of England or pay taxes. Before they left their ship, they wrote a contract for all to sign. This contract, called the Mayflower Compact, said that these settlers would write fair laws and choose leaders. They would do these things but remain loyal to the king. As their colony in Massachusetts grew, each church became a meeting place, and each person had a vote. These Pilgrims had the first ideas about democracy (rule by the people) in America. Other political ideas soon followed.

The *Mayflower* reached Massachusetts in 1620.

16 — The Colonists' Ideas

In other colonies people did not all vote as they did in the Pilgrim colony. The Jamestown colony was the first to have an assembly of representatives. This assembly, called the House of Burgesses, made decisions for the people. The people elected the representatives. The plan for the assembly did not come from the settlers, but was set up by England. England also sent a governor to rule.

The ideas of voting and electing representatives that began in these colonies were later used in modern American government. Today we elect representatives at all levels of government: city, county, state, and national.

★*Activity 6.* Number yor paper from 1 to 5. Choose the word or words to complete each sentence. Write your answer next to the number.

1. The Pilgrims left England because they did not want to belong to the _____ of England.
   (Assembly   Church   Democracy)
2. The Mayflower Compact was a contract written by _____.
   (the Pilgrims   the nobles   England)
3. The Mayflower Compact said that the Pilgrims would write laws and _____ _____.
   (collect taxes   choose leaders   meet daily)
4. The first assembly of representatives in the new country was formed in the _____ colony.
   (Athens   Pilgrim   Jamestown)
5. _____ were elected to serve in the assembly.
   (Monarchs   Representatives   English)

The First Constitution in America Was Written in Connecticut in 1639

Some of the people who were living in Massachusetts decided that the Puritan rule there was too strict for them. They moved away and settled in the Connecticut area. The leader of this group was Thomas Hooker. Hooker believed in a more democratic government that would give more control to the people.

Hooker and his followers drew up a constitution. A constitution is a written plan for government. It lists the powers of the government, as well as the rights of the people. In their constitution, the Connecticut group agreed to create an assembly with elected representatives. They agreed to elect a governor and judges.

This first constitution set an example. Soon other colonies were writing constitutions of their own. Massachusetts even set up a public school system which was paid for with tax money.

Years later, in 1787, the writers of the United States Constitution took many ideas from these early colonial constitutions.

The Idea of a Free Press

In colonial times there was a law in the New York area that said no one could publish anything that spoke out against the government. A newspaperman, John Peter Zenger, wrote an article that sharply criticized the governor. He was tried for breaking the law. The jury, however, decided against the law and said that Zenger was innocent. This was a big step toward the idea of a free press as we know it. Today it is no longer against the law to criticize the government or its leaders in a newspaper or other publication.

18 — The Colonists' Ideas

The Idea of Religious Freedom

Many colonists came to America to worship as they pleased. The Puritans came for this reason, but they would not give religious freedom to people living in their colony. People who disagreed with the Puritans were sent away, or left the Puritan colony.

Puritans at a Meeting

These people then set up colonies that *did* allow a few different religions. This idea of religious freedom soon spread throughout the colonies. It finally led to our system today, which guarantees people the right to worship as they please.

★*Activity 7.* Number your paper from 1 to 8. Each question has an answer that can be found on page 17 or 18. Write the answer next to the number.

1. Which of the early colonies had a very strict rule?
2. Who set up a colony with a more democratic rule than the Puritan colony?
3. What is a written plan for government called?
4. Which colony set up the first public school system?
5. Who wrote a newspaper article that criticized the governor?
6. What freedom permits people to worship freely?
7. What freedom permits people to publish critical remarks about the government?
8. What officers did the Connecticut group decide to elect?

1.7 AMERICAN COLONIES JOIN TOGETHER TO END ENGLISH RULE

England did not interfere with the government in the colonies for nearly a century. Then the English needed money to pay their debts. They tried to raise money from the colonies. By the middle 1700's, the colonists felt that England was trying to regain control. The colonists did not like the high taxes or the duties collected on certain goods. England passed the Stamp Act, which forced the colonists to pay a tax on all newspapers, pamphlets, legal documents, calendars, and playing cards. In order to end this taxation, representatives from the colonies met together in 1765. Other meetings followed, and gradually feelings against the English rule increased.

The First Continental Congress

In 1774, a large meeting called the First Continental Congress was held in Philadelphia. At this meeting the colonists decided to take action against England. They sent the King of England a list of the rights they demanded. They also said that they were refusing to buy all British goods, including tea.

This action of the First Continental Congress made no difference in the way England treated the colonists. Trouble continued between the colonists and England. The English soldiers (Redcoats) and the colonial soldiers (Minutemen) began shooting on April 19, 1775. The Revolutionary War was underway.

The Second Continental Congress

This Second Continental Congress met a few weeks after the shooting began. They organized an army led by George Washington. The colonists were ready to fight the British. The Second Continental Congress ran the government of the colonies and supported the colonists' cause during the war.

Soon the Continental Congress realized that the trouble with England would not end peacefully, but they wanted to end British rule once and for all. They also wanted to have a government run by the people — a democracy. They asked Thomas Jefferson to write down all their ideas to send to the king. This document was called the Declaration of Independence. It was the greatest contribution of the colonial period to the future form of democratic government in America.

The Declaration of Independence Told England That the Colonists Were Ending English Rule

The first part of the Declaration of Independence states that all people have certain rights, including "life, liberty, and the pursuit of happiness." It goes on to say that if a government denies these rights to the people, then that rule must end.

The middle section of the Declaration lists all the grievances, or complaints, the colonists had against the King of England, George III. The Declaration ends with an explanation of what the colonists have done to change the attitude of the English, but says that the English have been "deaf to the voice of justice..."

The very last paragraph of the Declaration says, in part:

"...That these united colonies are, and of right ought to be, free and independent States; that they are absolved from all allegiance to the British Crown, and that all political connection between them and the state of Great Britain, is and ought to be totally dissolved; and that as free and independent states, they have full power to levy war, conclude peace, contract alliances, establish commerce, and to do all other acts and things which independent states may of right do...."

The Top Portion of the Declaration of Independence

★**Activity 8.** Number your paper from 1 to 7. Choose the correct phrase to complete each sentence. Write the letter of that phrase next to the number.

1. By the middle 1700's, the colonists felt that England was (A) trying to regain control. (B) treating the colonists fairly.
2. The Stamp Act (A) helped the colonists. (B) forced the colonists to pay unfair taxes.
3. At the First Continental Congress, the colonists (A) decided to take action against England. (B) organized an army to fight the British.
4. The colonists sent England a list of the rights they demanded and said that they (A) would not buy British goods. (B) wanted to fight a war.
5. The group that ran the government of the country during the war between the colonists and the English was the (A) First Continental Congress. (B) Second Continental Congress.
6. The Declaration of Independence, which told England that the colonies were independent, was written by (A) Thomas Jefferson. (B) the Second Continental Congress.
7. The Declaration of Independence broke all ties with England and (A) listed the grievances the colonists had against the king. (B) wrote a new plan of government for the colonies.

SUMMARY OF CHAPTER 1

Government came into existence as the needs of people changed. Laws and customs were combined into governments that allowed people to lead safe, peaceful lives. American government began when the colonists realized they no longer wanted to live under British rule. They had to form their own government. Ancient governments, as well as English government, influenced the development of democratic government (rule by the people) in America.

Ideas from Ancient Governments

Greece and Rome contributed ideas to democracy in America. In Greece, free male citizens all had a say in the government. Because Rome was larger, representatives of the people were chosen to run the government. Rome had a group of senators who made laws, much as our senators do today.

Ideas from English Government

Our modern system of law has its roots in a system that began when Henry II was King of England. He appointed judges and provided jury trials.

The English Magna Carta put in writing, for the first time, the rights given to the common man by a government. The nobles could not be taxed without their consent. In colonial times when the colonists were being taxed without their consent, trouble began with England. It finally caused the colonists to break away from England and to form their own government.

In forming their own government, the colonists used ideas from the English Petition of Right and the Bill of Rights. Some of these ideas were: jury trials, the right to ask the government for help, and the right to be taxed fairly.

Ideas from the Colonies

Political ideas also came from the first thirteen colonies. The Mayflower Compact was drawn up by the Pilgrims before they landed in America. The Connecticut colony had the first constitution in the new land, with other colonies soon writing constitutions of their own. The idea of a free press began with John Peter Zenger. The idea of religious freedom began when some colonists fled the Puritan colony. The Puritans did not allow people to worship as they pleased, so many people set up colonies that allowed more freedom of religion. Today, freedom of the press and freedom of religion are two of our basic American rights.

By the middle 1700's, the colonists were ready to end British rule and form their own government. War was fought, and finally the Declaration of Independence was drawn up. This document said that the colonies were declaring themselves free and independent of England. It listed all the reasons the colonists were doing this. The Declaration of Independence was the most important document of the colonial era.

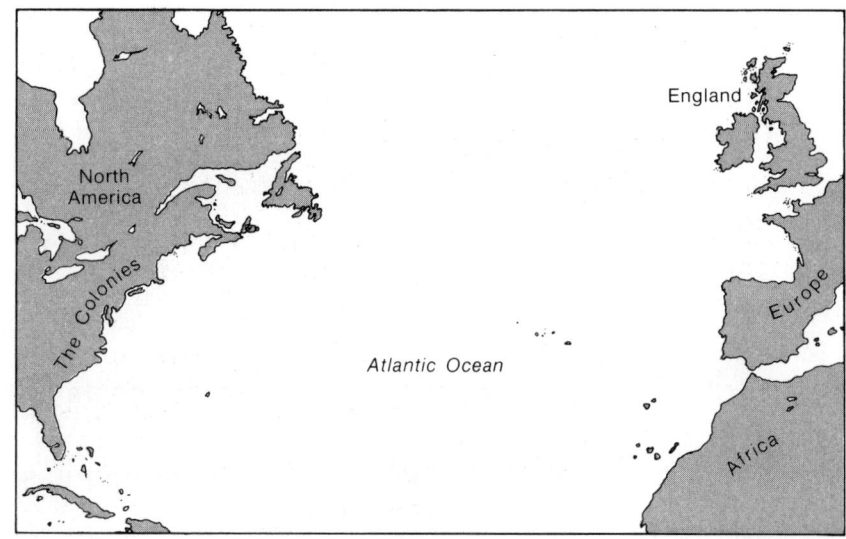

• CHAPTER REVIEW ACTIVITY •

Number your paper from 1 to 10. Choose the correct word or words from the box to complete each statement. Write the answers.

democracy	city-states
Parliament	republic
Magna Carta	representatives
Monarchy	Mayflower Compact
judges	Declaration of Independence

1. _____ was a group of nobles and common people who advised the king.
2. The most important document written in colonial times was the _____.
3. Henry II was the first king to appoint _____ to hear criminal cases.
4. Jamestown Colony had an assembly with elected _____.
5. _____ is a form of government where the rule is passed from generation to generation.
6. The citizens of Greece lived in _____ where all free males ran the government.
7. Because Rome had a representative form of government, it was a _____.
8. The word _____ is a Greek word meaning "rule by the people."
9. The _____ was a document written early in English history that granted rights to the common man.
10. The _____ was a contract signed by the Pilgrims when they arrived in America.

Chapter **2**

Creation of American Government

In the last chapter you learned that the Declaration of Independence broke all ties the colonies had with England. A new nation was formed, but it was a nation of separate and individual colonies. These colonies needed a form of government to join them together as a country.

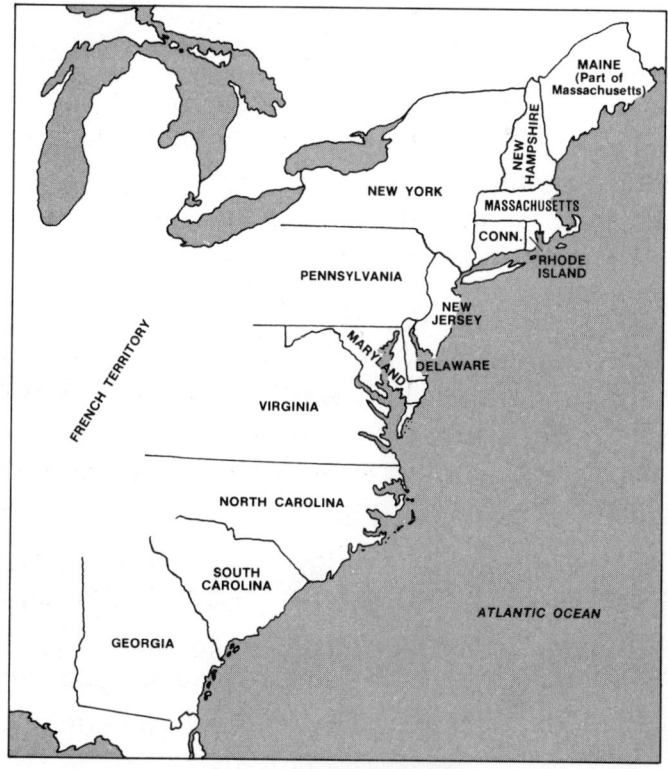

The Thirteen Colonies

2.1 JOINING THE COLONIES TOGETHER AS A COUNTRY

Words to Know:

Delegate — A person chosen to speak or act for another person or group.

Treaty — An agreement between two or more countries or states about trade, peace, or other matters.

Financial — Having to do with money.

Justice — Fair treatment; the use of authority to uphold what is right and lawful.

Satisfy — To convince; to fulfill certain requirements or conditions; to provide a solution for.

Revise — To improve; to bring up-to-date.

Safeguards — People or things that protect ideas or property against harm or loss.

Federal — A system of government in which power is divided between a central government and state governments.

At the Continental Congress, even before the Declaration of Independence was approved and accepted, a committee was working to write a plan for a government that would join the states together. This plan was called the Articles of Confederation.

Because of the great need, the Articles were quickly approved by all the states. It gave the thirteen states a plan for government. It was popular with the states because it did not make the national, or central, government too strong. The colonists remembered their dislike for the strong English rule.

The Articles of Confederation gave the government a national Congress made up of delegates from the thirteen states. This Congress could make war, agree to treaties with other countries, and take care of financial needs. Each state sent one delegate to the

Congress. The Articles did not provide for a president as a national leader, or for a system of justice.

At first most people were satisfied with the Articles. The Articles allowed the states a great deal of control over their own affairs. They limited Congress's power over the states. However, as time went on, the states saw that the Articles were too weak. The war that set the colonies free cost a great deal of money. The country owed 40 million dollars to foreign governments alone. Congress had no money of its own, and no way of raising money. Most of the money needed should have come from the states, but many states refused to pay. There was no system of law to force the states to pay. In addition, the Articles of Confederation did not provide for a system of law or justice.

Other financial problems, besides the war debt, were also facing the new nation. Businesses and farmers were out of money. Congress had no funds to pay an army and navy to defend the nation. Also, the soldiers who fought in the Revolutionary War had not yet been paid. Individual states were printing their own money. Something had to be done. A better government had to be worked out if the United States of America was to be a strong, rich country. Finally, a meeting was called to revise the Articles of Confederation. This meeting was held in Philadelphia in 1787, and became known as the Constitutional Convention.

2.2 THE CONSTITUTIONAL CONVENTION IN PHILADELPHIA

The delegates who attended the Constitutional Convention were all well-to-do, well-educated men, mostly from the cities. They all shared the same ideas about government, and they were important people in their own states. George Washington was their leader at the convention. At first the delegates worked to revise the Articles of Confederation, but soon they saw that a new plan for government would be necessary.

The colonists knew what they did not want. They did not want the states to lose control of the government. They did not want a king or a strong central government. Although the Articles of Confederation had provided these safeguards, that plan had failed. A new plan, with a stronger central government, was needed. The delegates worked for three and one-half months in secret to create a new plan for the country. This new plan for a national government was the Constitution.

Writing the Constitution

A federal government is one in which states join together to form a country. Some, but not all, power is given to a central government. The states are equal to each other in voting power, and are also given some responsibility to govern themselves. This federal type of government that the convention delegates finally worked out was the answer to the new nation's problems.

Several forms of federal government were suggested at first. The delegates looked at all the suggestions. Two plans were finally presented for discussion. They were as follows:

Virginia Plan. The Virginia Plan, suggested by the larger states, favored a strong central government. It called for one executive, and a two-part lawmaking body (legislature). The people would elect members of the legislature.

New Jersey Plan. The New Jersey Plan, suggested by the smaller states, favored greater power for the states. It offered a one-part legislature and two or more executives. All members of the legislature would be chosen by the states. The presidents would be chosen by the legislature.

Both plans provided for the federal government to be in charge of admitting new states to the union. Both plans favored a supreme court that would make final decisions concerning the law.

★*Activity 1.* Number your paper from 1 to 5. Choose the correct word or words in parentheses that make each statement true. Write your answer next to each number.

1. The Declaration of Independence (broke, began) all ties the colonies had with England.

2. At first, the Articles of Confederation were (unpopular, popular) with the people in the colonies because the Articles joined them together as a country.

30 — Constitutional Convention

3. The Articles of Confederation (did, did not) make the central, or national, government strong.

4. The Articles of Confederation (did, did not) provide for a president of the new country.

5. Congress (had, did not have) money to pay for an army and navy to defend the nation.

★*Activity 2.* Number your paper from 1 to 7. Match the definitions in Part A with the terms in Part B. Write the correct term by each number.

Part A, Definitions

1. Leader of the delegates at the Constitutional Convention.
2. Meeting held to revise the Articles of Confederation.
3. The people who attended the Constitutional Convention.
4. First plan of government that failed.
5. Plan that favored a strong central government.
6. Type of government which does not give all power to a national, or central, government.
7. Plan that favored greater power to the states.

Part B, Terms

Federal government
George Washington
Delegates
Constitutional Convention
Articles of Confederation
Virginia Plan
New Jersey Plan

2.3 COMPROMISES MADE AT THE CONSTITUTIONAL CONVENTION

Words to Know:

Separation — A division or parting.

Balance — To keep equal in power and influence.

Legislature — An official body of persons with power to make laws.

Judicial — Having to do with courts of law and justice.

Executive — A person or group having the power to carry out the plans and duties of a group; for example, a president.

Limited — Having a boundary.

Compromise — A settlement of differences in which each side gives up some of its demands.

Principle — A basic truth, law, or ideal of behavior.

Popular sovereignty — Rule by the people.

Compromising is a system of give and take used by opposing sides when an agreement cannot be reached. At the Convention, each side had to compromise, or give up some of its plan in order to reach an agreement. The people who favored the Virginia Plan, and those who favored the New Jersey Plan, worked out their differences. Four major compromises were made.

"Let's compromise."

Compromise One. The most important compromise was made by a group of delegates from Connecticut. It dealt with the problem of creating a legislature (lawmaking body) for the new government. These delegates said it should be a two-part legislature, in order to please both the larger and smaller states. The members of one part would be chosen according to population. The other part would have two representatives from each state, no matter how small.

Compromise Two. The second compromise settled a problem about slaves. The problem was whether the slaves should be counted the same as free men for tax collection and population purposes. The compromise said that every five slaves would count the same as three free men. This was called the Three-Fifths Compromise. Both the North and South accepted this plan.

Compromise Three. The third compromise had to do with commerce (trade). Everyone agreed that the states should control trade within their own borders. A question that remained was who would control foreign trade and trade among the states.

Compromise Four. Northerners wanted the new national government to have full power. The Southerners feared that the government might end slave trade. The fourth compromise gave the federal government power over foreign trade and trade among the states. It also said that slave trade could not be ended by the federal government for 20 years, or until 1808. This satisfied the Southern states.

By September 17, 1787, the compromises were agreed upon by all the delegates, and the Constitution was signed. The country had a new plan for government. The Constitution of the United States was, and still is, the foundation of the country's law.

★**Activity 3.** Number your paper from 1 to 5. Select the correct ending for each sentence from the two choices given. Write the letter of the ending next to each number.

1. A compromise is a system
    A) of give and take by each side in a disagreement.
    B) of rules and laws to run a country.

2. The delegates from Connecticut tried to settle the problems about
    A) a legislature.　　B) the slaves.

3. Everyone at the Convention agreed that the states should control
    A) their own trade.　　B) all foreign trade.

4. One compromise that the delegates agreed on was that slave trade could
    A) never be ended.
    B) not be ended by the federal government for twenty years.

5. On September 17, 1787, the compromises were agreed upon by
    A) all delegates.
    B) only some of the delegates.

2.4 GUIDING PRINCIPLES OF THE CONSTITUTION

The writers of the Constitution were careful to base this new plan on certain principles they felt were necessary for a democratic government. These principles are as follows:

1. **Popular Sovereignty Rule** — All power is held by the people because they elect the leaders of the national and state governments.

2. **Limited Government** — Government must obey the law and conduct business according to the principles of the Constitution. The government and its officers are never above the law. The Constitution has set limits on the power the government has.

3. **Separation of Powers** — The Constitution put the power into three different departments — the Congress, which is the legislative or lawmaking branch; the executive branch, which applies or enforces the laws; and the judicial branch, which interprets the laws made by Congress.

Congress alone can make laws. It cannot give anyone else the power to do so. It also must approve appointments made by the President. The President and the executive branch see that the laws are carried out. The President can also veto bills and appoint officials, such as ambassadors and judges.

The courts, with the Supreme Court as the most powerful court, can settle disagreements or disputes brought to them by the government or by private persons. The judicial branch interprets the laws (tells what they mean). It can tell whether or not the law follows the Constitution.

4. **Checks and Balances** — The three branches of government have separate duties, but they must act together in some cases. This balances the power and never allows one branch to become too powerful. There are limits placed on each branch. The following chart shows some of the ways each branch is limited in its power.

Limits of the Branches of Government

Presidential Limits	Congressional Limits	Judicial Limits
1. Congress can remove the President by impeachment.	1. President can veto (disapprove) bills of Congress.	1. President decides on all federal judges.
2. Congress can pass a bill even if the President vetoes it.	2. Supreme Court can say a law is unfair.	2. Congress must approve President's appointments of judges.
3. Congress must approve how money is spent.		3. Congress can remove a judge.
 4. Only Congress can declare war.		

Laws can never be made by the Supreme Court, but the court can decide if a law is unfair. The Congress then has to change the law or write a new law. The President cannot make laws on his own, but approves the laws Congress passes. In turn, the Congress must approve all money spent by the country. Congress must also approve presidential appointments of people to important government jobs.

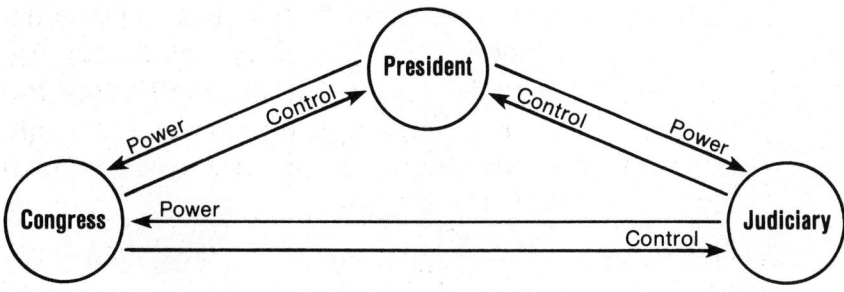

Each branch checks, or limits, the powers of the other two.

★**Activity 4.** Which principle of the Constitution is described in each statement below? Number your paper from 1 to 4. Write the correct principle by the number on your paper.

Basic Principles of the Constitution
Limited Government   Popular Sovereignty
Checks and Balances   Separation of Powers

---

1. The power of the federal government is held by three groups: Congress, the President, and a system of courts.
2. The three branches of the government work together and also check on the work of each other.
3. The government and its officers are never above the law. They cannot take away the rights of the people as guaranteed in the Constitution.
4. The people elect the leaders of the federal (central) and state governments.

Signing the Constitution

2.5 THE STRUGGLE FOR APPROVAL

After all work on the Constitution was complete, it had to be approved by the states. Most of the delegates at the Convention had signed the Constitution. These delegates worked hard to persuade the states to ratify (approve) it. Each state held a convention to study the Constitution. The approval of nine of the thirteen states was needed before the Constitution could be put into use.

It had been eleven years since the Declaration of Independence was signed. The people of the country were divided in their ideas about the Constitution. Some people favored the Constitution because it provided for a strong national government. These people were known as Federalists. The Federalists believed a strong central authority was necessary to defend the nation and keep it united. Alexander Hamilton strongly favored the Constitution and wrote essays in the newspapers to persuade people to vote for it. Another group, known as the Anti-Federalists, were opposed to the Constitution. They were mostly wealthy business people. They favored stronger state governments than the Constitution permitted. These people were afraid that a strong central, or national, government would take away some of their rights.

The Anti-Federalists were against the Constitution because they were afraid of losing individual rights. When a change giving people basic rights was suggested for the Constitution, many Anti-Federalists then favored it. This addition was made two years later and was known as the *Bill of Rights*. It guaranteed such rights as freedom of speech, religion, and of the press.

Discussions continued throughout the winter at the state conventions. Finally, by June, 1788, nine states had ratified the Constitution — enough to allow the Constitution to become the new plan for government. By 1790, all thirteen states had ratified the Constitution.

2.6 THE NEW NATION BEGINS UNDER THE CONSTITUTION

Congress began putting the Constitution into use as soon as it was ratified. The first action Congress took was to name New York as the temporary capital. Later it was moved to Philadelphia, and by 1800, to Washington, D.C., the present capital. The first elections were held, and George Washington was the popular choice for President. John Adams was elected Vice-President. Twenty-two senators and fifty-six representatives were elected from the states to serve in the new Congress. They met for the first time on March 4, 1789, in Federal Hall in New York.

★*Activity 5.* Number your paper from 1 to 5. Choose the correct answer for each blank from the three choices given. Write this answer by the number.

1. The _____ favored the new Constitution.
   (Federalists   Anti-Federalists   Congress)

2. The Federalists favored a _____ central, or national government.   (strong   weak   complete)

3. The Constitution had to be approved by _____ of the thirteen states in order to be ratified.
   (eight   nine   ten)

4. The _____ favored strong state governments.
   (Anti-Federalists   Federalists   Constitution)

5. Finally, by 1790, _____ of the thirteen states had ratified the Constitution.   (all   some   ten)

SUMMARY OF CHAPTER 2

The colonists finally broke all ties with England when the Declaration of Independence was approved. The next step was to write a plan for the government that would join the thirteen separate states together as a country. While the Declaration was still being written, another group of people began writing a plan for running the government of the new country.

A First Plan. This first plan to unite the states into a country was called the Articles of Confederation. It provided for a Congress made up of representatives from all the states. The Articles were quickly accepted by the states, but soon the weaknesses of the Articles were seen. Under the Articles of Confederation, the government did not have the power to raise money to run the country or to pay the nation's war debt. The states were asked to help pay the debt, but some of them refused. The Articles did not provide for a system of laws to force the states to pay their share.

A Second Plan. Another meeting was soon called to revise the Articles of Confederation. At this meeting, known as the Constitutional Convention, the delegates decided that a new plan for government was necessary. They felt the country needed a stronger central, or national, government. A federal form of government was agreed upon, with some of the power, but not all, going to a central government. All of the delegates did not agree completely with the way this federal government would be formed or run. The larger states favored a plan with very strong central government (Virginia Plan). The smaller states favored greater power for the individual states (New Jersey Plan). After about three months of discussions and making compromises, the new Constitution was ready. It became our new plan for government, and is still in use today.

Guiding Principles. The Constitution was written based on certain principles, or ideals. These principles are:

1. *Popular Sovereignty* — All power is in the hands of the people because they elect the leaders.

2. *Limited Government* — Leaders and government are not above the law and must follow the principles of the Constitution.

3. *Separation of Powers* — Power is divided among the three branches of government: the legislative, the executive, and the judicial.

4. *Checks and Balances* — The three branches work together, but also have separate duties to perform. Each branch must also check on the other's work so that one branch does not become too strong.

Ratification. After the Constitution was finished, it had to be approved, or ratified, by the states. Each state held a convention. The Federalists, who favored a stronger central government, approved of the Constitution. They were opposed by the Anti-Federalists, who said the states should have more power. The Anti-Federalists felt the Constitution would take away their individual rights. Some people suggested that a Bill of Rights be added to the Constitution to guarantee people's rights. When the Bill of Rights was suggested, many Anti-Federalists changed their minds and voted for the Constitution. After almost a year of discussions at the state conventions, nine states ratified the Constitution, and it became the new plan for government. New York was chosen as the temporary capital, and George Washington was elected President. Soon every state in the country had ratified the Constitution, and the new, independent nation was established.

• CHAPTER REVIEW ACTIVITY •

Number your paper from 1 to 10. Next to each number, write the word or phrase that is missing. Select the words from the box below.

1. The _____ was written by the colonists to break all ties with England.
2. The Articles of Confederation were written as the _____ for the new country.
3. The Articles of Confederation did not provide for a _____ or a system of law or justice.
4. In a _____ form of government, some power is given to a central government, and some power is given to the states.
5. The _____ states at the Constitutional Convention favored more power for the individual states.
6. Many _____ were made at the Constitutional Convention before the delegates approved the Constitution.
7. _____ means that power is in the hands of the people because they elect the leaders.
8. The separation of powers among the _____ branches of the government was provided for by the Constitution.
9. _____ of the thirteen states had to ratify, or approve, the Constitution before it could be used.
10. When the Constitution was ratified, it was put into use _____.

compromises	Nine	Declaration of Independence
smaller	three	Popular sovereignty
right away	federal	first plan of government
national leader		

Chapter 3

A Look at the Constitution

The Constitution, written in Philadelphia and approved by the states, became the new plan for government for the United States of America. It contained a Preamble, or introduction, and seven articles that explained how the new government should be set up and run. Later, when there was a need, amendments, or written changes, were added to the Constitution. The first ten amendments, known as the Bill of Rights, were added just two years after the Constitution was ratified.

The Constitution has been in use for two hundred years. It has remained strong even though the country has changed from a small agricultural, or farming, nation to a powerful, modern nation with many industries and businesses.

The First Part of the Constitution

The Constitution of the United States

Preamble — Goals and Purpose

Article I — Legislative

Article II — Executive

Article III — Judicial

Article IV — States

Article V — Amendments

Article VI — Supreme Law

Article VII — Ratification

Amendments 1 through 10, The Bill of Rights (1791)

1. Freedom of religion, speech, press, and petition
2. Right to bear arms; states to have militia
3. Freedom from having to quarter soldiers in time of peace
4. No unreasonable searches and seizures
5. Grand jury, double jeopardy, and due process
6. Fair trial in criminal cases
7. Jury trial in most civil cases
8. Reasonable bail, fines, and punishment
9. Protection of rights not written in Constitution
10. Power to states or people if not given to federal government

Amendments 11 through 26

11. Protection of states from federal lawsuits (1795)

12. Separate ballots for President and Vice-President (1804)

13. End of slavery in all states (1865)

14. Citizenship for blacks (1868)

15. Voting rights for blacks (1870)

16. Income tax (1913)

17. Direct election of senators in their own states (1913)

18. Prohibition of liquor (1919)

19. Voting rights for women (1920)

20. Dates for Congress to begin and for President to take office (1933)

21. The end or repeal of Prohibition (1933)

22. Limits a President to two elected terms (1951)

23. Voting rights for citizens of Washington, D.C. in presidential elections (1961)

24. End of poll tax (1964)

25. Filling the offices of President and Vice-President if they become vacant (1967)

26. Eighteen-year-olds may vote in all elections (1971)

3.1 THE PREAMBLE AND THE FIRST THREE ARTICLES

Words to Know:

Article — One of the parts of a written document.

Justice — Fair and equal treatment under the law.

Convention — A formal meeting called for a special purpose.

Majority — The greater number or part of something; more than one-half of the total.

Preamble — An introduction or short statement of purpose.

Vested — Given to or placed under someone's authority.

The Preamble, which is the short introduction to the Constitution, begins with these words: "We the people of the United States, in order to form a more perfect Union..." It goes on to explain the goals and purpose of the Constitution. The people of the United States, living under the Constitution, could expect justice, peace, and safety at home, and protection from other countries. All these things would be provided by the new Constitution.

The first three articles clearly show how the principle of separation of powers would be followed. Three branches of the federal government would be set up with certain powers and duties.

Article I (One): The Legislative Branch

> **Section 1.** All legislative powers herein granted shall be vested in a Congress of the United States, which shall consist of a Senate and House of Representatives.

This means Congress has the power to make laws. It further says that the Congress has two parts—a Senate and a House of Representatives.

Article II (Two): The Executive Branch

> *Section 1.* (1) The executive power shall be vested in a President of the United States of America. He shall hold his office during the term of four years, and together with the Vice-President, chosen for the same term, be elected...

The many duties of the office are explained in this article, including the power to appoint ambassadors to foreign countries, and judges to the Supreme Court.

Executive Powers

The executive branch's job is to carry out the law. Through the Constitution, the President:

- Is Commander in Chief of the armed forces.
- Has the ability to make treaties, provided two-thirds of the senators agree.
- Shall nominate ambassadors, judges of the Supreme Court, and other public officers.
- Shall give to the Congress information on the State of the Union, and recommend measures for them to consider.

Article III (Three): The Judicial Branch

> *Section 1.* The judicial power of the United States, shall be vested in one Supreme Court, and in such inferior courts as the Congress may from time to time ordain and establish...

The types of cases which come under the federal courts are outlined in Article III.

3.2 ARTICLE IV (Four): HOW THE STATES SHOULD TREAT EACH OTHER

The laws and other legal rulings of one state must be recognized by all other states. This principle is clearly explained in Article IV (Four) of the Constitution. Article IV also says that the rights a citizen has in one state will be respected in all states. Finally, in this article concerning the states, the federal government guarantees each state a form of government which includes three separate branches of organization, just as the federal system has: legislative (state legislature), executive (governor), and judicial (courts).

★*Activity 1.* Number your paper from 1 to 7. Read each statement. Decide which article of the Constitution made this provision. Write the article number (one of the first four articles) beside the number.

1. A Congress is established or set up.
2. A citizen's rights are respected in all states.
3. Congress shall consist of a Senate and House of Representatives.
4. Each state has three separate branches of government.
5. A President will hold his term of office for four years.
6. The highest judicial power of the United States shall be vested in (given to) the Supreme Court.
7. The President has the power to appoint ambassadors to foreign countries.

3.3 ARTICLE V (Five): MAKING AMENDMENTS TO THE CONSTITUTION

Any change to the Constitution is called an amendment. The writers of the Constitution knew that changes might have to be made from time to time in this important document. Often words had to be added or taken out of the Constitution. Article V (Five) was added so that changes could be made when necessary.

Amendments are proposed in order to make corrections or to add something new. These changes are not easily made. By one method, an amendment is suggested in Congress. This suggestion must then be approved by a two-thirds (2/3) majority vote in both the Senate and House of Representatives. This suggestion for a change is then sent to all the states. Three-fourths (3/4) of the state legislatures (lawmaking bodies) must ratify, or approve, the change. If this happens, the change is added to the Constitution as an official amendment.

By using another method for making an amendment, Congress can order special meetings of state conventions. Three-fourths of these conventions must vote "yes" to approve a new amendment.

Through the years, more than 6,000 amendments have been suggested, but only twenty-six have been added to the Constitution since it was written in 1787. All but one of the amendments have been approved by state legislatures. The one exception was the 21st Amendment, which ended Prohibition, the law that banned the manufacture, use, or transportation of alcoholic beverages. This amendment was approved by constitutional conventions in three-fourths of the states.

Articles VI and VII — 49

3.4 ARTICLES VI (Six) AND VII (Seven)

Article VI (Six) of the Constitution declares that the Constitution is the supreme, or highest, law of the land. All officials of both the federal and state governments are sworn under oath to support and obey the Constitution.

Article VII (Seven) tells how the ratification of the document will take place. It says that the thirteen states should hold conventions. At least nine of the states must approve the Constitution before it may be used.

★*Activity 2.* Number your paper from 1 to 7. Read each statement. Select an answer from the box below which completes that sentence. Write your answer beside each number.

1. The Constitution contains _____ articles.
2. Amendments can make corrections or add _____.
3. The Constitution was written in the year _____.
4. An amendment can be suggested in _____ or a _____.
5. Article _____ says that a citizen's rights in one state must be respected by other states.
6. Article _____ made the Constitution the supreme law of the land.
7. In order for the Constitution to be ratified, _____ states had to vote for it.

seven	state convention
Congress	something new
1787	Six
Four	nine of the thirteen

3.5 IN 1791, THE BILL OF RIGHTS WAS ADDED

The Constitution was not approved at first because it did not guarantee the rights of individuals. A promise was made at the Constitutional Convention to add a part that would guarantee people the rights they wanted, including the right to worship as they pleased and the right of free speech. This promise caused many people to vote in favor of the Constitution.

James Madison, then a member of the House of Representatives, made the first move to see that a list of rights was added to the Constitution. He suggested nine amendments that would strengthen the Constitution. Other suggestions were also made, and finally Congress wrote twelve amendments. These were sent to the states for approval. It took two years for the states to ratify the new amendments, and then only ten of the twelve were approved. These first ten amendments, known as the Bill of Rights, were added to the end of the Constitution. They guaranteed to the people most basic freedoms, including freedom of religion, freedom of speech, and trial by jury.

The First Amendment

Words to Know:

Express — To make known one's thoughts, ideas, or feelings.

Opinion — A belief or judgment of an individual or group.

Circulate — To pass out or distribute widely; for example, to *circulate* a newspaper.

Assemble — To come together as a group.

Petition — A formal written document, or legal paper, asking for a right or benefit from someone in authority.

The purpose of the First Amendment is to allow people to express themselves. This right of free expression is considered by many to be the most important freedom guaranteed by the Constitution.

> **"Congress shall make no law respecting an establishment of religion, or prohibiting the free exercise thereof; or abridging the freedom of speech, or of the press; or the right of the people peaceably to assemble, and to petition the Government for a redress of grievances."**

First of all, the First Amendment guarantees people the right to worship as they please, or not to worship at all. Also, the government may not favor religion over no religion by giving public tax money or other support to any one religion.

Second, the First Amendment guarantees to all people the right to express themselves either by the spoken or written word. When some people express themselves, their words offend others; but in a free country, this is allowed. The writers of the amendments felt that by allowing the freedom of speech, many different opinions would be heard. The best opinions could be accepted by the people.

There are a few ways our country stops people from speaking freely. We have laws against slander (spoken false statements) and libel (written false statements), which may hurt someone's reputation. There are restrictions against using speech to promote violence or to endanger public safety.

Freedom of the press is the third guarantee in the First Amendment. This means that not only can people speak freely, they can write down their opinions. These opinions can then be circulated in newspapers, magazines, pamphlets, and on radio and television. People also have the right to be informed. In the United States, the press is not owned by the government, but is owned by private individuals or groups of persons. The press can print what it believes to be true and fair.

The fourth guarantee in the First Amendment is the right to assemble in groups in a peaceful way and for peaceful purposes. In some countries this is not allowed. Any interest group in our country has the right to hold meetings, whether its ideas are popular or not. Outdoor or indoor meetings and demonstrations are permitted. If these events take away the rights of any other citizen, then they are stopped.

The fifth and last guarantee in the First Amendment is the right to petition. This means that government officials may be asked to do something or to stop doing something. These petitions, or requests, may come from individuals or from groups. They may be letters or formal written requests. Group petitions may also be prepared and signed by many people and sent to government officials. The petitions may ask a senator, for example, to work to get a certain law passed. People often send petitions to ask that something be stopped, such as the building of a highway or a shopping center.

★**Activity 3.** Number your paper from 1 to 6. Choose the correct word from the two given in each sentence. Write the correct word by the number.

1. The government (may, may not) favor one religion over another.
2. We have laws in this country (for, against) slander and libel.
3. The press (is, is not) owned by the government in our country.
4. Interest groups in our country (can, cannot) hold meetings if their ideas are unpopular.
5. Group petitions (may, may not) be sent to government officials.
6. Many people consider the First Amendment to be the (most, least) important amendment to the Constitution.

The First Amendment guarantees freedom of religion.

The First Amendment and Supreme Court Decisions

Questions come up from time to time about the First Amendment and its guarantees of individual rights. The Supreme Court has the job of deciding what the First Amendment means in certain cases. Freedom of religion was questioned in the issues of school prayer and financial aid to parochial (religious) schools. When the issues were brought to the Supreme Court, it ruled that it is unconstitutional (illegal) to have students recite a prayer, even if it was written by school officials and did not favor any one religion. The Court said this went against the separation of government and religion as stated in the First Amendment. On the issue of financial aid, the Court ruled that money may be given to parochial schools only for non-religious things, such as lunches, bus rides, textbooks, and counseling.

Freedom of speech has been limited by the law during wartime. During World War I, Congress passed a law forbidding disloyal speech about the government, Constitution, army, navy, the flag, or uniforms. The Supreme Court ruled that this law was legal and constitutional.

Students who write for high school newspapers were being denied freedom of the press. School officials would not allow certain things to be printed if the ideas criticized the school. The Supreme Court said, "Students do not shed their constitutional rights of free expression at the schoolhouse gate." This means that students do have the freedom to express their ideas.

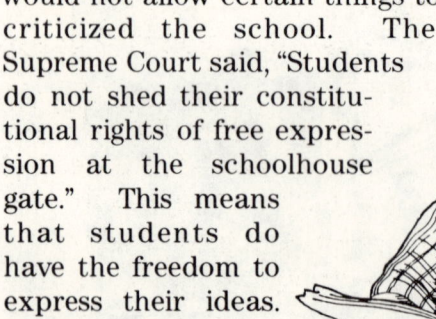

The Second and Third Amendments: Weapons and Militia

Words to Know:

Warrant — A written, legal order authorizing something, such as a search, seizure, or arrest.

Indict — To accuse or charge with a crime; usually done by the grand jury.

Evidence — The objects and statements gathered and used to judge a person accused of a crime.

Grand jury — A group of people who decide if there is enough evidence to have a trial for the accused person.

Witness — Someone who has seen or heard something; a person who is called to testify, or tell what he knows, in court.

Civil — Having to do with citizens; a civil law case does not involve a crime but deals with the rights of private citizens.

The next two amendments to the Constitution were added to protect Americans from things that had happened in the past. During the Revolutionary War, the British tried to take weapons away from the colonists. This made the colonists feel helpless because they needed the guns to serve in their state militias. A militia is an organized group of citizens who serve as soldiers during a war. The Second Amendment not only gives the people the right to bear arms (weapons), but also the right to use them when serving in the militia. This amendment also permits a state to train and keep a militia for protection in time of need.

Another thing the British did during the war was to force the colonists to quarter (house) soldiers in their homes. Many colonists did this against their will. The Third Amendment protects people from this. It states:

> "No soldier shall, in time of peace be quartered in any house,..."

The Fourth Amendment: Searches and Seizures

In the early days of our country, the people in authority felt free to enter and search private homes. Sometimes the searchers were looking for stolen or smuggled goods. Many times they were acting on "hunches," and innocent people were made to look guilty. People remembered this and wanted to feel safe and secure in their homes. The Fourth Amendment does not completely stop searches and seizures, but it does set definite rules about how they are to be done. The amendment makes it illegal, except in certain cases, to search someone's house without a warrant. This warrant must describe the place to be searched and what things might be seized.

Wiretapping and "Bugging"

When the words "unreasonable searches and seizures" were written in the Fourth Amendment, there were no telephones. Later, private telephone conversations could be tapped (secretly listened to) when evidence was needed for a criminal case. Some people felt that this tapping was illegal because it was an "unreasonable search." The Supreme Court ruled in 1928 that phone-tapping was legal, but all the justices did not agree. Some said people had the "right to be let alone....no intrusion by the government on privacy...." It took many years, but finally in 1967, the Court ruled that the Fourth Amendment protects people, not just buildings, against "unreasonable searches and seizures." No wiretapping or electronic "bugs" are now permitted unless the court orders it in advance.

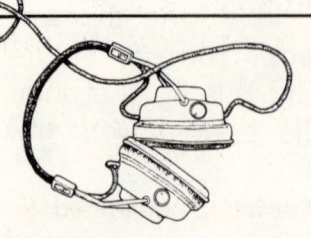

Amendments Five, Six, Seven, and Eight: Rights of People Accused of Crimes

The Fifth Amendment states, in part:

> "No person shall be held to answer for a capital, or otherwise infamous crime, unless on a presentment or indictment of a grand jury,..."

When a person is accused of a serious (capital) crime, he is first brought before a grand jury. This jury listens to the charges made against the person and studies the evidence given. If the citizens serving on the grand jury decide there is enough evidence, the person is indicted and stands trial for the crime. A person cannot stand trial until the grand jury indicts him.

> "...nor shall any person be subject for the same offense to be twice put in jeopardy..."

When a person goes on trial for a crime, it is said that his life or freedom is in jeopardy or danger. According to this amendment, a person does not have to go through this danger a second time, because he may not be tried twice for the same crime. It protects citizens from double jeopardy. This amendment also guarantees "due process of law." This means that a person must be given a fair trial according to all the rules and procedures set down in the Constitution. The last part of the Fifth Amendment states that the government may not seize a person's land, money, or other property for public use without paying for it.

The Sixth Amendment protects a person's right to defend himself in a federal court trial. The accused person has the right to:
1. A speedy, public trial before a fair jury in the state where the crime took place.
2. Be told of the crime of which he is accused.

3. Have a lawyer to argue the case.
4. Question all witnesses.
5. Have witnesses appear, by legal force if necessary, to tell the accused's side of the case.

The Seventh Amendment applies to civil lawsuits. A civil case does not involve a crime. It is usually a dispute between two or more parties over rights or duties. According to this amendment, if the value being disputed is more than twenty dollars, the civil lawsuit is brought to trial before a jury.

The Eighth Amendment was added to limit the amount of bail set by a judge, or fines a person must pay for breaking certain laws. Bail is a sum of money that an accused person must deposit for the privilege of staying out of jail while waiting for the case to come to trial. The judge decides on the amount of bail, usually according to the seriousness of the crime, and the reputation of the accused. The reason for bail is to be sure that the person will appear for his trial. This money is returned to the person when the trial begins.

This amendment also states, "...nor cruel and unusual punishments inflicted." This means that punishments such as torture are not allowed. A military court has stopped an old Navy punishment of three days on bread and water because the punishment was "cruel and unusual."

Amendments Nine and Ten
Amendments Nine and Ten were added so that all rights not listed directly in the Constitution would belong to the people or to the states. The following words of the Tenth Amendment assure people of these rights and make the people and the states partners in our federal system of government.

> "The powers not delegated to the United States by the Constitution, nor prohibited by it to the states, are reserved to the states respectively, or to the people."

The list of rights in the Bill of Rights is not complete, and Americans also have other freedoms: the right to live and travel anywhere, the right to hold a job, the right to receive an education and marry, and the right to join a political party or other group.

★*Activity 4.* Number your paper from 1 to 7. Match the sentence beginning in Part A with the correct sentence ending in Part B. Write the letter of the correct ending next to each number.

Part A

1. A person accused of a serious, or capital crime...
2. "Due process of law" means...
3. The Fourth Amendment says that in order to search someone's home,...
4. A militia is an...
5. The Third Amendment protects people from...
6. According to the Fifth Amendment, a person tried for a crime may not...
7. Under the Fifth Amendment the government may not seize...

Part B

a. the authorities will need a search warrant.
b. is first brought before a grand jury.
c. housing soldiers in their home during peacetime.
d. organized group of citizens who serve as soldiers.
e. be tried for the same crime again (double jeopardy).
f. an accused person must be given a fair trial.
g. private property for public use without paying for it.

60 — Amendments Eleven through Fifteen

★*Activity 5.* Number your paper from 1 to 7. Match the definition in Column B to the correct word or words in Column A. Write the letter next to each number.

Column A
1. Witness
2. Civil case
3. Bail
4. Lawyer
5. Fair jury
6. Cruel and unusual
7. Judge

Column B
a. Argues the case for the accused person.
b. Money deposited to stay out of jail before the trial.
c. Dispute between two citizens where no crime is involved.
d. Someone who has seen or heard something important to a case.
e. Accused person's trial held before this group.
f. This kind of punishment is not allowed.
g. Decides amount of bail.

3.6 AMENDMENTS ELEVEN THROUGH FIFTEEN

Words to Know:

Sue — To bring legal action against a person; to satisfy a claim or complaint.

Candidate — A person who seeks or is named to run for an office.

Debate — An argument or dispute between persons who have different views.

Up until 1860, only two amendments were added to the Constitution. The Eleventh Amendment denied the federal courts, including the Supreme Court, the right to make rulings in state affairs. The matter arose when the state of Georgia was sued by two citizens of South Carolina. The federal government stepped in to force Georgia to pay. Georgia refused to pay.

The state said that the federal government was taking away some of its power by ruling in the case. As a result of this case, and to ensure that it would not happen again, the Eleventh Amendment was added to the Constitution.

The Twelfth Amendment changed the system for electing a President and Vice-President. According to this amendment, separate candidates for each office had to be chosen. In the past, all candidates for both offices were on the same list. The candidate getting the highest number of votes was elected President. The second-place candidate was elected Vice-President. Problems arose with this system, and one election resulted in a tie. The addition of the Twelfth Amendment, calling for separate candidates for each office, solved this problem. The House of Representatives chooses a winner if neither candidate receives a majority of votes.

Slavery in the United States

In 1863 and at the end of the war between the North and South (Civil War), President Lincoln declared that the slaves in the Confederate States (Southern states) were free men. Congress wrote the Thirteenth Amendment to end slavery. The issue of slavery had been one of the causes of trouble between the North and South. Congress felt it needed to end the dispute once and for all. By the end of 1865, the amendment was ratified and added to the Constitution.

Slaves were now free, but there was still a debate over whether the slaves and other black people could be citizens. The passage of the Fourteenth Amendment settled this debate. The amendment says that all people born in the United States and under its rule are citizens. Foreign-born persons who live in the United States can also become citizens by following certain steps. The Fourteenth Amendment also says that the states must follow "due process" and give all citizens "equal protection," just as the federal government does.

The Fifteenth Amendment was the last of the amendments that was passed soon after the Civil War ended. It gave all male Americans the right to vote. The Northern states approved the amendment right away, but the Southern states, except for Tennessee, would not obey the amendment. Congress, using military force, made the Southern states hold conventions. They had to rewrite their state constitutions so that blacks were guaranteed the right to vote.

★*Activity 6.* Number your paper from 1 to 10. Complete the following paragraph with words from the box. Write the correct word by the number on your paper.

Civil War	President	vote
Vice-President	citizens	Constitution
courts	ended	slavery
affairs		

Until 1860, only slight changes were made in the 1)_____. Amendment Eleven said the federal 2)_____ could not make rulings in state 3)_____. Amendment Twelve changed the system for electing a 4)_____ and 5)_____. After the 6)_____, three amendments were added, having to do with 7)_____. The Thirteenth Amendment 8)_____ slavery in all states. The Fourteenth Amendment said all slaves and black persons could be 9)_____. The Fifteenth Amendment gave the right to 10)_____ to all males, even former slaves.

3.7 AMENDMENTS SIXTEEN THROUGH TWENTY-SIX

After 1870, forty-three years passed before any more additions were made to the Constitution. Starting in 1913 and ending in 1971, eleven more amendments were added to the Constitution. The following chart gives the amendments and the reasons they were added.

Amendment	Reasons for Adding
Sixteen (1913)	To allow Congress the power to pass income tax laws and to collect taxes.
Seventeen (1913)	To allow direct election of senators by the people of their states.
Eighteen (1919)	To end (ban) the making and selling of alcoholic beverages. This was called Prohibition.
Nineteen (1920)	To give women the right to vote.
Twenty (1933)	To set new dates for Congress to begin; to set January 20 as day President takes office.
Twenty-one (1933)	To end Prohibition; to give states the decision on whether to ban liquor.
Twenty-two (1951)	To limit the term of President to two elected terms.
Twenty-three (1961)	To allow the citizens of Washington, D.C. to vote for national officials.
Twenty-four (1964)	To end the poll tax (tax paid to vote) in federal elections.
Twenty-five (1967)	To decide who will fill the positions of President and Vice-President if these persons leave or become disabled.
Twenty-six (1971)	To set the voting age at 18 in all states.

★**Activity 7.** Number your paper from 1 to 10. Read the statements below. Select the correct answer from the box below. Write that answer beside the number on your paper.

1. Amendment Twenty-six set voting age in all elections at _____.
2. A President may be elected to that office no more than _____ times.
3. The Nineteenth Amendment gave women the right to _____.
4. The _____ Amendment allowed the citizens of the nation's capital to vote in national elections.
5. Prohibition banned the making and selling of _____ beverages.
6. Amendment Twenty-four put an end to the _____ tax in federal elections.
7. Amendment _____ put an end to Prohibition.
8. Because of the _____ Amendment, Congress now has the power to pass income tax laws.
9. January _____ is the day the President takes office.
10. So far we have _____ amendments added to the Constitution.

Twenty-six	20
vote	Twenty-third
Twenty-one	poll
Sixteenth	18
two	alcoholic

SUMMARY OF CHAPTER 3

When the Constitution was ratified by nine of the states, it became the plan of government for the new country. The Preamble states the purpose and goals of the Constitution. The first three articles tell how the federal, or national, government is set up with legislative, executive, and judicial branches. Article Four explains how the states should treat each other. Article Five says that changes can be made in the document when necessary. Article Six declares the Constitution the supreme (highest) law of the land. Article Seven says the Constitution had to be ratified by nine of the thirteen states before it could be put into effect.

The Bill of Rights

Two years after the Constitution was ratified, the first ten amendments were added. These were the guarantees of individual rights that were promised at the Constitutional Convention. These first ten amendments are known as the Bill of Rights. Many people consider the First Amendment the most important. It allows people freedom of religion, freedom to express themselves in spoken or written word, and the freedom to assemble peacefully in groups. It also allows people to petition the government for any reason.

Because each state wanted and needed a trained militia made up of citizens who could bear arms, the Second and Third Amendments were added. The Fourth Amendment protects people in their homes. The next four amendments have to do with the treatment of people accused of crimes. An accused person has to be indicted, then be given a speedy and fair trial, with a lawyer to defend him. Cruel punishment and high fines or bail are not allowed. The last two amendments of the Bill of Rights give to the states and the people any power not given to the national government.

Other Amendments

After the Bill of Rights was added, several years passed with only slight changes in the Constitution. When the Civil War ended in 1865, three important amendments dealing with slavery were approved. The slaves were freed by the Thirteenth Amendment, given their citizenship by the Fourteenth, and then given the right to vote by the Fifteenth.

Another 43 years passed, and in the years between 1913 and 1971, Amendments Sixteen through Twenty-six were added to the Constitution. Some of the important changes brought about by these amendments are: 1) women were allowed to vote; 2) alcohol was banned, and then later the ban was removed; 3) a President's term of office was limited to two elected terms; 4) the poll, or voting, tax was removed; and 5) the voting age was reduced to 18 in all elections.

• CHAPTER REVIEW ACTIVITY •

Number your paper from 1 to 10. Choose a word from the box to complete each sentence. Write the correct word next to each number.

Rights	Preamble	women
articles	freedoms	freed
President	amendments	ratified
accused		

1. The purpose and goals of the Constitution are stated in the _____.
2. The first three _____ tell how the federal government is set up.
3. Article V (Five) said that changes, or _____, could be made when necessary.
4. The Constitution was _____ by nine of the thirteen states.
5. The first ten amendments are known as the Bill of _____.
6. The First Amendment of the Bill of Rights gave people many _____.
7. There are four amendments that have to do with how people _____ of crimes should be treated.
8. The Thirteenth Amendment _____ the slaves.
9. One important amendment gave _____ the right to vote.
10. An amendment was added that said the _____ may be elected to office for only two terms.

Chapter 4

The Legislative Branch

4.1 THE THREE BRANCHES OF GOVERNMENT

The federal government of the United States is divided into three separate branches, or parts. Each part has special powers granted to it by the Constitution. One branch of the federal government is the executive branch. The executive branch includes the President, Vice-President, and the President's assistants, or his Cabinet. Another branch is the judicial branch, which is made up of the courts and the judges. The third branch is the legislative branch, which is Congress.

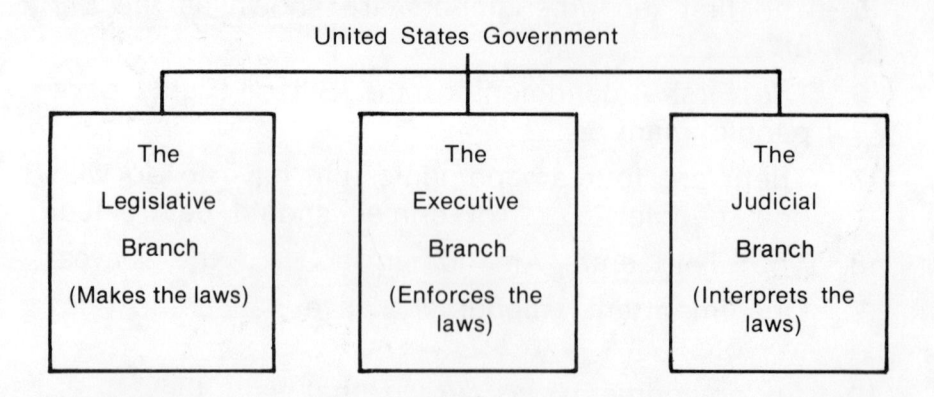

United States Government

The Legislative Branch (Makes the laws)	The Executive Branch (Enforces the laws)	The Judicial Branch (Interprets the laws)

In this chapter you will find out how Congress is organized, what the powers of Congress are, and how Congress does its work.

4.2 THE LEGISLATIVE BRANCH

Words to Know:

Federal government — The national government that has certain powers to run the whole country.

Washington, D.C. — The capital city of the United States, located between Maryland and Virginia. The federal government carries on its work from Washington, D.C.

Legislative branch — The branch of the federal government that has the power to propose new laws that are needed for the whole country.

Executive branch — The branch of the federal government that is in charge of carrying out the laws.

Judicial branch — The branch of the federal government that reviews laws and makes decisions about the laws.

District of Columbia — An area of land given by Maryland and Virginia for our nation's capital.

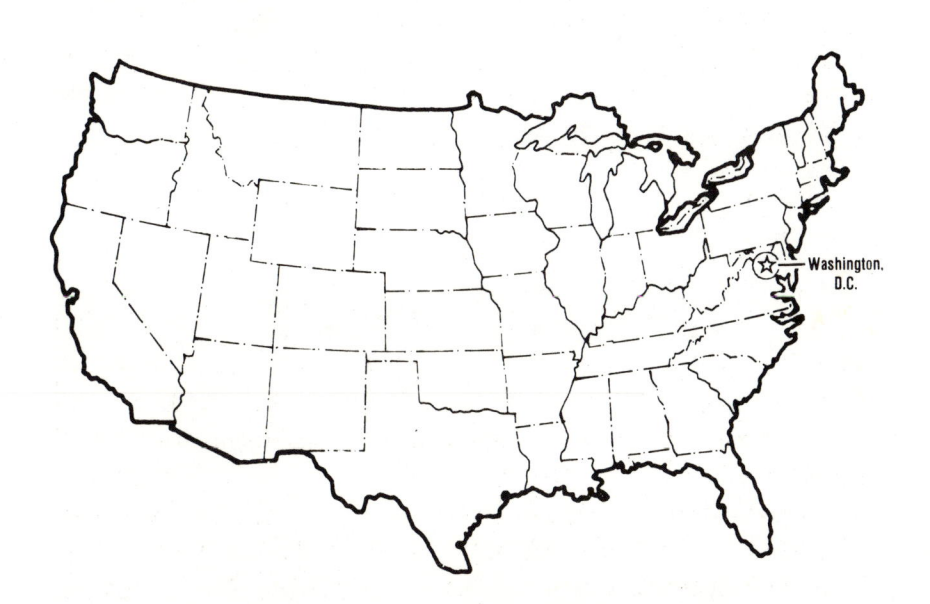

Washington, D.C. is located between the states of Maryland and Virginia.

Where the Legislative Branch Works

Most of the people who run the federal government meet and work in the capital city, Washington, D.C. The letters *D.C.* stand for the words *District of Columbia*. Washington, D.C. is located between the states of Maryland and Virginia. The work of the legislative branch is carried on, for the most part, in the United States Capitol Building.

★*Activity 1.* Number your paper from 1 to 7. Next to each number, write the word that completes the sentence. Use words from the box below.

1. The _____ branch of the federal government includes the President and Vice-President.

2. The legislative branch of the federal government has the power to make _____.

3. Another name for the federal government is the _____ government.

4. The courts and judges are part of the _____ branch of the federal government.

5. The men and women who are elected to run our federal government meet and work in _____.

6. The _____ was written by the citizens of the United States when it was a new country.

7. The work of the legislative branch is carried on in Washington, D.C. at the United States _____ Building.

Washington, D.C.	executive
national	laws
Constitution	judicial
Capitol	

4.3 HOW CONGRESS IS ORGANIZED

Words to Know:

Congress — Large group made up of men and women who are elected by the voters of their own states. They make laws that are needed for all the states. There are two parts of the Congress: the House of Representatives and the Senate.

House of Representatives — The larger of the two houses of Congress. The number of representatives from each state is based on the population of the state.

Representative — A person who is a member of the House of Representatives.

Represent — To act in place of others; to take care of the interests of other people.

Senate — The smaller of the two houses of Congress. There are one hundred members of the Senate. Each of the fifty states elects two senators.

Senator — A person who is a member of the Senate.

Majority — The greater part of anything; more than half.

Public official — A person who holds an office.

The Congress of the United States is divided into two parts: the House of Representatives and the Senate. The writers of the Constitution did not want one group of officials to become too strong, so they made two parts to the Congress. The men and women who work in these two houses of the Congress are elected by the voters in each state. Every new bill for our country must be passed by a majority of votes in both the Senate and the House of Representatives. In this way, both houses can carefully study each bill and make better decisions.

The Senate

The writers of the Constitution wanted to be sure that every state would be represented equally in the

Congress. Each of the fifty states elects two senators to serve in the Senate. Each state, no matter how large or how small its population, has the same number of votes in the Senate as any other state. There are one hundred senators serving in the Senate.

The Vice-President of the United States serves as the president of the Senate. The Vice-President does not take part in the debates. He votes only in case of a tie.

The House of Representatives

The House of Representatives is set up to reflect the size of each state's population. States that have more people living in them send more representatives to Congress than states that have fewer people. Each state is divided into districts that have about the same number of people, as nearly as is possible. Each district elects its own representative. In this way all citizens are represented equally, no matter what the size of their state's population. There are 435 representatives serving in the House of Representatives.

The leader of the House of Representatives is known as the Speaker of the House. The Speaker is one of the representatives who is elected by the majority party members to serve for two years. The Speaker has a strong position, and uses his power to run the House's business.

★**Activity 2.** Number your paper from 1 to 5. Write the answer to each question. The sum of your answers should equal 590.

1. How many states are in the United States?
2. How many senators are in the Senate?
3. How many branches of the federal government are there?

How Congress Is Organized — 73

4. How many representatives are serving in the House of Representatives?
5. How many parts does Congress have?

House   **Senate**

The U.S. Capitol Building in Washington, D.C.
This is where Congress makes the laws.

★**Activity 3.** Number your paper from 1 to 8. Next to each number write the word that is missing. Use answers from the box below.

The House of 1)_____ was set up by the Constitution so that all people, even those in heavily populated areas, would be represented fairly in Washington, D.C. The states are divided into 2)_____ according to population. Each district elects one representative. There are 3)_____ representatives in all. The leader of the House of Representatives is called the 4)_____ of the House. Each state elects two 5)_____. There are 6)_____ senators serving in the 7)_____. The leader of the Senate is the 8)_____. He does not take part in the debates.

| districts | 100 | Representatives | senators |
| Senate | 435 | Vice-President | Speaker |

4.4 WHO CAN BE A MEMBER OF CONGRESS?

Words to Know:

Citizen — A person given certain rights, duties, and privileges because he or she was born in, or chooses to live in, a city, state, or country.

Legal — Allowed by law.

Serve — To spend a period of time carrying out a duty.

Term — A period of time for carrying out a duty.

Requirement — Something that is needed to do other things.

Qualify — To meet the requirements for doing a job or task.

Requirements for Representatives

A member of the House of Representatives serves only a two-year term. All of the members of the House are elected in a national election held in November of each even-numbered year. A representative must be at least twenty-five years old. He or she must have been a citizen of the United States for at least seven years. The representative must also be a legal resident of the state he or she represents. He or she is also expected to live in the district he or she represents.

Requirements for Senators

A senator serves a six-year term. Only one-third of the Senate membership are elected at any one time. To run for the Senate, a candidate must be at least thirty years old. He or she must have been a United States citizen for at least nine years. He or she must be a resident of the state he or she represents.

★**Activity 4.** Number your paper from 1 to 5. If the statement is about a representative, write *Representative*. Write *Senator* if the statement is about a senator.

1. Mr. Jacks is twenty-eight years old. He has been serving the voters of his district for one year.

2. Mr. Todd has been working in Congress for four years. He ran for re-election two years ago when his first term ended.

3. Mrs. Ellis is fifty. She is a member of the smaller house of Congress. There is one other person from her state who serves with her.

4. Ms. Lee is from the large state of California. There are more than forty people from her state serving in the same part of Congress with her.

5. John Smith has worked in his part of Congress for six years. He has to run for re-election for the first time this November.

4.5 HOW CONGRESS CARRIES ON ITS WORK

Words to Know:

Session — The period of time each year when Congress works.

Bill — A proposed new law.

Permanent — Lasting a long time.

Adjourn — To bring a meeting to an end.

Introduce — To bring into use; to make known.

Consider — To examine or to think over.

Veteran — A person who has served in the armed forces.

Reject — To refuse to accept or use.

Foreign — Belonging outside one's own country.

System — A set of rules; a way of doing things.

Political — Having to do with the affairs of government.

Encourage — To give courage, hope, or confidence to.

Seniority — Special place in a group because of longer service.

Congress Meets in January

The Senate and House of Representatives both begin their sessions in Washington, D.C. early in January of each year. The sessions last until the work is completed. Each year Congress takes longer and longer to finish its job. Sometimes Congress does not adjourn until late fall. Near the end of the sessions, the senators and representatives vote on a day to adjourn. If a serious problem comes up after Congress has adjourned, the President may ask Congress to come back and hold a special session. Such a special session would last until the problem was solved.

Congress's Duties

The most important duty of Congress is to make laws. It has other powers or duties given to it by the Constitution. Congress may suggest amendments to the Constitution. The process, however, is not an easy one. The final decision rests with the consent of the states. Congress can investigate or check on the other two branches of the federal government. This investigation may take place if one of the departments of the government is thought to be doing something wrong. Taxes, the armed forces, trade, and certain crimes are some of the other things taken care of by our Congress.

Floor Leaders

In order for the Senate and House to do their work well, they must have good leaders. Floor leaders are chosen during the early part of the sessions. These floor leaders are very important because they tell other senators and representatives about the new bills that will be voted on. They also encourage the other members to take part in the voting. They work closely with the Speaker of the House and the president of the Senate to manage debates and committee business.

The Work of Congress — 77

Bills Are Plans for New Laws

During every session of Congress, the members study a great number of bills. A bill is an idea for a new law or a change in an old law. The idea can come from a citizen who writes a senator or a representative with the suggestion. An idea can come from special groups, such as businessmen, veterans, or parents' groups. The President of the United States can also suggest ideas for bills. Senators and representatives themselves can suggest ideas for new laws.

Bills Are Numbered

A new bill can be introduced in either the Senate or the House. It is carefully typed, and each line is numbered. In this way every part of the bill is easy to find if it needs to be changed. The whole bill is also given a number and letters. For example, H.R. 505 means that the bill was introduced in the House of Representatives and that it is the five hundred fifth bill to be studied during that session.

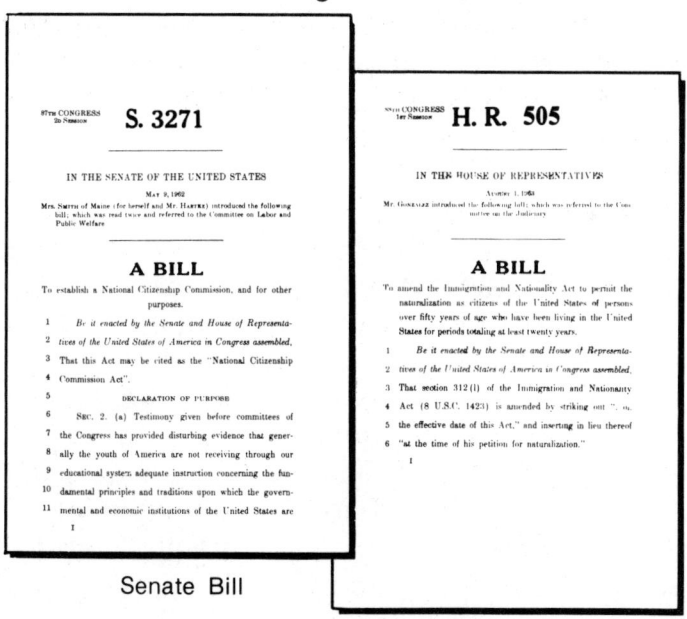

Senate Bill

House Bill

Work Is Done in Committees

Thousands of bills have to be studied and considered by Congress each year. It would not be possible for all of the members to look at all these bills. Therefore, the work of studying the bills is turned over to many smaller groups, or committees. Committees decide which bills are important enough to send to the House or Senate for all members to consider. Many bills are rejected by committees and never given further consideration.

Each part of Congress has a number of permanent committees called *standing committees*. Each considers a specific topic, such as how we get along with foreign governments. Another committee takes care of the needs of the armed services. Another decides how to raise money for running the federal government. This committee is called the Ways and Means Committee.

There are also special committees which are formed just for certain purposes and then dismissed. A few committees are made up of members from both the Senate and the House of Representatives. These are called *joint committees*.

All Members of Congress Serve on Committees

Each senator and representative must serve on at least one standing committee. He or she is asked to serve on a committee by special groups from political parties. Members of Congress always hope to be put on important committees, such as the Foreign Affairs, Ways and Means, and Armed Services. Some members serve on two or three committees. The longer a member serves on a committee, the more likely he or she is to become its leader, or chairperson. This practice was called the seniority system. Even though changes in this system were made in the 1970's, seniority is still very important.

★**Activity 5.** Number your paper from 1 to 9. Choose the correct ending for each sentence from the two endings given. Write the letter you choose next to each number.

1. During every session of Congress (a) thousands of bills are studied, (b) about ten bills are studied.

2. A bill is (a) an idea for a new law, (b) a list of charges from a special group.

3. The idea for a bill (a) can come from a citizen, groups, or members of Congress, (b) cannot come from members of Congress.

4. Each member of Congress (a) decides whether or not to serve on a committee, (b) must serve on at least one standing committee.

5. Committees of senators or representatives who study the bills (a) can never change anything in a bill, (b) may amend a bill, if necessary.

6. Committees decide if the bills are important enough to send to (a) the President, b) other members of the Senate or House.

7. Standing committees (a) study bills about matters like the armed services and taxes, (b) make bills into law.

8. The chairperson of a committee is usually (a) the oldest member of the committee, (b) the member who has served the longest on the committee.

9. Senators and representatives are asked to serve on committees (a) by groups from political parties, (b) by the committee chairperson.

4.6 HOW A BILL BECOMES LAW

Words to Know:

Express — To put an idea into words.

Congressional Record — A list of all business carried on by Congress. It is published four times a year (quarterly).

Debate — A discussion or argument.

Pigeonhole — To put a bill aside to be studied at a later date.

House calendar — The dates set for introducing different bills, as decided upon by the representatives.

Veto — The power of the President to reject a bill sent to him by Congress.

Two-thirds majority — Two-thirds of the members of the Senate or the House.

State of the Union Message — A speech given by the President yearly before both parts of Congress.

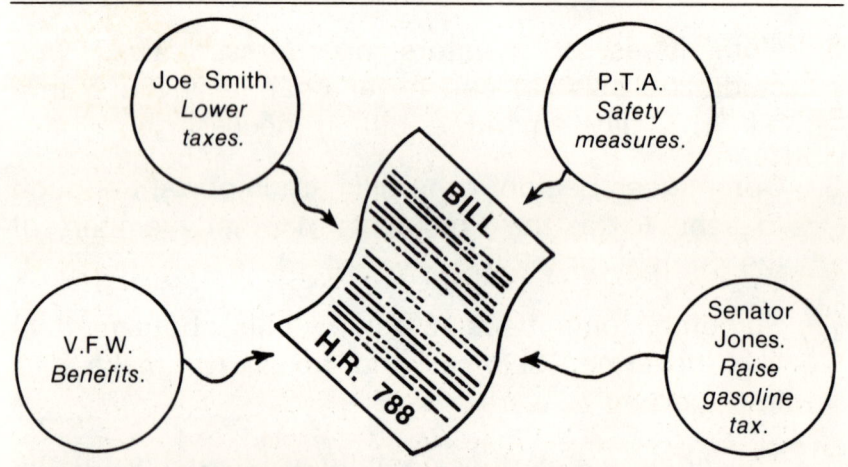

A Bill Is Introduced

Anyone may suggest the idea for a new law to a member of the House of Representatives or Senate. Members of Congress may give ideas for new bills. The President often expresses to Congress his feelings about the need for new laws in his State of the Union Message. This speech is given at the start of each new session of Congress in January.

If an idea for a new bill begins in the House of Representatives, a representative writes out a proposed bill and gives it to the Clerk of the House. The Clerk assigns it a number and reads the title to the members. The title is printed in the *Congressional Record*. This action is called the *first reading*. The Clerk sends the bill to be printed so that all members and interested persons may have copies. The bill is then sent by the Speaker of the House to the proper standing committee for study. The committee may change it if necessary, or put it aside for awhile (pigeonhole it). If the committee likes the bill, it will approve it and send it back to the House with a good report. The bill is given a date when it will be acted on and then put on the House calendar. On that date, the bill is given the second of three readings.

Action on a Bill

A bill may begin either in the House or in the Senate. It goes to a committee, and then to the entire House or Senate to be discussed and debated. The members of Congress can change the bill, send it back to the committee for more changes, or pass it. A bill must be read for the third time before the final vote takes place. It is passed by either part of Congress when a majority of its members vote in favor of it.

The bill is then sent to the other house of Congress and given a number. The same procedures are followed as in the first house.

The Difference Between Senate and House Action

A new bill follows the same steps to become a law, whether it starts in the House or in the Senate. There is a difference, however, in the amount of time allowed for debate. House debate is limited, but senators may debate as long as they wish. A senator can delay voting on a bill by talking on and on, sometimes for many hours. This way of putting off a vote is called *filibustering*.

A senator may filibuster for a long time.

Conference Committee

Sometimes a special conference committee, made up of members from both houses, is asked to work on a bill. After the conference committee irons out their differences, and both houses pass the bill, it is sent to the President.

The President Acts

When a bill reaches the President's desk, he has several choices.

1. He can accept and sign the bill. This makes the bill a law.
2. He can do nothing. He can simply let the bill become a law without signing it. The bill automatically becomes a law after ten working days, if Congress is still in session.
3. He can reject the bill and refuse to sign it. This is called a *veto*. If the president vetoes a bill, it can still become a law if it is voted on by a two-thirds majority of the members of both houses of Congress.

How a Bill Becomes Law

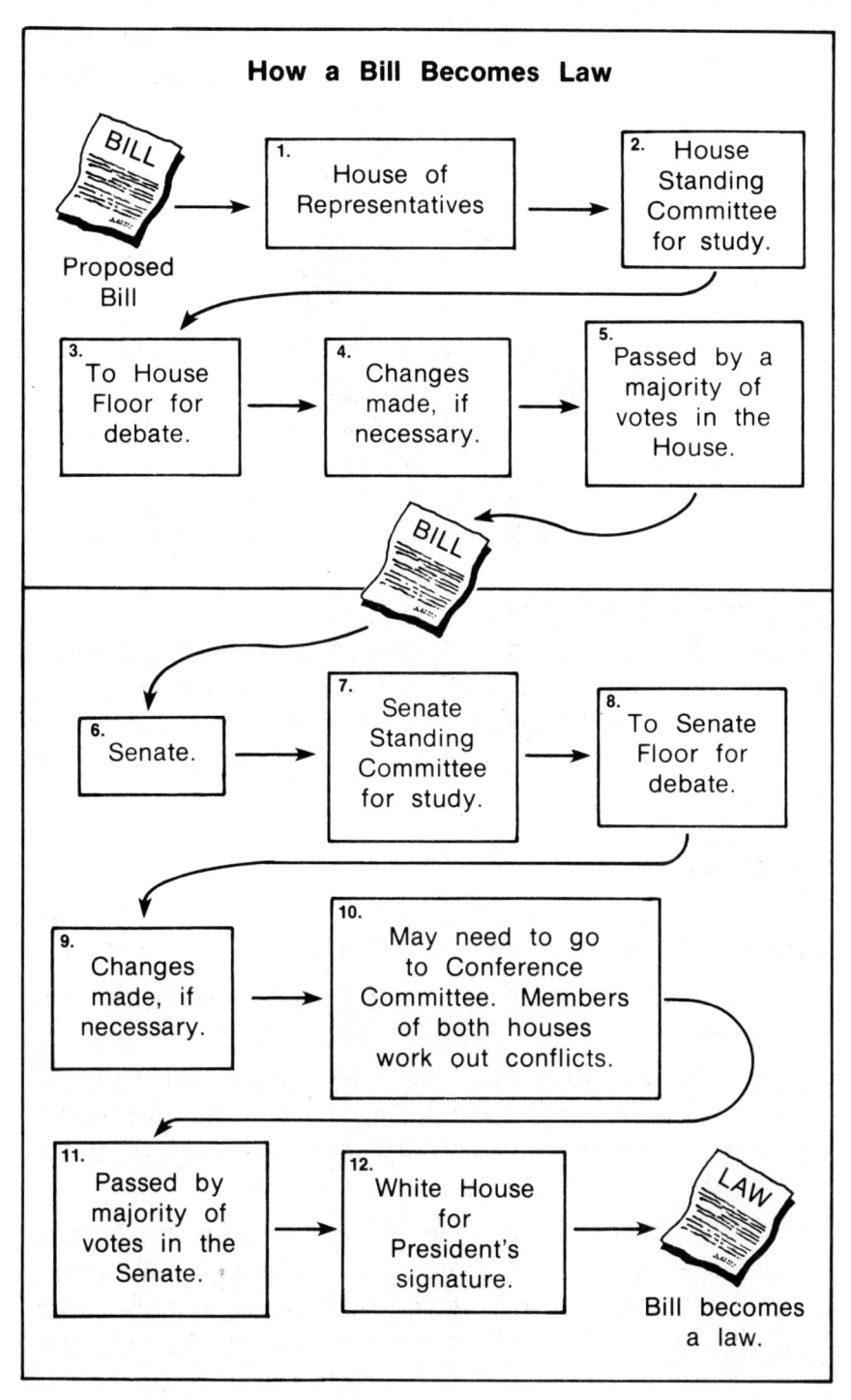

Proposed Bill → 1. House of Representatives → 2. House Standing Committee for study.

3. To House Floor for debate. → 4. Changes made, if necessary. → 5. Passed by a majority of votes in the House.

6. Senate. → 7. Senate Standing Committee for study. → 8. To Senate Floor for debate.

9. Changes made, if necessary. → 10. May need to go to Conference Committee. Members of both houses work out conflicts.

11. Passed by majority of votes in the Senate. → 12. White House for President's signature. → Bill becomes a law.

84 — How a Bill Becomes Law

★*Activity 6.* Every bill must follow certain steps through the House and the Senate. These steps are given below in the wrong order. On your paper write the steps in the correct order.

In the House of Representatives:
- The bill is printed and copies are sent to a standing committee.
- A suggested bill is numbered and approved for study.
- A standing committee studies and acts on the bill.
- The bill is passed and sent to the Senate.

In the Senate:
- The bill goes to the President for consideration.
- A standing committee studies and acts on the bill.
- The bill is given to a standing committee to be studied.
- The bill is voted on and passed by the Senate.

4.7 POWERS OF CONGRESS

Words to Know:
Power — Ability to take action; the right to decide.
Limit — Something that restricts or forbids.
Admit — To allow or permit to enter.
Elastic — Able to change; flexible.
Defend — To protect from attack or harm.
Nobility — A social class of people known for rank, wealth, or power.

Article I, Section 8 of the Constitution lists the powers of Congress. Some of those powers are described on page 85.

1. Congress can raise and collect taxes. The federal government needs a great deal of money to carry on its work. Government employees must be paid. Government property must be taken care of. The government also has programs that care for the poor, old, sick, and handicapped.

2. Congress watches over trade and business. Congress passes laws to protect business and customers. Congress runs the system of national highways. These roads help businesses in our country move their products across the whole nation.

3. Congress defends the nation against enemies. It can declare war. It has set up our army and navy.

4. Congress may set standards of weights and measures.

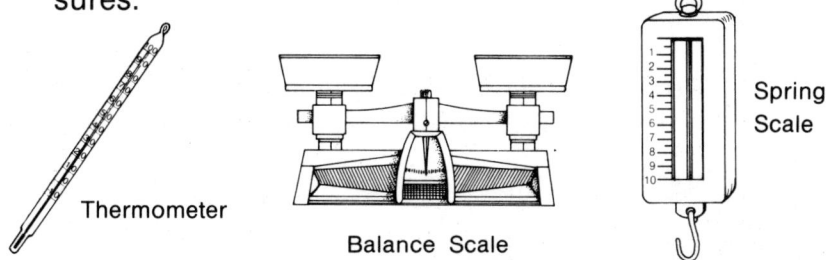

Thermometer

Balance Scale

Spring Scale

5. Congress passes laws to tell people from other countries how they may become citizens. Congress decides how new states are admitted to the United States.

★*Activity 7.* Copy the words below on your paper. Next to each word write the number of the item above that tells about that power of Congress.

a. war
b. taxes
c. new states
d. citizens

e. customers
f. weights
g. roads
h. army

i. navy
j. trade

Powers of Congress

★**Activity 8.** Number your paper from 1 to 10. Choose the best word to complete each sentence. Write the word next to the number on your paper.

1. The _____ is a set of rules and laws that has granted Congress its powers. (Amendment, Constitution, capital)

2. The federal government needs a great deal of money to operate our capital, _____. (Congress, Washington, D.C., District)

3. Congress can raise and collect _____ to pay the employees of the federal government. (roads, taxes, programs)

4. The government has special _____ that care for the sick, poor, and handicapped. (needs, crimes, programs)

5. Congress may set the standards for weights and _____. (temperatures, measures, heights)

6. Through its power, Congress has set up the army and navy to _____ our country. (collect, defend, declare)

7. Congress set up a system of national highways through the _____ given to it by the Constitution. (place, power, nation)

8. Congress has the power to _____ war. (weigh, declare, raise)

9. People from other countries may want to become _____ of the United States. (citizens, Congress, nobility)

10. _____ can decide how new states are admitted to our country. (Washington, D.C., Congress, Capital)

Limits on the Congress

The writers of the Constitution restricted the power of Congress. For example, Congress might pass a bill and it is signed into law. Then, if the Supreme Court says that the law goes against the Constitution, the law is taken away.

Congress cannot make laws about such things as elections, education, or marriage. The Constitution gave the states the power to control those things.

Congress cannot make laws that take away the rights of citizens. These rights were granted by the Bill of Rights. The Bill of Rights is made up of the first ten amendments to the Constitution. The Bill of Rights guarantees to citizens the basic rights, such as freedom of religion, freedom of speech, and freedom of the press.

Congress cannot take money from the federal government without passing a law to do so. It cannot grant titles of nobility (king, queen, prince) because the American people believe that "all men were created equal."

The "Elastic Clause" of the Constitution Stretches the Power of Congress

The writers of the Constitution knew that problems would come up that were not mentioned in the Constitution. Therefore, the Constitution has an "elastic clause." The last part of Article 1, Section 8 tells Congress that it can make all laws necessary for carrying out its duties. For example, Congress was given the power to set up an army and navy to protect the citizens. After a few years, Congress saw that in order to have the best army and navy, we would need military colleges to train officers for services. Congress passed a law that gave money to set up and run military colleges. Two of the best known are the U.S.

Military Academy at West Point, New York, and the U.S. Naval Academy at Annapolis, Maryland. These are examples of how Congress used the "elastic clause" of the Constitution to stretch its power.

★*Activity 9.* Number your paper from 1 to 7. Answer the questions below. Write *Yes* or *No* next to each number.

1. Does the "elastic clause" tell Congress it can make any laws necessary for carrying out its duties?
2. Does Congress have the power to set up an army and a navy?
3. Does the Constitution put limits on Congress?
4. Can Congress make laws about marriage?
5. Can Congress give a person the title of "King" or "Queen"?
6. Can the Supreme Court decide whether a law passed by Congress is constitutional or not?
7. Can Congress get money from the government by just asking for it?

SUMMARY OF CHAPTER 4

In this chapter you learned that the *legislative branch* is one of the three branches of the federal, or national, government. The other two branches are the *executive* and the *judicial*.

The main job of the legislative branch is to propose legislation that affects all of the states, and the country as a whole. Each state in the United States can also make certain laws for itself. The Constitution has given the legislative branch the power to make laws.

The lawmaking body of the legislative branch is called the Congress. Congress is divided into two separate parts: the Senate and the House of Representatives. The people of this country elect the men and women who work in the Senate and the House. The citizens of each state elect their own senators and representatives, who represent them in Congress.

Every January, all of the senators and representatives go to Washington, D.C. to begin their work. Leaders, such as the Speaker of the House, are chosen for each part of Congress. In order to carry out their tasks, the senators and representatives work in committees. The committees study all of the new bills that are given to them. Usually changes are made in the bills before they are voted on. After one part of the Congress passes a bill, it must be passed by the other part of Congress. Then the President must consider it. If the President signs the bill, then it becomes a law for our country.

Congress is an important group of people. The Constitution granted Congress special powers. Some of these powers include collecting taxes, taking care of trade, and providing for defense.

The writers of the Constitution did not want Congress to become too powerful. Therefore, they limited the powers of Congress. Congress cannot do the following: pass laws that take away individual rights given by the Bill of Rights, interfere with state laws, or take money from the government without passing a law.

To make sure that Congress had the power to do everything needed to carry out its duties, an "elastic clause" was included in the Constitution. This gives Congress the power to take action as times change, even if this power is not written in the Constitution. However, this action cannot take away states' rights, or a person's rights.

• CHAPTER REVIEW ACTIVITY •

In the box are ten words from the chapter. Use them to complete the paragraph below about the legislative branch. Number your paper from 1 to 10. Write the correct word next to each number.

vote	elected	considered
reject	veto	introduced
population	majority	committee
session		

The number of representatives from each state is determined by the size of the state's 1)_____. There are two senators from each state. Senators and representatives are 2)_____ by voters in their own states. These congress-members meet in January each year to begin a 3)_____. Each senator and representative must serve on at least one 4)_____ during a session. Thousands of new bills are 5)_____ in Congress each year. After a bill is 6)_____ by a committee, two things may happen to it. The committee can 7)_____ the bill. They will do this if they find the bill of little use. The committee can accept the bill and give it to the whole Senate or House to consider and 8)_____ on. If a 9)_____ of the members vote in favor of the bill, the bill is sent to the other house of Congress to be considered. The bill must be passed by both houses of Congress before it can go to the President. The President may accept or 10)_____ the bill. A bill that is vetoed goes back to Congress for more discussion. Congress may vote to override the veto, and the bill becomes law. If not, the bill is set aside and rejected.

Chapter **5**

The Executive Branch

5.1 WHAT IS THE EXECUTIVE BRANCH?

The executive branch is one of the three departments of the federal government. The executive branch carries out, or enforces, the laws made by the legislative branch. The President is in charge of the executive branch.

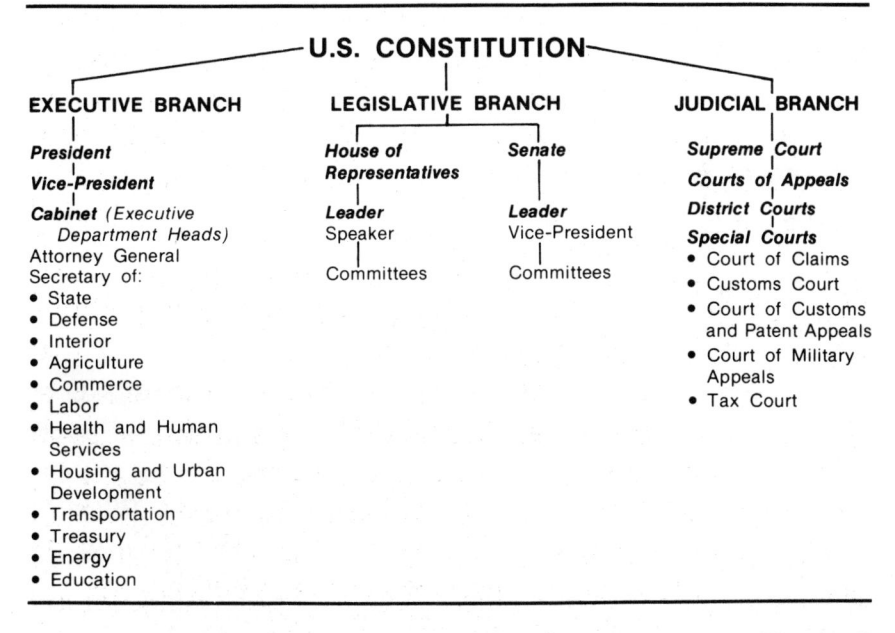

U.S. CONSTITUTION

EXECUTIVE BRANCH

President
Vice-President
Cabinet (*Executive Department Heads*)
Attorney General
Secretary of:
- State
- Defense
- Interior
- Agriculture
- Commerce
- Labor
- Health and Human Services
- Housing and Urban Development
- Transportation
- Treasury
- Energy
- Education

LEGISLATIVE BRANCH

House of Representatives *Senate*

Leader *Leader*
Speaker Vice-President

Committees Committees

JUDICIAL BRANCH

Supreme Court
Courts of Appeals
District Courts
Special Courts
- Court of Claims
- Customs Court
- Court of Customs and Patent Appeals
- Court of Military Appeals
- Tax Court

In this chapter, you will learn about the office of the presidency and how it works as part of the executive branch.

91

5.2 THE PRESIDENT IS THE LEADER OF THE EXECUTIVE BRANCH

Words to Know:

Responsible — Can be depended upon; able to answer for the actions of a department or agency.

Adviser — A person who gives information, advice, or help.

Staff — A group of people who advise or assist a chief officer or executive.

Agency — A division within the executive branch that serves a special purpose.

The President of the United States is not only the leader of the nation, but is also the leader of the executive branch. He is sometimes called "the Chief Executive." His job is difficult because he is responsible for everything that is done by the different groups who work in this branch of the government.

The President needs many assistants in the executive branch to help him carry out the laws. His main helper is the Vice-President. The Vice-President becomes President if for any reason the President cannot carry out his duties. The President also has a staff of advisers that he depends upon. These advisers do everything from answering the mail to planning the President's busy schedule.

There are many departments and agencies within the executive branch. The men and women in these special groups carry out the day-to-day work. The President has to know what goes on in all his departments and agencies. He has the final responsibility for all that happens in the executive branch.

**Departments and Agencies
of the Executive Branch**

The President

Executive Office
Office of Management and Budget
National Security Council
Council on Economic Policy
Council of Economic Advisers
White House Office
Community Services Administration
Special Action Office for Drug Abuse Prevention
Energy Resources Council
Council on Wage and Price Stability
   (and many others)

Cabinet
Department of State (1789)
Department of the Treasury (1789)
Department of Defense (1789)
Department of Justice (1870)
Department of the Interior (1849)
Department of Agriculture (1862)
Department of Labor (1913)
Department of Commerce (1903)
Department of Housing and Urban Development (1965)
Department of Transportation (1966)
Department of Energy (1977)
Department of Health and Human Services (1979)
Department of Education (1979)

Agencies and Commissions
Federal Reserve System
Federal Communications Commission
Federal Trade Commission
Interstate Commerce Commission
United States Information Agency
Environmental Protection Agency
Veterans Administration
   (and many others)

★**Activity 1.** Number your paper from 1 to 8. Next to each number, write the word or words that complete the sentence. Use words from the box below.

1. The part of the federal government that carries out the laws of the nation is the _____ _____.
2. The Vice-President is the President's main _____.
3. The _____ is in charge of all parts of the executive branch.
4. The President is sometimes called the _____ _____.
5. The Vice-President is _____ by the voters of the United States.
6. The _____ becomes President if for any reason the President cannot carry out his duties.
7. The President has a staff of _____ to help him with with his busy _____.
8. There are many _____ and _____ to carry out the work of the executive branch.

assistant	executive branch	agencies
President	Chief Executive	schedule
elected	Vice-President	
departments	advisers	

The White House, Home of the President

5.3 THE PROCESS WE USE TO ELECT A PRESIDENT

Words to Know:

Elector — A person chosen by a political party to vote for the President and Vice-President.

Electoral College — Name of the group of electors from all the states.

Qualification — A skill or quality; a condition that must be met to fill a job or position.

Election — The process of electing or choosing a person by voting.

Vacant — Empty; not occupied by an individual.

Resign — To give up an office or position; to quit one's office.

Select — To choose carefully.

Definite — Certain, exact, or without doubt.

Modern — Up-to-date; related to the present.

Candidate — A person who hopes to be elected to an office, such as the presidency.

With just a few words, the writers of the Constitution set up the powerful office of President. Article II of the Constitution begins:

Section 1. **(1) The executive power shall be vested in a President of the United States.**

The Constitution goes on to explain, in more detail, the full power of the President. Throughout the years much has been added to Article II to make the duties of the President more definite.

Qualifications of a President

The Constitution says that a candidate for President must have certain qualifications. They are:
1. He or she must be a native-born American citizen.
2. He or she must be at least 35 years of age.
3. He or she must have been a resident of the United States for at least 14 years.

We Elect Our President Every Four Years

Every four years on the Tuesday following the first Monday in November, the people of the United States vote for the President and Vice-President. This day is called Election Day. After campaigns that last many months, it is then time for the people to vote for their choices. Each person is guaranteed the right to vote in secret. This is done in the privacy of a voting booth.

Article II and the Twelfth Amendment describe how the President and Vice-President are to be elected. Votes for the President and Vice-President are really votes for electors. Each state has the same number of electors as it has Senators and Representatives. They are selected by political parties, each of which names candidates. As a group these electors are called the Electoral College. A count of votes on or shortly after the election day shows who will be President and Vice-President. However, the Electoral College must meet in January and make the election official by voting for the candidates they have promised to support.

A President May Not Be Elected to More Than Two Terms of Office

The limit of two terms of office was set by the Twenty-second Amendment to the Constitution. Before this was passed, Franklin Roosevelt had been elected

Electing a President — 97

four times, starting in 1932. This was the main reason a limit was put on the number of times a person could run for President. George Washington, our first President, had the chance to run for a third term. He refused because he believed changing the presidency was for the good of the country. He believed new ideas would keep the country strong.

★*Activity 2.* Number your paper from 1 to 5. Write the answer to each question. The sum of your answers should equal 77.

1. At least how old must a candidate for President be?
2. For at least how long must a candidate for President have been a resident of the United States?
3. For how many terms may a President be elected to office?
4. What is the number of the Amendment that tells about the number of terms of office for a President?
5. How many terms was Franklin Roosevelt elected to office?

★*Activity 3.* Number your paper from 1 to 6. Write the word that completes each sentence.

1. The voters of the United States elect a President and Vice-President every _____ years.
2. The Constitution, in Article _____, set up the office of the President.
3. Election Day is in the month of _____.
4. We elect a President according to the rules stated in the _____ and in the Twelfth Amendment.
5. People are guaranteed the _____ to vote in secret.
6. Votes for the President and Vice-President are really votes for the _____ from each state.

5.4 THE DUTIES OF THE PRESIDENT

Words to Know:

Commander — A person who has full control of a group.

Ambassador — A person appointed by the President to represent the United States in a foreign country.

Budget — A plan that lists the amount of money to be taken in and the ways the money is to be spent.

Military — Having to do with war or the armed forces.

Legislator — A person who makes or passes laws.

Representative — One who is given the power to act for others.

Scandal — Anything that leads to shame or brings dishonor upon someone.

Accused — Blamed; charged with an offense or crime.

Commander in Chief

As the leader of the executive branch of the government, the President may send armed forces anywhere in the world. For this reason, he is known as the Commander in Chief of the armed forces. He does not actually lead American forces into battle. However, he stays in close touch with the military leaders.

Chief Diplomat

The President is also our chief diplomat. He is responsible for the way our nation treats other nations in the world. He tries to keep our country on friendly terms with other countries. The President appoints ambassadors to represent the United States in foreign countries. He also welcomes foreign representatives when they visit the United States. Many Presidents have traveled around the world to speak to important leaders. They have done this to develop better understanding with the leaders of foreign countries.

Chief Legislator

The President is our chief legislator, even though he is not a member of Congress. All bills passed by the Congress must be sent to the President for him to act on. He can also suggest new laws to Congress. Once each year he makes an important speech to both parts of the Congress. This is called the "State of the Union Message." In this talk, he tells Congress and the whole nation about the condition of the country. He points out what he believes the country will need in the following year. He tells how the government is planning to make any important changes.

The President must also prepare a budget for the nation each year. This budget goes before Congress. The members of Congress study it carefully. If they approve it, the President may use this budget in carrying out his plans for running the government.

United States Budget — Sources of Receipts

Individual Income Taxes
Corporation Income Taxes
Social Insurance Taxes and Contributions
Excise Taxes
Estate and Gift Taxes
Customs Duties
Deposits of Earnings — Federal Reserve Banks

Political Leader

When the voters elect a President, they also choose a plan for running the government. This plan is made up by the President's political party. For this reason, we may call the President the chief of the party. The President is expected to follow these plans of his party. He tries to get Congress to put his party's plans into action. The President can use his power to appoint people to jobs important to running the nation. He usually chooses these people from his own political party.

World Leader

Smaller nations of the world look to the leaders of powerful nations for help and guidance. This makes our President a world leader. What he does is followed and studied by people of other countries and by their leaders. In his role as a world leader, the President must act in the interest of peace. By keeping the United States at peace with other countries, he sets an example for foreign leaders. It was President Franklin Roosevelt who was a leader in planning the United Nations. President Carter acted as a peacemaker when Israel and Egypt were having trouble in 1978. He brought the leaders of these two nations together to discuss a peace plan.

Power to Grant Pardons

A pardon is a legal order given by the President. If a person is guilty of breaking a federal law, the President can pardon that person. This is done only in special instances. Then the person will not be punished for the crime. Persons breaking state laws cannot receive a pardon from the President. A pardon is usually granted after the person has been found guilty in court. But the President may pardon a person before the person is tried in court. This happened in 1974 when President Gerald Ford granted a full pardon to ex-President Richard Nixon. Nixon had resigned when he was about to be tried. Gerald Ford, the Vice-President, became President. Nixon had been involved in a scandal called "Watergate," and had been accused of breaking the law. He was never tried because he resigned first. When Ford became President, he granted Nixon a full pardon. This meant he could not later be tried for the same crime.

★*Activity 4.* Number your paper from 1 to 7. Choose the best word for each sentence. Write your answers.

1. The President is the leader of his _____ party. (political Constitution annual)
2. The President tries to get the _____ to put his plan into action. (Congress courts Vice-President)
3. The President is the leader of one of the most _____ nations in the world. (undeveloped powerful lawless)
4. The President can _____ people in his political party to jobs. (elect appoint force)
5. Because the President is head of a strong country, other countries follow what he does. This makes him a _____ leader. (limited weak world)
6. The President uses his power to try to keep _____ in the world. (peace power war)
7. The President can _____ a person guilty of breaking a federal law. (accuse pardon represent)

5.5 THE OFFICE OF PRESIDENT MAY BECOME VACANT

There are several reasons why the office of President may become vacant. This has happened at least six times since 1900. President McKinley was shot, and he died in 1901. President Woodrow Wilson was disabled by a stroke in 1919. Presidents Harding and Franklin Roosevelt died while in office. John F. Kennedy was assassinated in 1963. In 1974, Richard Nixon resigned. He has been the only President to resign.

Amendment Twenty-five of the Constitution provides for filling a vacancy in the office of President or Vice-President.

102 — The Presidency

> ***Section 1.*** **In case of the removal of the President from office or of his death or resignation, the Vice-President shall become President.**
>
> ***Section 4.*** **Whenever there is a vacancy in the office of the Vice-President, the President shall nominate a Vice-President who shall take office upon confirmation by a majority of both houses of Congress.**

The Vice-President resigned in 1973. This was Spiro Agnew. The President at the time, Richard Nixon, named Gerald Ford as Vice-President. This action had to be approved by Congress. As it turned out, Ford himself became President when Richard Nixon resigned the office. Now the office of Vice-President was vacant again, and President Ford named Nelson Rockefeller as Vice-President. This happened in a short period of time. The country had two men in the two most powerful offices, and neither one had been elected by the people. This had never happened before in our history.

★***Activity 5.*** Write the sentences below on your paper. Fill in each blank with the correct word.

1. The office of President has become vacant at least _____ times since 1900.
2. Gerald Ford became President when _____ resigned.
3. _____ President has resigned his office.
4. If the office of President becomes _____, the Vice-President takes over.
5. When Ford and Rockefeller were President and Vice-President, it was the first time that the two offices were filled by men who had not been _____ by the voters.

5.6 PEOPLE WHO ADVISE THE PRESIDENT

Words to Know:

Cabinet — People who head the executive departments and who advise the President.

Security — Safety and protection.

Environment — Surroundings.

Economy — Manner of handling money and business.

Natural resources — Raw materials given to us by nature, such as coal, water, soil, minerals.

Labor — Work that produces goods or services.

Air pollution — Making the air dirty and unsafe.

The Members of the Cabinet

The President has a group of advisers called "the Cabinet." The Cabinet is made up of the heads of the thirteen executive departments. The Cabinet members are in charge of their special departments, and they also offer advice to the President. They are all called Secretaries except for the head of the Justice Department. He is called the Attorney General.

Members of the President's Cabinet

Secretary of State
Secretary of the Treasury
Attorney General
Secretary of the Interior
Secretary of Agriculture
Secretary of Commerce
Secretary of Defense
Secretary of Energy
Secretary of Education
Secretary of Transportation
Secretary of Housing and Urban Development
Secretary of Health and Human Services
Secretary of Labor

The President appoints the Secretaries and the Attorney General. Special qualifications are carefully considered for each job. The Secretary of Agriculture, for example, is usually a farmer or has a background in agriculture. The Secretary of the Treasury should have financial experience. The Secretary of Housing and Urban Development almost always has experience in "big-city" matters.

The Cabinet meets with the President whenever the President decides it is necessary. The meetings usually take place once a week. Reports are made by the Secretaries about important happenings within their departments. Advice is offered to the President at these meetings. Also present at the meetings are the Vice-President and the heads of some of the agencies of the Executive Office. The meetings are closed to the press and the public.

The Executive Office

The President is assisted by a large group of individuals and agencies called the Executive Office of the President. These people work in offices in the White House and in nearby buildings.

The White House Office. The people closest to the President are in the White House Office. These special assistants advise the President about such important things as foreign affairs, defense, money matters, and the business of Congress. There is a press secretary whose job it is to give all of the White House news to the press. There is an assistant who writes the President's speeches. The President also has a personal doctor.

The National Security Council. The National Security Council keeps the President informed about security, or safety, matters in our country. The very secret Central Intelligence Agency works under this council. Its job is to gather information that has to do with our country's security. Agents of the CIA work in all parts of the world and report their findings to the National Security Council.

The Office of Management and Budget. The Office of Management and Budget (OMB) is in charge of preparing the federal budget. This budget is prepared yearly and lists all the money that is expected and the ways it will be spent by the government. When the budget is ready, the President presents it to the Congress for approval. In addition to writing the budget, the OMB studies how the executive branch is run. It makes suggestions for improvements and changes to the President.

Council of Economic Advisers. There are several other agencies within the Executive Office that keep the President informed and advised about important matters. The President needs information about the nation's economy. He gets it from the Council of Economic Advisers. This small group reports to the President about money matters and also suggests needed programs. The President uses this information in his work and in his reports to Congress and to the American people about our economy.

Council of Environmental Quality. The condition of the environment is of great importance to the President. Clean water, clean air, and careful use of natural resources are controlled by the government. This is done, in part, by the Council of Environmental Quality.

Other Groups. Several other councils inform the President about foreign trade and labor matters. He is also told about the latest developments in science.

Presidential Advisers

★**Activity 6.** Number your paper from 1 to 5. Choose the best word to complete each sentence. Write your answers.

1. The head of the Department of _____ is called the Attorney General.
    (Labor   Justice   Interior)
2. The heads of all the other departments have the title _____.
    (President   Adviser   Secretary)
3. The heads of the executive departments make up the President's _____.
    (Cabinet   Council   Agency)
4. The Secretary of _____ usually has a background in farming.
    (Defense   Education   Agriculture)
5. The Cabinet members give advice to the _____.
    (environment   President   voters)

★**Activity 7.** Number your paper from 1 to 5. Match the name of each agency in the box with the work it does. Write the name of the agency next to the number.

> National Security Council
> White House Office
> Office of Management and Budget
> Council of Economic Advisers
> Council of Environmental Quality

1. Gives White House news to the press.
2. Gathers information having to do with security.
3. Aids the President in money matters.
4. Informs the President about air pollution.
5. Helps prepare the nation's budget.

SUMMARY OF CHAPTER 5

The executive branch of government carries out the laws made by the Congress. The President of the United States is in charge of the executive branch. He is responsible for everything that takes place in this part of government.

Every four years we elect a President. In order for a person to be a candidate for President, he or she must be at least thirty-five years of age, a native-born American citizen, and a resident of the United States for fourteen years. The Vice-President is next in line if the office of the President becomes vacant.

The presidency is the most powerful office in the land. In his job the President has to fill many roles. As leader of the executive branch, he is also Commander in Chief of the armed forces. He acts as chief diplomat by keeping our country on friendly terms with other nations. As chief legislator, he must respond to all the actions of Congress and make suggestions to the Congress. Because he is elected by the voters of his party, he becomes head of his political party. He tries to put his party's plans into action. He appoints people to fill jobs. Many of the people of the world look to the President for guidance. This makes him a world leader.

The President's Cabinet is a group of close advisers. They are the heads of the thirteen executive departments. They meet regularly with the President to keep him informed about matters within their department. The President appoints the heads of these departments.

Directly under the President is the Executive Office. Working within this group is the press secretary, a speech writer, and other assistants who help the President.

• CHAPTER REVIEW ACTIVITY •

In the box are ten words from the chapter. Use them to complete the paragraphs below about the President. Number your paper from 1 to 10. Write the correct word next to each number.

Vice-President	Cabinet	advisers
environment	Office	electors
responsible	budget	security
appointed		

The President holds the most powerful office in the country. He is 1) _____ for everything that happens in the executive branch of government. If the office of President becomes vacant, the 2) _____ takes over. The President is elected every four years. He is really elected by 3) _____ who are chosen from each state.

The President has many 4) _____ who assist him in carrying out his duties. The heads of the executive departments are known as the President's 5) _____. The Cabinet members are 6) _____ by the President. They meet about once a week to advise and inform the President about matters within their departments. The closest advisers to the President are the members of the Executive 7) _____ of the President. Some of the matters taken care of by this group have to do with the nation's safety, or 8) _____. Another agency within this office helps the President prepare a plan for taking in and spending money. This plan is called a 9) _____. Another agency informs the President about the conditions of the nation's 10) _____, including water, air, and land.

Chapter 6

Departments of the Executive Branch

6.1 THE FIRST DEPARTMENTS

George Washington, our country's first chief executive, did not have all of the assistants that a President now has. The Constitution said that the President should ask for and have the help he needed. Congress provided three departments to meet Washington's needs: State, War, and Treasury. There was also an Attorney General to help with matters concerning the law.

George Washington, our first President, had a small Cabinet.

The Secretaries of the departments, the Attorney General, and the Vice-President often met together with President Washington. This group was the beginning of what later came to be known as the President's Cabinet.

6.2 HOW THE DEPARTMENTS CHANGED AND INCREASED

Words to Know:

Interior — Having to do with the inside; the business within the country.

Commerce — The buying and selling of large amounts of goods.

Welfare — Having to do with good health, happiness, and financial well-being.

Urban — Having to do with living in a city.

Today the President's Cabinet is made up of the heads of the thirteen executive departments our country now has. They are appointed by the President, but they must be approved by Congress before they can serve.

Through the years, more departments were added as they were needed. Some departments were done away with, or combined with others. Between 1798 and 1965, eight departments were added. They were: Navy, Agriculture, Justice, Commerce, Post Office, Labor, Interior, and Health, Education, and Welfare (HEW). HEW has since been divided into two departments: Education, and Health and Human Services. The Defense Department came into being after World War II when the Departments of War and Navy were combined.

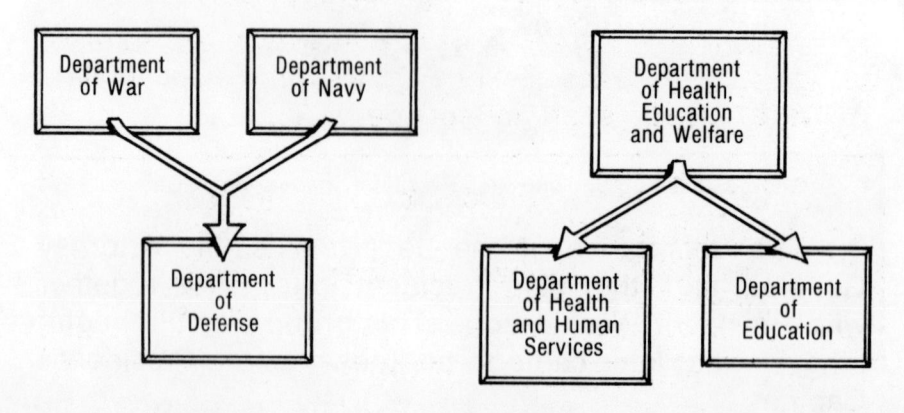

```
Department      Department              Department
of War          of Navy                 of Health,
                                        Education
                                        and Welfare
       ↓           ↓                    ↓           ↓
      Department              Department       Department
         of                   of Health            of
      Defense                 and Human        Education
                              Services
```

Since 1965, three other departments have been formed. They are the Department of Housing and Urban Development, the Department of Transportation, and the Department of Energy. In 1971, the Post Office Department was done away with. It was formed into an independent agency, the U.S. Postal Service.

★*Activity 1.* Number your paper from 1 to 8. Choose the correct word to complete each sentence below. Write your answer next to the number.

1. There are _____ members of the President's Cabinet.
2. After the President appoints a Cabinet member, he or she must be approved by the _____.
3. Between 1798 and 1965, _____ departments were added.
4. The Department of _____ and the Department of _____ were formed from the Department of Health, Education, and Welfare.
5. The Departments of War and Navy were combined to make the Department of _____.
6. Since 1965, _____ more departments have been added.
7. The Department of Housing and Urban Development was formed to help solve problems of the _____.
8. The U.S. Postal Service, once the Post Office Department, is an independent _____.

three	Education	thirteen
Congress		cities
Health and Human Services		agency
eight		Defense

6.3 DUTIES OF THE DEPARTMENTS

There are many people in the executive departments who work with the Secretaries as they carry out their duties. Each department is made up of smaller units called bureaus, offices, services, or divisions. These offices are not all in Washington, D.C. They are scattered throughout the country where they are needed to serve the people. The Department of Agriculture, for instance, has offices in every state, so it can help farmers and consumers through its many food services.

Department of State, Established in 1789

The Department of State is concerned with how the United States gets along with other countries. This department sends people to places all over the world to represent our government. *Ambassador* is the title given to a person who serves our country for the State Department in a large foreign country. In a smaller country, the title is *Minister*. A *Consul* is a representative sent to a foreign city. His or her office is called a *consulate*. A consulate can be found in almost every large foreign city in the world. Consuls and their staffs try to build up foreign trade and commerce for our country. They also protect American citizens who travel, work, or own property in foreign countries.

The State Department is in charge of passports, which give permission to Americans to travel in foreign countries.

Seal of the State Department

Department of the Treasury, Established in 1789

The Department of the Treasury collects taxes, borrows money when it is needed, and pays back the money. It prints and coins money. It is responsible for letting the President know about the financial standing of our country. The Treasury Department makes sure that government money is spent as Congress had decided it should be spent.

Some important duties are taken care of by smaller units of the department:

- The Internal Revenue Service (IRS) collects taxes from individuals and from businesses.
- The Customs Service collects import taxes on goods that are brought in from foreign countries.
- The Secret Service protects the President, his family, and certain other people. It also safeguards against the use of counterfeit money.

The Treasury Building in Washington, D.C.

Department of Justice, Established in 1870

The Department of Justice enforces federal laws. It argues all suits in the Supreme Court that involve the United States government. There are several important agencies of the Justice Department. When a federal law is violated, or broken, an investigation is carried out by the Federal Bureau of Investigation (FBI), which is part of this department. This agency can arrest anyone who is accused of committing a crime against the federal government. The Immigration and Naturalization Service patrols our nation's borders to keep people from coming into the country illegally. The Bureau of Prisons is responsible for all persons convicted of federal crimes and sent to prison. It also runs all of the federal prisons and other institutions that house prisoners.

★*Activity 2.* Number your paper from 1 to 10. For each description below, write the name of the correct department: *State, Treasury,* or *Justice.*

1. Prints money
2. Guards our nation's borders.
3. Is concerned with how the United States deals with other countries.
4. The Attorney General is head of this department.
5. Lets the President know financial standing of the country.
6. Helps protect Americans overseas.
7. The Customs Service is part of this department.
8. Is in charge of passports.
9. The Secret Service is part of this department.
10. The Bureau of Prisons is part of this department.

Department of the Interior, Established in 1849

It is the responsibility of the Department of the Interior to see that our country's natural resources are used wisely. These resources include land, water, and minerals, as well as fish and wildlife. The Interior Department also looks after national parks and dams built by the federal government. There are many divisions of the Interior Department. Examples of these are the National Park Service, the Bureau of Indian Affairs, and the Fish and Wildlife Service.

Department of Agriculture, Established in 1862

The well-being of our country and people is in many ways dependent upon farmers. They have the important job of producing much of the food needed by our country. Our leaders have always felt that the federal government should help farmers in raising and selling crops.

There are agencies within the Agriculture Department that aid farmers in planning and using the best farm methods. These agencies keep farmers informed about the market for livestock and crops. They also try to help farmers get the money they need to do their work. Two agencies which tend to these farm concerns are the Soil Conservation Service and the Farmers Home Administration.

There is the school lunch program which provides states with funds that help furnish lunches to students from low income families. Food stamps are available to needy persons to assist them in purchasing food. The Department of Agriculture is responsible for inspecting and grading meat, poultry, and dairy products.

The Department of Agriculture places seals on food packages.

Department of Commerce, Established in 1903

Business and trade are important to the welfare of our country. The Department of Commerce is concerned with business and trade in this country and in foreign countries. The department is made up of a number of agencies dealing with these matters. For instance, the Census Bureau reports on the population count in the United States. Inventors, people who create new products or ideas, are protected by the U.S. Patent Office. The U.S. Weather Bureau gathers information about storms, frosts, floods, and earthquakes. This information helps protect farmers, pilots, and sea-going vessels from the dangers that could be caused by violent weather.

★*Activity 3.* Number your paper from 1 to 7. Match the department or office in Part A to the correct description in Part B.

Part A
1. Farmers Home Adminstration
2. Census Bureau
3. U.S. Patent Office
4. U.S. Weather Bureau
5. Department of Commerce
6. Department of the Interior
7. Department of Agriculture

Part B
a. Protects inventors.
b. Lends money to farmers.
c. Gathers information about storms, earthquakes, and floods.
d. Concerned with business and trade.
e. Oversees the use of natural resources.
f. Reports population count.
g. Helps farmers in raising and selling crops.

Department of Labor, Established in 1913

The Department of Labor offers many services to American workers. It sees that federal laws concerning labor are carried out, such as those on child labor and minimum wages. The Labor Department is made up of a number of agencies. The Bureau of Labor Statistics publishes information about the nation's work force, such as wages, prices, living conditions, and the size of the work force. The Occupational Safety and Health Adminstration (OSHA) sets standards for good work environments. The Employment and Training Administration helps people find jobs. Included in the Labor-Management Services Administration are the Office of Pensions and Welfare Services and the Office of Labor-Management Relations Services. These are only a few of the divisions within the Labor Department.

Department of Defense, Established in 1947

In 1947 Congress decided to combine the War Department and the Navy Department into one organization called the Defense Department. At that time, all of the country's armed forces were put under the control of this one department. The Secretary of Defense is a civilian, and each branch of the armed forces has a Secretary who is also a civilian. There is a Secretary of the Army, Secretary of the Navy, and Secretary of the Air Force. None of these Secretaries have Cabinet rank. They advise the President about matters having to do with the military.

The Defense Department looks after many peacetime projects, too. An example is the branch of the Army called the Corps of Engineers. The Corps of Engineers helps with improving rivers and harbors and promoting flood control. Among the Defense Department's responsibilities are the schools that train officers for military service. They are the Naval Academy at Annapolis, Maryland; the Military Academy at West Point, New York; and the Air Force Academy at Colorado Springs, Colorado.

Department of Housing and Urban Development, Established in 1965

As the cities in our country grew, so did their problems. There was an increase in the number of low-income families in the big cities. The cities needed help in providing homes and community development, in repairing buildings, and in protecting consumers. The Department of Housing and Urban Development was established to help the cities. It deals with all types of urban, or city, problems, including aid in financing housing, promoting water conservation, and protection against air pollution.

Department of Transportation, Established in 1966

For a nation to prosper, the easy movement of goods and services from place to place is important. The citizens of a country also need to travel easily. As our nation and its population have expanded, more highways, railroads, airports, and even waterways have been needed. The Transportation Department was created to make all methods of travel more economical and efficient. It also sets safety standards for vehicles.

The Coast Guard is operated by the Department of Transportation in peacetime. The Coast Guard protects life and property at sea. It also enforces federal maritime, or shipping, laws.

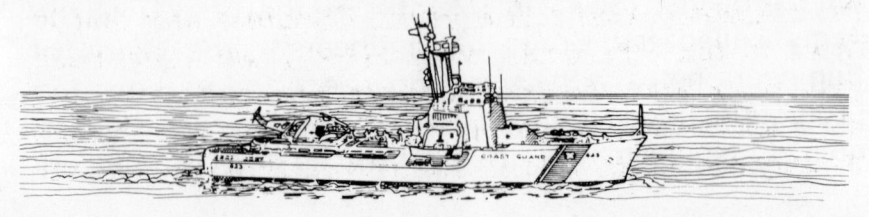

★**Activity 4.** Number your paper from 1 to 10. Write the word that completes each sentence below.

1. The Labor Department publishes information about the nation's _____.
2. The Department of Defense was established in _____.
3. In recent years, the number of low-income families in the cities has _____.
4. The Secretary of Defense is a _____.
5. The military is the main concern of the Department of _____.
6. The Labor Department has many smaller _____ within it.
7. HUD deals with all kinds of _____ problems.
8. The Defense Department operates the _____ academies.
9. The Department of Labor helps the _____ find jobs.
10. The Department of _____ sets standards for highway safety.

civilian	work force	urban
military	unemployed	Transportation
Defense	grown	1947
agencies		

Department of Energy, Established in 1977

The Department of Energy came into being to find and protect sources of energy, such as water power, oil, and natural gas. It also regulates the sale of fuel and electricity.

The United States has long depended on other countries for petroleum. Our leaders saw that we needed to protect our decreasing supply of oil. Federal programs have been set up to experiment with new ways to produce energy. Solar energy, or energy from the sun, is being used in some homes and industries. Nuclear power is another energy source. Its use has been limited because of the concern of many people who fear radioactive leaks. Other ways to produce power for automobiles are also being investigated. The Department of Energy works to meet our country's energy needs.

Gas

The Sun and Wind

Electricity

Coal   Oil   Nuclear Power

Department of Health and Human Services, Established in 1979

The Department of Health and Human Services is second in size only to the Defense Department. It was formerly part of the Department of Health, Education, and Welfare. That department was established in 1953. In 1979, it was split into the Department of Health and Human Services and the Department of Education. It handles the social welfare programs of our country.

An agency within this department, the Social Security Administration, is probably the best known of its services. Health care for the elderly is handled by the Social Security Administration. This service is called Medicare. Other services included in this department are aid to the handicapped, research into the treatment and cures for diseases, and the enforcement of laws concerning pure food, drugs, and cosmetics.

Department of Education, Established in 1979

Before 1979, educational matters were looked after by the Department of Health, Education, and Welfare. Since that time the Department of Education has been concerned with the well-being of the country's educational systems. It offers financial help for all levels and types of education. Elementary schools, high schools, colleges, and educational programs for the handicapped, disadvantaged, and the gifted may receive aid from this department. Statistics about schools are gathered and published. The department encourages experimental programs to improve education.

★*Activity 5.* Number your paper from 1 to 8. Match each term in Column A to the correct description in Column B.

Column A

1. Department of Energy
2. Department of Health and Human Services
3. Solar energy
4. Fuel
5. Department of Education
6. Social Security
7. Medicare
8. Nuclear energy

Column B

a. Handles social welfare programs.
b. Gas and oil.
c. Benefits for people who have retired from work.
d. Conserves our country's electricity and fuel.
e. Power from splitting atoms.
f. Provides support for schools.
g. Power from the sun.
h. Health services for the elderly.

SUMMARY OF CHAPTER 6

The executive departments have grown in number through the years. The Constitution stated that the President should have the help he needed to run the country successfully. When the country was new, three departments were set up to help George Washington, the country's first President. They were the Departments of State, War, and the Treasury. Secretaries who headed these departments were the first three members of what was to become the President's Cabinet. The Cabinet is made up of the heads of the executive departments. Today there are thirteen such departments.

To protect our country's natural resources, the Interior Department was set up in 1849. The Department of Agriculture came into being in 1862 to help farmers. In 1870, the Justice Department was established to see that federal laws were obeyed.

The Department of Commerce's main concern is business and trade in our country and in foreign countries. It was established in 1903. Ten years later, in 1913, the Department of Labor was established to look after the welfare of American workers.

The Defense Department was an outgrowth of the Departments of War and Navy. It was established after World War II, in 1947. All of the armed forces are under its control.

In more recent years, five departments have come into existence. The Department of Housing and Urban Development was set up in 1965 to help with housing and other problems of big cities. In 1966, the Department of Transportation was created to help with our country's highways, railroads, airports, and waterways. The Department of Energy was established in 1977 to protect our sources of energy and to see that those sources are used wisely.

In 1979, the Department of Health and Human Services was established. It handles the social welfare programs of the country. The newest of the departments is the Department of Education, which is concerned with the well-being of schools.

• **CHAPTER REVIEW ACTIVITY** •

Number your paper from 1 to 10. Write the answers.

1. What are the names of the thirteen executive departments?
2. What were the first three departments to be established?
3. Which department collects taxes?
4. Which department is concerned with the quality of schools?
5. Which department looks after community development projects?
6. Which department is in charge of the military?
7. To which department does the FBI belong?
8. Which department runs the National Park Service?
9. Which department sends ambassadors to foreign countries?
10. Which department does research on growing crops?

Chapter **7**

The Independent Agencies

7.1 THE FIRST INDEPENDENT AGENCY

In the 1880's, some of the problems that citizens and businesses were having could not be handled directly by the three branches of government. For example, farmers needed to use the railroads to transport animals and harvested crops. The farmers and the railroads could not agree about fair business practices. So Congress set up the Interstate Commerce Commission to regulate the railroads. The Interstate Commerce Commission (ICC) was the first independent agency.

The Seal of the Interstate Commerce Commission

7.2 HOW THE INDEPENDENT AGENCIES WORK

Words to Know:

Regulate — To control or direct.

Regulatory agency — An agency that controls an activity according to certain rules and regulations. The agency can enforce these rules and penalize violators.

Service agency — An agency that helps, serves, or assists the public.

Independent agencies are created by Congress. They have definite powers to deal with certain matters which no other department of government handles. Even though they are spoken of as "independent," these agencies do not stand completely alone. They are involved with the three branches of the government. The President, head of the executive branch, appoints the heads of the agencies. In the legislative branch, the Senate must approve the President's appointments, and Congress must approve the budgets of the agencies. Also, the agencies must file reports with Congress once or twice a year. Sometimes the judicial branch reviews the decisions the other branches make concerning the independent agencies.

Some of the agencies are regulatory. They have the authority to make rules about the activities they supervise. They also enforce their rules and regulations. Other agencies focus more on giving service to the public.

There are dozens of independent agencies. In this chapter you will find out about ten of these government agencies that regulate industry and serve citizens.

7.3 SOME REGULATORY AGENCIES

Words to Know:

Interstate — Between or connecting two or more states.

Free enterprise — The freedom of private business to operate without interference from the government; the freedom of a business to compete with other businesses in its own way.

Communication — A message sent by radio, mail, telephone, or by other means.

Frequency — Has to do with the position or location on the air waves that radio and television stations use. Each station or channel must broadcast at its own frequency.

Misuse — To use something wrongly or incorrectly.

Nuclear — Having to do with energy produced from the use of atoms.

Radioactive material — Material that gives off radiation that can be harmful to people.

The Interstate Commerce Commission (1887)

The ICC was established to regulate the railroads. The railroads did not always treat the public fairly; therefore, when the government stepped in, it saw to it that rates and schedules were planned for the public good. In this century, the commission has overseen the commercial surface transportation between states. This includes all companies that move goods and passengers from state to state by trucks, trains, buses, or boats. These companies are required to get a permit from the ICC to operate. Interstate moving vans must have their rates approved by the ICC. They must also obey the ICC safety rules about lights, brakes, and rest stops.

The Federal Trade Commission (1914)

The Federal Trade Commission (FTC) was set up to prevent unfair trade practices and competition that would harm the free enterprise system in our country. The commission enforces laws that protect the public from such things as price fixing, false labeling, and advertising that makes untrue claims. The FTC also sees that products put on the market are safe for people to use. For instance, the commission makes sure that materials that burn easily and might harm people are not available for purchase. This agency also assures that labels on products are truthful so that a buyer knows what he or she is buying.

A Clothing Label

Lining:	80% Cashmere
	20% Nylon
Outer Shell:	81% Nylon
	19% Spandex

The Federal Communications Commission (1934)

The Federal Communications Commission does not control programs seen on television or heard on the radio. However, it does decide who can have a license to broadcast and what frequencies may be used. The FCC limits the number of commercials per hour. It also requires some public service broadcasts. It decides how much use can be made of the communication satellites (man-made objects that go around the earth). The commission sees to it that the nation's communication systems can take care of emergencies. For instance, in case of a natural disaster such as an earthquake or flood, communication is very important. This agency sees that good communication is available to the public.

The Environmental Protection Agency (1970)

The United States has become more and more populated, and the land has become more crowded with people and industry. Years ago, when our country was younger, few people worried about overused land or cities becoming too crowded. There was always more land to move to. This is no longer true. People and industry can pollute air and water and misuse the land. The purpose of the Environmental Protection Agency is to guard the country's environment. It enforces laws that Congress has passed to keep air and water clean and to prevent pollution.

Part of a label on a can of disinfectant spray. The manufacturer complies with EPA regulations.

Active Ingredients:
0-Phenylphenol 0.1%, Ethyl Alcohol 79.0%
Inert Ingredients: 20.90%.
Includes CO_2 Propellant and N-Alkyl (C_{18} 92%; C_{16} 8%)-N-Ethyl Morpholinium Ethylsulfates.

Environmental Protection Agency
Reg. No. 777-53-AA
EPA Est. 777 IL1 NJ2
EPA Est. 11525 RI1 IL01 (See Bottom)

The Nuclear Regulatory Commission (1974)

After World War II, this country became interested in the development of nuclear power for peaceful uses. Several agencies have served this purpose. In 1974, the Nuclear Regulatory Commission was established. The NRC exists to see that nuclear power plants operate safely. It gives permission for radioactive material to be stored or transported for civilian use. The commission studies ways to make working with nuclear material safer all the time. It may shut down any nuclear plant that is a danger to public health.

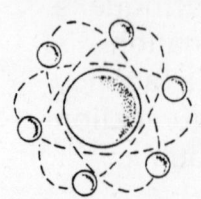

★**Activity 1.** People often refer to the independent agencies by their initials. Write out the full name of each of these agencies.

1. FTC
2. ICC
3. NRC
4. FCC
5. EPA

★**Activity 2.** Number your paper from 1 to 10. Read each description. Decide which agency it fits. Write the name of that agency.

1. Gives licenses to radio and television stations.
2. Is responsible for safety at nuclear power plants.
3. Enforces laws that are meant to prevent pollution.
4. Approves rates used for interstate shipping.
5. Protects the consumer from untruthful advertising claims.
6. Gives permission for radioactive materials to be transported.
7. Was the first independent agency to be set up.
8. Sees that products on the market are safe to use.
9. Decides on how communications satellites may be used.
10. Carries out research on ways to keep the air clean.

A Communications Satellite

7.4 SOME SERVICE AGENCIES

Words to Know:

Aeronautics — The science of designing, building, and flying aircraft.

Humanities — Studies that deal with human thought, such as literature, history, music, and art.

Endowment — A gift, given to a person or organization, which provides income for that individual or group.

Great Depression — A period during the 1930's, when many businesses, banks, and factories closed down, and millions of people lost jobs.

Bankrupt — Without money; legally unable to pay one's bills; ruined.

Efficient — Acting to get results with the least amount of effort or waste.

Civil servants — Persons who work for the government, except those in the armed forces or those elected or appointed to office.

Social work — Work that is done to improve the health and living conditions of the poor, aged, handicapped, or ill.

Ghetto — A section of a city where many members of some minority group live.

National Aeronautics and Space Administration (1958)

No government agency is better known to more people than the National Aeronautics and Space Administration, or NASA. Since it came into being in 1958, the American people have followed its many projects with great interest. It was established to help develop peaceful uses of space.

A reusable spaceship is launched.

NASA has put satellites and astronauts into space and made it possible for men to walk on the moon. It has done research for the creation of Skylab, which will be used by scientists for experiments as it orbits high above the earth. Its space shuttle program has allowed people to go into space and return in the same vehicle. NASA's programs also have helped in research for industry and medicine.

National Foundation on the Arts and the Humanities (1965)

Unlike the governments of many other countries, the United States government had not done a great deal to encourage the development of its arts and humanities. When Congress became aware of the importance of supporting the arts of the country, it set up this foundation. Two groups, the National Endowment for the Arts and the National Endowment for the Humanities, do the work of the agency. These endowments make grants available to theaters, museums, music groups, talented individuals, and groups who best promote the arts and humanities in our country. The agency's purpose is to support the cultural life of the citizens.

Federal Deposit Insurance Corporation (1933)

During the Great Depression of the 1930's, more banks failed at one time than at any other time in the history of our country. Congress saw a need to protect people's money and to protect the banks from bankruptcy. It set up the Federal Deposit Insurance Corporation. This agency pays back to people any money, up to $100,000, that they may lose when a bank fails.

Because of this, people are not afraid to put their money in banks. This money helps the country's economic growth. Banks have more money to lend for homes, industry, and businesses. When businesses borrow money, they can create more jobs, and the community prospers.

United States Postal Service (1971)

Until 1971, the United States Post Office was an executive department. Because this department usually lost money, the government saw a need to make the mail service more efficient, and the new service agency was created. The Postal Service is now run like a private business. It has a board headed by the postmaster general. The postmaster general, the deputy postmaster, and a board of nine governors are appointed by the President. These appointments must be approved by the Senate. Postal workers are no longer civil servants. They have a union just as workers have in many other industries.

The Postal Service has certain powers to enforce laws concerning the mails. These laws make it illegal to send certain items, such as firearms or liquor through the mails. There is also a law against mailing lottery tickets, which are a form of gambling. If any such offense is found, the case is turned over to the justice department.

Even though the Postal Service is run like a business, if it loses money, Congress must help pay for this service to the American people.

The Pony Express

A short but exciting period in the development of the nation's mail service happened when the Pony Express was in operation. It started in April of 1860, and continued for about eighteen months. Brave young men on horseback carried the mail between the cities of St. Joseph, Missouri, and Sacramento, California. Then an ocean-going steamer would carry the mail to San Francisco, California. The system worked something like a relay race.

The riders would ride very fast — sometimes 25 miles an hour — from station to station. At the stations, which were about twelve miles apart, they would quickly pick up the mail and change horses. A rider would go about 75 miles before another rider would take over. This went on day and night, no matter how bad the weather might be.

The Pony Express proved to be faster than the stagecoach for delivering the mail. However, the telegraph, or wireless, method of sending messages came into use across the country in 1861. This was a much faster way of communication to distant places. At this time, the Pony Express came to an end. The people who invested in this mail delivery service lost their money.

ACTION (1971)

ACTION is an agency that was set up as an organizer and supervisor of many volunteer programs sponsored by the government. The Peace Corps is the best known of these programs. A 1961 law established this program. The goal of the Peace Corps is to bring about peace and friendship between the United States and other countries. American citizens who wish to volunteer as teachers, farmers, engineers, or for other selected jobs, are carefully chosen, trained, and sent to areas in foreign countries where their job skill is needed and requested.

Another well-known program is VISTA (Volunteers in Service to America). It serves needy citizens of our own country. VISTA workers are often found volunteering their time in such places as inner-city ghettos, Indian reservations, and migratory labor camps.

The success of these two programs inspired the creation of others. Through the Foster Grandparents Program, volunteer grandparents offer their time and interest to children who have little or no family. The Retired Senior Volunteer Program gives retired citizens the chance to use their work experience to help others in their jobs. The Senior Companion Program brings together, on an individual basis, people who can help each other.

ACTION offers programs to young people. The University Year for ACTION lets students earn college credit while living and doing social work in poverty-stricken areas. The National Student Volunteer Program and the Youth Challenge Program are set up to train young people for volunteer service. These programs develop skills and allow the volunteers to serve where they are most needed.

Service Agencies — 135

★**Activity 3.** Number your paper from 1 to 10. Complete the sentences by matching the sentence beginning in Part A with the correct sentence ending in Part B. Write the correct letter by the number.

Part A

1. NASA was established...
2. NASA has put...
3. Many governments support the arts and the humanities more...
4. Skylab will be used by scientists...
5. The space shuttle has allowed men and woman...
6. The purpose of the National Foundation on the Arts and the Humanities is...
7. Endowments makes grants available...
8. The greatest number of bank failures at one time...
9. The FDIC was set up to protect...
10. The insurance corporation Congress set up...

Part B

a. for experiments as it orbits above the earth.
b. happened during the Great Depression of the 1930's.
c. to theaters, museums, music groups, and talented individuals.
d. to support the cultural life of the country for the enjoyment of the people.
e. guarantees to pay back all money (up to $100,000) that depositors may lose when a bank fails.
f. people's money and the banks from bankruptcy.
g. than the United States government has done.
h. to go into space and return in the same spaceship.
i. astronauts and satellites into space.
j. to help establish peaceful uses of space.

136 — Service Agencies

★**Activity 4.** Number your paper from 1 to 6. Each statement below tells about the Postal Service or ACTION. Write the correct agency by each number.

1. The Foster Grandparents Program and the Retired Senior Volunteer Program are part of this agency.
2. This agency has certain powers to enforce laws concerning the mails.
3. The Peace Corps is a part of this organization.
4. This agency was an executive department until 1971, when it was reorganized as a private business.
5. VISTA workers often volunteer their services in ghettos and on Indian reservations.
6. This agency's workers used to be civil servants, but now are union members.

7.5 THE FEDERAL BUREAUCRACY: WHERE AGENCIES FIT

The Executive Office of the President, the executive departments, and the many government independent agencies make up what is known as the *federal bureaucracy*. We may think of the federal bureaucracy as a large pyramid. The bottom part, or foundation, is made up of many agencies which form the largest part of the federal government. Next come the executive departments, which are fewer in number. Each one is represented by a secretary, who serves in the President's Cabinet. Next comes an even smaller group which makes up the Executive Office of the President. These individuals and agencies directly assist the President.

At the very top of the pyramid is the President of the United States, who has the highest position in the country. It is his responsibility to see that all parts of the government function as they should. It is important that each part of this pyramid does its job, if the government is to work well for the good of every citizen.

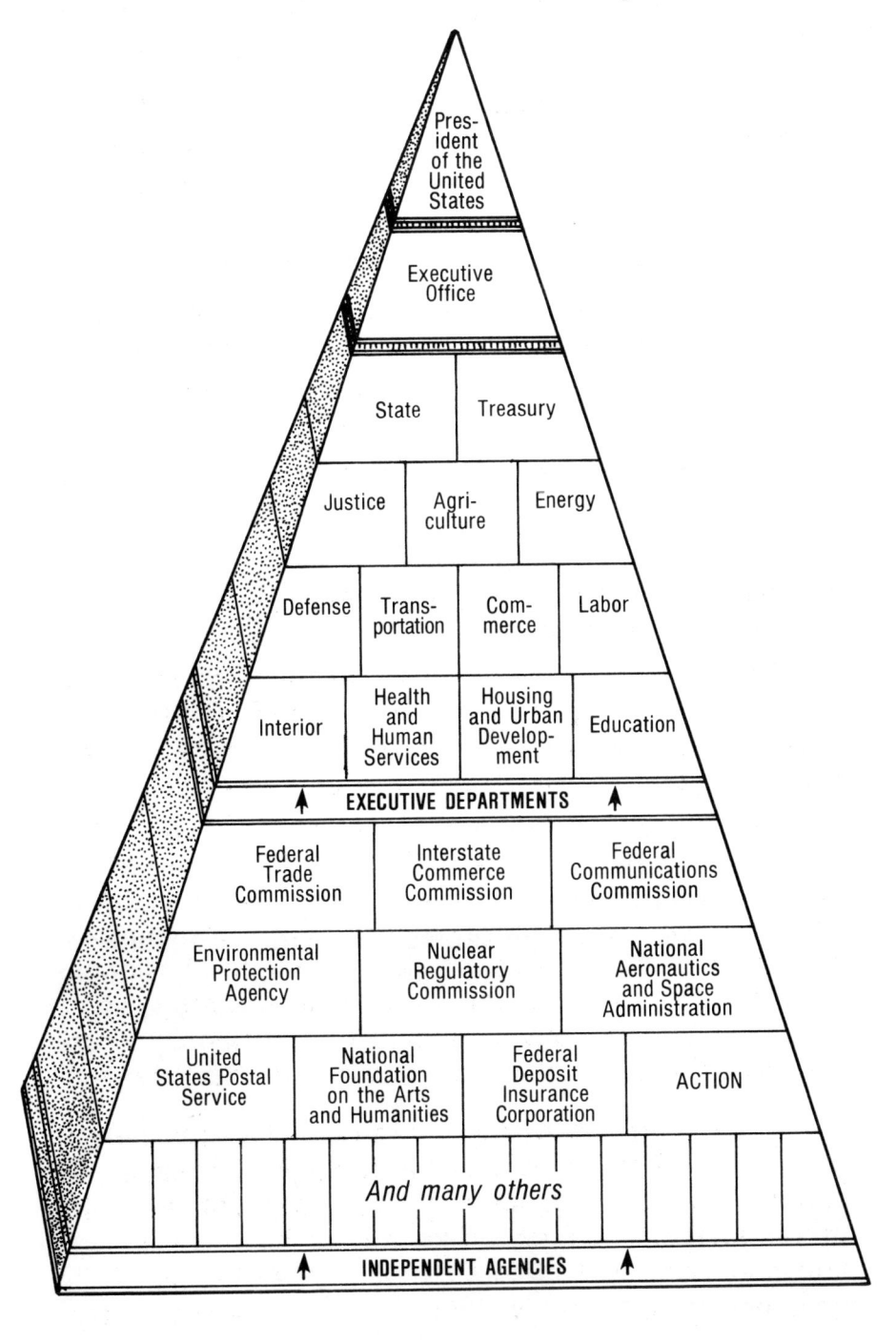

The Federal Bureaucracy — 137

The Federal Bureaucracy

- President of the United States
- Executive Office

EXECUTIVE DEPARTMENTS
- State
- Treasury
- Justice
- Agriculture
- Energy
- Defense
- Transportation
- Commerce
- Labor
- Interior
- Health and Human Services
- Housing and Urban Development
- Education

INDEPENDENT AGENCIES
- Federal Trade Commission
- Interstate Commerce Commission
- Federal Communications Commission
- Environmental Protection Agency
- Nuclear Regulatory Commission
- National Aeronautics and Space Administration
- United States Postal Service
- National Foundation on the Arts and Humanities
- Federal Deposit Insurance Corporation
- ACTION

And many others

SUMMARY OF CHAPTER 7

Congress created the first independent government agency in 1887. An agency's purpose is to deal with some matter that is not being handled by any other part of the government. Even though the agencies are called *independent*, they are involved with the three branches of government: legislative, executive, and judicial.

There are dozens of independent agencies. Some are regulatory. They make rules and regulations about the activities they supervise. Other agencies perform services, either for the government, or for the general public.

The regulatory agencies have many different concerns. One oversees the workings of surface interstate transportation. Another helps prevent unfair trade practices and competition. Other agencies supervise the nation's communication systems—radio and television, enforce laws to protect the environment, and help develop safe and peaceful uses of nuclear power.

The independent service agencies are also concerned with a number of matters. NASA is developing peaceful uses of space. Support for the arts—music, dance, theater, and museums—is made available by one service agency. Other agencies insure the money people deposit in banks, operate the nation's mail service, and supervise volunteer programs sponsored by the government.

• CHAPTER REVIEW ACTIVITY •

Number your paper from 1 to 10. Read each statement. Decide which type of agency is being described. Write *Regulatory* or *Service* next to each number.

1. Enforces laws intended to protect the environment.
2. Works to develop peaceful uses of space.
3. Supports the arts, including music, dance, and theater.
4. Has set up standards for buses that carry passengers to other states.
5. Insures the money that people put in banks.
6. Gives permission for a radio station to broadcast.
7. Sees that nuclear power plants are operated safely.
8. Supervises volunteer programs sponsored by the government.
9. Delivers mail.
10. Enforces rules about the kinds of labels that may be put on consumer goods.

Number your paper from 1 to 7. Copy these agencies on your paper. For each agency, find its description in the activity above. Write the description next to the agency.

1. The Environmental Protection Agency
2. The Federal Trade Commission
3. ACTION
4. Federal Deposit Insurance Corporation
5. The Interstate Commerce Commission
6. The Federal Communications Commission
7. United States Postal Service

Chapter 8

The Judicial Branch

Article III of the Constitution describes the third branch of our government, the judicial branch. The judicial branch includes all of the federal courts. The highest and most powerful of all these courts is the Supreme Court.

The Bench and Chairs Used by the Nine Justices of the Supreme Court

8.1 LAWS ARE INTENDED TO PROTECT THE RIGHTS OF ALL CITIZENS

Words to Know:

Innocent — Free from evil; not guilty of a crime.

Appeal — A request for help; in law, to ask a higher court for help.

Customs — Taxes placed on goods coming into the country.

Patent — An official document granting the right to make and sell an invention.

All laws that are passed must follow the ideals written in the Constitution. Every American citizen is responsible for knowing these laws. Laws guarantee our property and our basic rights. If a citizen does not obey a law, he or she can be arrested and tried. When this happens, the person still has certain rights. A person charged with violating the law has the right to a fair trial in a public court of law.

Only Courts of Law Can Decide If a Person Is Guilty

The Constitution says that a person is innocent until proven guilty. Only a court of law can decide that the person is guilty. Most cases are heard in lower courts, such as traffic courts, juvenile courts, and small claims courts. If the case involves a federal law, then the case is heard within the federal court system. The federal court system includes district courts, courts of appeals, and the Supreme Court. There are other special federal courts that take care of taxes, customs, and patents.

8.2 FEDERAL COURTS HEAR CERTAIN CASES

Words to Know:
Authority — The power or right to make final decisions.
Stationed — Assigned to work in a certain place.
Disagreement — A quarrel; a difference of opinion.

State courts hear cases of persons who are charged with breaking the laws of the state. Most trials are heard in state courts. The federal courts hear only certain cases. The Constitution gives federal courts the authority to hear the following kinds of cases:

1. Of any person disobeying any part of the Constitution, including the amendments.
2. Of any person accused of breaking laws passed by Congress, such as tax laws, mail laws, banking laws, or military law.
3. Of a foreign nation suing the United States or a citizen of the United States.
4. Of any ambassador accused of breaking a law of the country in which he is stationed.
5. Of any crime committed on American ships at sea.
6. Of any crime committed on federal property.
7. Of any disagreement between states.
8. Of any lawsuit between citizens of different states.

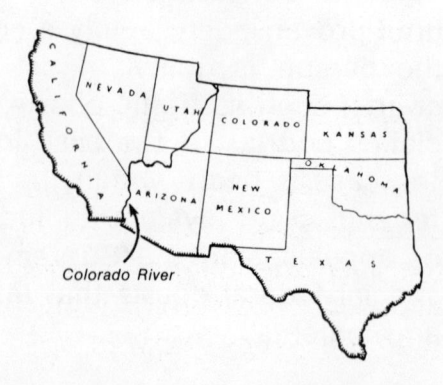

For years California and Arizona argued over rights to Colorado River water. The case was heard in a federal court.

Colorado River

8.3 DISTRICT COURTS

Words to Know:
Entitled — Given a right or privilege.
Random — Having no particular order or pattern.

A district court is the place where federal cases are heard. There is at least one district court in each state. Some larger states are divided into two or more districts. Each district has district court. Several judges are assigned to each district court. District courts are the only federal courts which use juries.

> **Jury Trial**
>
> The Constitution, in the Sixth Amendment, provides that an accused person is guaranteed a speedy, public trial by a jury in the state where the crime took place. He is to be told of the charge against him. He is entitled to have a lawyer to defend him.
>
> The trial jury is made up of twelve persons who live in the community. They are chosen at random from lists of voters or taxpayers. They must decide, after hearing both sides of the case, whether a person is guilty or not guilty. All twelve members must agree on the guilt or innocence of the accused.

District Court Judges

District court judges are appointed for life. There is a Chief Judge for each district and one or more other judges. One duty of the judge is to explain to the jury the nature of the law that the defendant is accused of breaking. If the person is found guilty, then the judge decides on a sentence, or punishment.

District court judges hear a wide variety of cases that may include bank robbery, kidnapping, counterfeiting, or tax evasion (refusing to pay taxes).

★**Activity 1.** Number your paper from 1 to 8. Choose the correct ending for each sentence from the two endings given. Write the letter you choose next to each number.

1. A district court is the only federal court
   (a) in which a jury trial is held.
   (b) that is in the federal court system.
2. District courts are found
   (a) in every state.   (b) only in the larger states.
3. An accused person is guaranteed a speedy, public trial
   (a) in the state where the crime took place.
   (b) in Washington, D.C.
4. An accused person must be told
   (a) nothing about the charge against him.
   (b) about the charge against him.
5. The trial jury is made up of
   (a) twelve persons who live in the community.
   (b) people chosen by the accused.
6. The decision as to whether a person is guilty or not must be agreed upon by
   (a) all twelve members of the jury.
   (b) a majority of the jury members.
7. The district court judge explains to the jury
   (a) the law involved in the case.
   (b) why the accused person is guilty or not guilty.
8. The sentence given to a person found guilty of a crime is decided by the
   (a) jury.   (b) judge.

8.4 UNITED STATES COURTS OF APPEALS

Words to Know:
Review — To look over; to examine again.
Final — The very last; definite and without change.

If an accused person feels that his trial was unfair in a district court, he may *appeal* his case, or ask a higher court to review his case. This review would then take place in a court of appeals.

The United States Courts of Appeals were set up by the Congress in 1891. These courts handle almost every appeal from the district courts. The nation is divided into eleven large judicial areas known as *circuits*. In each circuit there is a United States Court of Appeals. The number of judges varies from circuit to circuit. There may be from three to fifteen judges who serve in a circuit. These judges are appointed for life.

When a court of appeals gets a case to review, the judges study the history of the case. At least three judges take part in the review. They do not decide whether the person is guilty or innocent. There is no jury trial. The reason for review is largely based upon the question of legal procedures or interpretation of the law. The judges listen to the lawyers from each side. They carefully check written records from the district court. When all the facts are presented, the three judges vote. If the judges decide that justice was not done, and the trial was not fair, the case is sent back to the district court for a new trial. The judges may decide that justice was done. Then the verdict that was reached by the district court will stand firm. This decision made by the court of appeals is final in most cases.

★*Activity 2.* Number your paper from 1 to 7. Choose the best word to complete each sentence. Write the correct word next to each number.

1. The U.S. Courts of Appeals were set up by the _____ in 1891.
   (Constitution, Congress, Senate)
2. The nation is divided into eleven large judicial areas called _____.
   (courts, circuits, appeals)
3. Every circuit has a court of appeals that reviews decisions made in _____ _____.
   (higher courts, state courts, district courts)
4. The courts of appeals do not have _____ _____ for the cases they review.
   (jury trials, circuit courts, good records)
5. The judges in the court of appeals listen to arguments presented by the _____ from each side.
   (accused, judges, lawyers)
6. A case may be sent back to a district court for a new trial if the judges decide that _____ was not done.
   (justice, argument, an appeal)
7. If the court of appeals decides that justice was done, the _____ of the district court will stand.
   (judge, argument, decision)

8.5 THE SUPREME COURT

Words to Know:

Challenge — To question the truth or accuracy.

Unconstitutional — Not in agreement with the rules set down in the Constitution.

Apportion — To divide and assign something according to a plan.

Segregation — The act of separating a group, such as a race or class, from a larger group.

The Supreme Court of the United States is the highest court in the nation. Its decisions are final and cannot be appealed.

The Supreme Court Building

In most instances, the Supreme Court receives cases after they have passed through a district court and a court of appeals. Someone has to challenge the law involved in the case before the case can come to the Supreme Court. The Supreme Court alone has the right to decide whether or not it will review the case. Once it decides to hear the case, the Court then makes a decision about the law involved. It rules whether the law is constitutional or unconstitutional. If the intent of the law is ruled unconstitutional, it means that the law has gone against the Constitution.

Justices of the Supreme Court

There are nine justices, or judges, on the Supreme Court. Congress has the power to change this number and has done so several times in history. The total number of justices serving on the Supreme Court has varied from four to the present number, nine, which was set in 1869. There is a Chief Justice and eight associate justices.

Supreme Court justices are appointed by the President for life. These appointments must be approved by the Senate. A justice may serve as long as he or she feels able to do so. Justices may resign at any time. If they are accused of wrongdoing, they may be *impeached*, or brought to trial by the Congress.

A justice may retire with full pay at age sixty-five if he or she has served as a judge for at least fifteen years. Justices may retire at age seventy if they have at least ten years service.

Supreme Court Sessions

The Supreme Court works in Washington, D.C. Its term, or period of work, begins the first Monday in October each year and continues until late June. For the first two weeks, the justices hold public sessions, or sittings. All justices are present and listen to the facts of each case. The Chief Justice sits in the middle of the group. Lawyers from both sides are given a limited amount of time to explain their case. The justices may question the lawyers.

For the next two weeks, the justices study the facts of the cases presented, and the lawyers provide them with briefs (written statements about a case). This period of study is called a *recess*. Throughout the rest of the term, the justices follow this pattern of sittings and recesses.

Chief Justice John Marshall and His Influence

In 1801, President Adams appointed John Marshall as Chief Justice. He remained in this role as head of the Supreme Court for 34 years. During his term, the Court made decisions in more than 500 cases. He helped establish the Supreme Court as a powerful influence for justice. Before his term, the Supreme Court was poorly respected. It was difficult to get men to serve as justices.

Marshall's decisions established three basic ideals that are followed today by the Supreme Court. They are as follows:

1. The Supreme Court *does* have the power to declare a law unconstitutional. A law that goes against the Constitution must be changed.

2. The Supreme Court may set aside (overrule) *state* laws if they are against the Constitution.

3. The Supreme Court may *reverse* (change) the decisions of any court, even state courts.

Through the years these principles, or ideals, followed by the Supreme Court mean that the Court has the final word in deciding what the Constitution means. The Supreme Court interprets, or explains, the Constitution for us.

150 — The Supreme Court

★**Activity 3.** Number your paper from 1 to 10. From the list of words at the bottom, select the correct word for each blank. Write the word beside the correct number.

1. The Supreme Court is the _____ court in the nation.
2. The Supreme Court usually receives cases after they pass through the district court and a court of _____.
3. The Supreme Court may decide whether or not to _____ a case.
4. The Supreme Court may decide that a law is _____.
5. There are _____ associate justices on the Supreme Court.
6. The _____ is the head of this highest court.
7. The justices are appointed for a _____ term.
8. An appointment of a Supreme Court justice must be approved by the _____.
9. A session of the highest court lasts from October until _____.
10. The time when the justices study and consider the cases they have heard is called a _____.

appeals	highest
unconstitutional	review
eight	Chief Justice
Senate	life
June	recess

How Supreme Court Decisions Are Reached

The decisions made in the Supreme Court are reached by a majority vote of the nine justices. Six justices must be present to call for a vote. After the court has voted, it writes an opinion. This is a carefully worded statement that explains why the decision was made. The writing of an opinion takes a long time. Both the opinions for and against the decision are written down. These opinions are then published in a series of books titled *United States Reports*.

Is the Supreme Court Too Powerful?

As you learned earlier, the decisions of the Supreme Court are final. Early in the history of our country, Thomas Jefferson and some other Americans did not agree with all the decisions the Supreme Court made. They thought the Supreme Court had become too powerful because it could decide that a law was unconstitutional. This meant that the law had no force. In case after case, laws were ruled against and said to be unconstitutional.

However, not all Americans felt the way Jefferson and others did. Many people thought these rulings were good because laws were improved while people's rights were protected. They could see that these changes kept our laws up-to-date.

In spite of the disagreements among officials since Jefferson's time, the Supreme Court has continued to use its power to change laws.

Supreme Court Decisions Can Lead to Changes in the Constitution

In the past some Supreme Court decisions have even brought about changes in the Constitution. The Constitution states in Article I, Section 9 that direct taxes must be apportioned according to the population of each state. This means that taxes must come equally from every state. In 1895, the Supreme Court ruled that income taxes were unconstitutional because they did not come evenly from each state. As a result of this decision, the Sixteenth Amendment was written, passed by all states, and added to the Constitution. It stated that Congress was allowed to tax incomes without apportionment among the states.

★*Activity 4.* Number your paper from 1 to 9. Match the term in Column A with its description in Column B. Write the correct letter next to each number.

Column A	Column B
1. Opinion	a. Thought the Supreme Court had become too powerful.
2. Majority vote	b. A written statement that explains why a decision was made.
3. Six	c. To come equally from all parts of the population.
4. Unconstitutional	d. Supreme Court Justice who set high ideals.
5. John Marshall	e. Number of justices needed to vote on a case.
6. Thomas Jefferson	f. A printed list of decisions made by the Supreme Court.
7. Apportioned by population	g. Needed for justices to reach a decision.
8. Sixteenth Amendment	h. Goes against the Constitution.
9. *United States Reports*	i. Allows Congress to collect income tax.

The Supreme Court May Change Its Mind

The Supreme Court can make a decision that is exactly the opposite of an earlier decision. This happened with the issue of segregated schools, which were separate schools for black and white children. In the 1880's, many southern states set up separate schools for blacks and whites. Some Americans declared that these segregated schools were unequal, and that therefore they went against the Fourteenth Amendment. The Fourteenth Amendment states in part:

> "...**Nor shall any state deprive any person of life, liberty, or property, without due process of law; nor deny to any person within its jurisdiction the *equal* protection of the laws.**"

There was a case in 1896 calling for the end of segregated schools because some people said these schools did not give equal education to all students. The Supreme Court was asked to make a decision whether or not these schools violated the intent of the Constitution. The Court ruled in favor of segregated schools, saying that they were equal even though they were separate. The Court was saying that the schools did not go against the Constitution and therefore could remain segregated.

In 1954, another case concerning segregated schools came before the Supreme Court. The National Association for the Advancement of Colored People (NAACP) sued the Board of Education of Topeka, Kansas. The NAACP argued that the separate schools operating in Topeka were illegal. They claimed that the white schools were better equipped and therefore not equal to the black schools. The NAACP said that this went against the Fourteenth Amendment. This time the Supreme Court ruled that the segregated schools were illegal because they went against the idea of equality stated in the Fourteenth Amendment. The Court said the schools should be desegregated immediately. The Supreme Court had changed its mind.

Some Supreme Court Decisions May Not Be Popular

Because of the decision in the case concerning the schools of Topeka, segregated public schools became illegal. Although the Supreme Court said segregation in schools must be stopped, many American schools remained segregated. The Court's decision was not liked by many, and some Americans refused to accept it. Finally, in the 1960's, laws approving segregation were removed one by one. Laws supporting black voting rights were passed. The civil rights of all citizens were beginning to be enforced in the United States.

Other Federal Courts and the Cases They Handle

Congress has set up a number of other federal courts to handle special cases. Some of these are:

1. *Court of Claims* — Hears cases involving money claims against the federal government. A decision in favor of the person bringing the suit usually results in a sum of money being given to that person.
2. *Customs Court* — Hears cases from individuals and businesses about tariffs and taxes collected by customs officials on imported goods.
3. *Court of Customs and Patent Appeals* — Hears cases appealed from Customs Court. Also hears cases from people applying for patents and from people whose patent rights have been violated.
4. *Territorial Courts* — Hear cases of the people who live in territories of the United States overseas (Guam, the Virgin Islands, the Marianas, and Puerto

Rico). These courts work the same as the federal district courts.

5. *Tax Court* — Hears appeals concerning payment of federal taxes. Does not hear criminal cases, but settles arguments about the amount or type of tax.

★*Activity 5.* Number your paper from 1 to 5. Match the type of case with the court in which it would be heard. Write the letter of the correct court by the number.

1. Application for a patent
2. Disagreement over the amount of federal tax
3. Disagreement over amount of tax on goods imported into the country
4. Bank robbery case in the territory of Guam
5. Claim against the government for damages caused by waste products

a. Court of Claims
b. Customs Court
c. Court of Customs and Patent Appeals
d. Territorial Court
e. Tax Court

SUMMARY OF CHAPTER 8

In this chapter, you learned about the judicial branch, which is the third part of the federal government. It includes all the federal courts and judges. If people are accused of breaking the law in our country, the Constitution says that they are innocent until proven guilty. Each case is tried in a court of law. If the case involves a federal law, then it is tried within the federal court system.

There are three main courts in the federal court system: district courts, courts of appeals, and the Supreme Court. District courts are located in every state and hold jury trials. The decision of the district court can be questioned, or appealed, in a court of appeals. The case does not receive another jury trial in this court, but is reviewed by the judges. From the court of appeals, a case may be taken to the Supreme Court, if the Supreme Court agrees to hear it.

The Supreme Court is the only court in the country that can decide which cases it will hear. The decision of the Supreme Court is final. The Supreme Court has the power to decide if the law involved in a case it hears is constitutional. If the justices decide that it is unconstitutional, then the law has no force and must be changed. The Supreme Court alone has the power to interpret, or explain, the Constitution for the citizens of our country. Sometimes the Supreme Court changes its mind and reverses an earlier decision, as it did with public school segregation.

The Congress also has set up a number of other special federal courts. There is a court to handle appeals about taxes. Another court hears cases from individuals and businesses who make property or money claims against the federal government. Still other courts handle cases involving customs laws and patent appeals and violations.

All of the courts mentioned above have judges who are appointed by the government. The nine Supreme Court justices, or judges, are the most important and have the most power. The head of these justices is the Chief Justice of the United States.

• CHAPTER REVIEW ACTIVITY •

Number your paper from 1 to 10. From the word box below, select the word which correctly completes each sentence. Write the correct word beside each number.

final	nine	Constitution
judges	innocent	reversed
district	appealed	three
chooses		

1. There are _____ levels of federal courts.
2. A person in our country is _____ until proven guilty by a court of law.
3. The only federal courts that hold jury trials are _____ courts.
4. A decision from a district court may be _____.
5. A case taken to the court of appeals is reviewed by a panel of _____ to see if the law was fairly applied.
6. The Supreme Court is the highest court in the nation, and its decisions are _____.
7. There are _____ justices serving on the Supreme Court, and they are all appointed by the President.
8. The Supreme Court _____ which cases it will hear.
9. The Supreme Court has _____, or changed, its decisions from time to time.
10. Supreme Court decisions have sometimes brought about changes in the _____ itself.

Chapter 9

State Government

Thirteen states existed as separate governments before the federal government was formed. In 1787, the Constitution was written by the original states to give certain powers to the federal government. All other powers were kept by the states. The new federal government was modeled after the government of the original states. The thirty-seven states that were admitted later were modeled after the federal government.

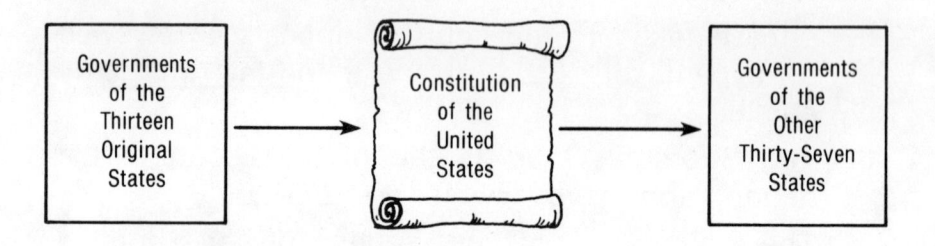

Governments of the Thirteen Original States → Constitution of the United States → Governments of the Other Thirty-Seven States

The name, *United States of America*, means a group of states joined by the rule of the federal government in Washington, D.C. The individual states share the same goals and ideals. Although our fifty state governments are similar in many ways, each state has some rules which are different because of its location, population, and local industry. Each state also grants smaller, local areas within the state the power to rule themselves.

9.1 THE COUNTRY GROWS FROM THIRTEEN TO FIFTY STATES

Words to Know:

Admitted — Allowed to enter. (Alaska was *admitted* as a state in 1959.)

Treaty — An agreement between two or more countries or states; a pact or bargain.

Statehood — The condition of being a state; having all the rights and benefits of belonging to the United States of America.

Eligible — Meeting all the requirements for a certain position or rank, such as statehood. (Hawaii was *eligible* to become a state.)

Independent — Free from the control of others; not connected with a larger group. (Texas was an *independent* republic before it became a state.)

In 1788, when the Constitution went into effect, the country was made up of thirteen states. By 1959, when Alaska and Hawaii became states, the country had grown to fifty states. Most states entered the country before 1900. Only five states were admitted after 1900.

The Last Five States Admitted

State	Year Admitted	Number
Oklahoma	1907	Forty-sixth
New Mexico	1912	Forty-seventh
Arizona	1912	Forty-eighth
Alaska	1959	Forty-ninth
Hawaii	1959	Fiftieth

Congress Has the Power to Admit States

The United States Constitution gives Congress the power to admit states. Over the years Congress has acted thirty-seven times to admit new states to the country. Some states were formed by dividing old states. Maine was once a part of Massachusetts. Texas was an independent republic before it joined the country in 1845. Other states were formed from land the United States had bought or had gained by wars and treaties with other countries.

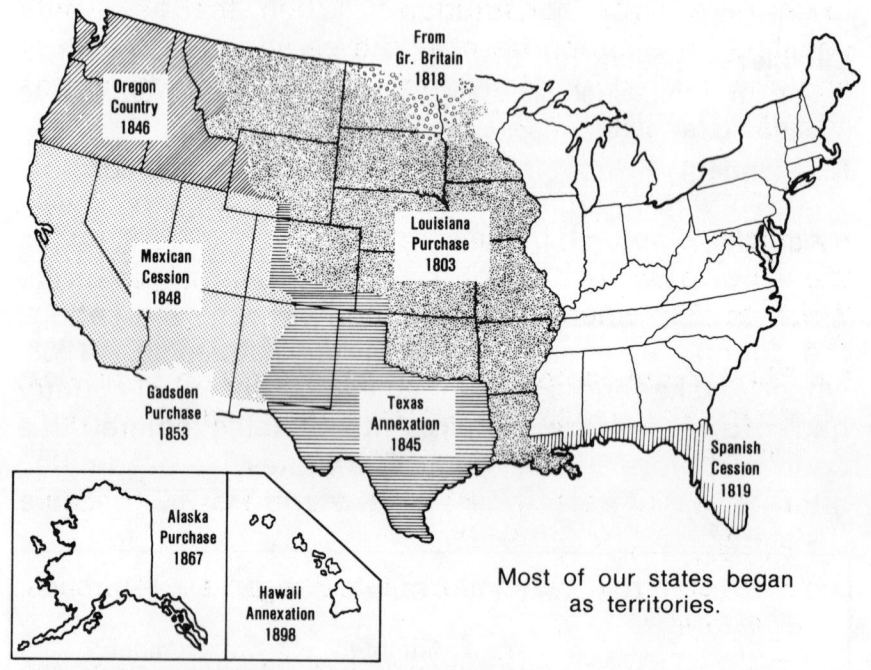

Most of our states began as territories.

Most States Began As Territories

The thirteen original colonies joined together to form the United States when they approved the Constitution. Most of the other states were territories first. A territory is an area that has to follow the rules and laws of the government.

The territories followed a certain procedure to become states. Officials were appointed by Congress to rule the territories. If a territory wanted to become a state, it had to petition, or ask, Congress for statehood. The territory needed to have at least five thousand male voters to elect its lawmaking body. When the entire population of the territory reached sixty thousand voters, it was eligible to become a state.

If Congress agreed that a territory was ready to become a state, it passed a special act. This act, called an *enabling act*, asked the people of the territory to write a state constitution. When the new state constitution was approved by the people of the territory and the United States Congress, this new state was admitted to the United States.

★*Activity 1.* Number your paper from 1 to 7. Choose the word to complete each sentence from the two given. Write this word next to the number.

1. The United States of America is a group of (states, countries) joined by the rule of a federal government.
2. Our two newest states, Alaska and Hawaii, became states in (1900, 1959).
3. Most states in the United States began as (republics, territories).
4. The territories were governed by officials appointed by the (Constitution, Congress).
5. A territory needed sixty thousand (people, voters) before it could ask Congress for statehood.
6. A state (constitution, Congress) had to be written and approved before statehood was granted.
7. The state constitution had to be approved by the people of the territory and by the (Congress, President).

9.2 EACH STATE HAS ITS OWN CONSTITUTION

Words to Know:

Document — An official paper that gives information, such as a mortgage or a will.

Reserved — Held aside for a special reason; for example, the states *reserved* some power for themselves.

Borough — A small community that governs itself, usually smaller than a town.

The original thirteen colonies wrote their constitutions after the Declaration of Independence set them free from England in 1776. Until that time, these colonies were ruled by charters, which were similar to constitutions. Charters were documents, given by England, which allowed each colony to govern itself. As each of the other thirty-seven states was admitted to the United States, it wrote its own constitution.

Most state constitutions are long and detailed, much longer than the United States Constitution. One reason for this is that people have always been afraid of giving too much power to a government. In order to prevent the misuse of power by the state government, many rules and regulations were put in the state constitution.

Amendments to state constitutions are often made, which add to their length. In some of the older constitutions, there are laws and regulations that no longer apply but which have never been removed.

Basic Principles of Our Constitutions

1. Popular Sovereignty
2. Separation of Powers
3. Checks and Balances
4. Limited Government

The United States

A Single State

All State Constitutions Are Based on the Principles in the United States Constitution

Because the state constitutions were modeled after the United States Constitution, the same basic ideals or guidelines were used. These basic principles are:

1. **Popular sovereignty.** People control their government because they elect the leaders.
2. **Separation of powers.** Each of the three branches of state government has separate and definite powers. This keeps any one branch from becoming too powerful.
3. **Checks and balances.** Each branch can check on the work of another branch. Certain actions and decisions must sometimes be approved by other branches. For example, judges appointed by the executive branch must be approved by the legislature.
4. **Limited government.** State and federal officials are not above the law. They must obey the Constitution. The government must never do anything that takes away from an individual's basic freedoms as explained in the Bill of Rights.

What State Constitutions Contain

The special needs of each state require that state constitutions be different in some ways. They may contain many laws to take care of these special needs. However, all state constitutions, no matter how large or small, are similar in certain ways. Each explains how the state government is to be set up and run. All state constitutions contain the following parts:

1. **Preamble.** A statement of goals and purposes.
2. **Bill of Rights.** A list of freedoms and rights given to each citizen.
3. **Organization of the government.** Lists the duties of the three branches of government.
4. **Election rules.** Explains how to handle elections and tells the qualifications for each office.
5. **Other regulations.** Gives guidelines for providing state education, keeping order, building and caring for highways and roads, operating businesses, and collecting taxes.
6. **Process for making amendments.** Tells ways to change or amend the laws and regulations that rule the state.
7. **Amendments.** The actual changes which have been made to the state constitution.

State Capitol Building in Annapolis, Maryland

★**Activity 2.** Number your paper from 1 to 10. Choose the correct ending for each sentence from the two given. Write the letter of that ending by the number.

1. The U.S. Constitution and the state constitutions were written (a) using the same basic principles as guidelines. (b) with different ideals or principles in mind.
2. *Separation of power* means that (a) all power is given to one branch of government. (b) power is divided among three branches of government.
3. The principle of *popular sovereignty* means people are in charge of their government because (a) they elect the leaders. (b) they sometimes do not have to obey the law.
4. The goals and ideals of a constitution are written in the (a) amendments. (b) preamble.
5. All state constitutions contain election rules which tell how (a) education is to be managed. (b) elections should be run, and lists the qualifications of candidates.
6. The list of rights and freedoms is called the (a) preamble. (b) Bill of Rights.
7. All state governments have (a) three branches — legislative, executive, and judicial. (b) only two branches to carry out the duties.
8. All state constitutions may be amended, which means that (a) they may be changed or added to. (b) they have no way of being changed.
9. The principle of *checks and balances* means that (a) the branches of government have nothing to do with each other. (b) each branch may check on the work of the other branches.
10. State and federal officials (a) must always obey the law. (b) can take away some basic rights.

States Have Reserved and Shared Powers

The states have certain powers that the federal government does not have. These are called *reserved* powers. The states reserved, or kept, these powers for themselves when they wrote and approved the United States Constitution.

Reserved Powers of the States

- To establish local governments.
- To regulate trade within the state.
- To run elections.
- To establish schools.
- To license professional workers, such as doctors and lawyers.
- To protect the lives and property of the people.

States also share responsibilities with the federal government. These *shared* powers mean that both the state and federal government can do some things at their own levels. For example, both groups collect taxes. People are usually required to pay taxes to both the state and federal governments.

Powers Shared by States and Federal Government

- To make laws.
- To enforce laws.
- To establish courts.
- To collect taxes.
- To borrow money.
- To spend money for the health and welfare of people.
- To establish banks.

State Government Affects the Daily Lives of People

Most laws and rules that affect the daily lives of people are made by state governments. Many of the laws that tell which actions are crimes are decided by the state. State laws also control guidelines for education, driving an automobile, and marriage.

State laws also explain how local governments — county, city, township, village, or borough — are set up and operated. It even decides how large school districts will be, although these districts are run by their own officials.

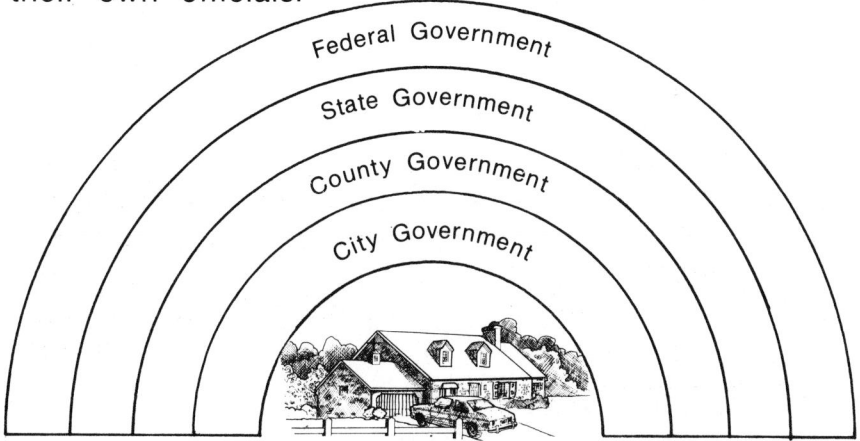

Americans live under several kinds of governments.

★Activity 3. Number your paper from 1 to 6. Match each word in Column A with its meaning in Column B. Write the correct letter next to each number.

Column A	Column B
1. Regulate	a. An official paper
2. Shared	b. A small community
3. Reserved	c. To direct
4. Document	d. Land or possessions
5. Property	e. Used together
6. Borough	f. Kept; held aside for a special use

9.3 STATE GOVERNMENTS NEED MONEY

Most state governments have yearly budgets of more than a billion dollars. Such large amounts are needed because states provide many services for their citizens.

In order to maintain such large budgets, states must get funding from many sources. Among those sources are personal income taxes, sales taxes, federal funds, and gasoline taxes. The graph at the right shows where one state gets its money.

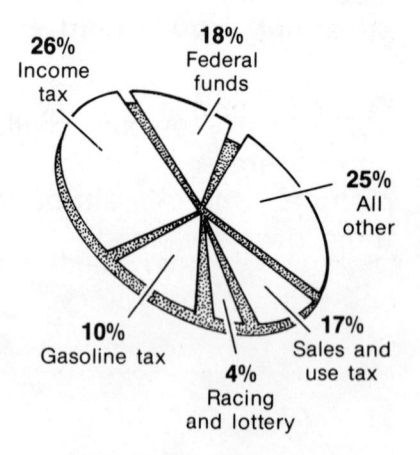

26% Income tax
18% Federal funds
25% All other
17% Sales and use tax
4% Racing and lottery
10% Gasoline tax

Where One State's Money Comes From

Personal Income Tax

About forty-three states collect a personal income tax from their citizens. A personal income tax is a tax which state residents must pay on the money they earn from a job or from a business they own. If citizens live in one state and work in another, they pay the state income tax in the state where they work. Income taxes usually account for about twenty-five percent of the total money needed for a state to operate.

Sales Tax

The second largest source of income for many states is their sales tax. A sales tax is a set percentage of money that people pay on goods or services they buy. Sales taxes vary from state to state. The amount may be as little as two percent (two cents on each dollar) to as much as seven or eight percent (seven or eight cents on a dollar).

In most states, some items like milk, bread, and other necessities are not taxed. Other items, such as gasoline, cigarettes, and alcoholic beverages, have special taxes. Some states charge a tax on restaurant meals, hotel and motel rooms, and admission to theaters and amusement parks.

Federal Funds

Some of the money the federal government collects in taxes is used to aid the states. The amount of federal funds varies from state to state, and from year to year. In some states, federal funds might make up one-fifth of the budget. Federal support to a state is often given as a grant. Such grants must, by law, be used in certain ways. The state must follow guidelines set by the federal government. For example, a federal grant for state education must follow rules set by the national government which do not permit discrimination. Discrimination is unfair treatment of any person or group of individuals because of their race, beliefs, sex, or age. Buildings or highways built with federal money must follow certain requirements set by the national government.

Other Taxes and Fees

In addition to personal income tax, sales tax, and federal funds, other fees are collected by the state. Citizens pay for driver's licenses and for automobile registration and tags. There are fees for recording certain official papers, such as titles to property. Most businesses and many professionals pay fees to be licensed to perform their work. Some states charge tolls for using certain roads and bridges. Some states permit racing or lotteries and receive a percentage of the money that is taken in from these activities.

9.4 STATES SPEND MONEY

The graph at the right shows how one state spends its money.

Education

In most states, the largest part of the budget is spent on public education. Much of the money is used to operate the state colleges and universities. Some money pays for new school buildings, education for the handicapped, and education for very young children. Only a small portion of money goes to elementary and secondary schools because they are operated mainly on local tax money. Although the state sets some rules for schools, most of the decisions are made by local school officials. The state may decide how many days schools should be in session each year. The state also requires teachers to meet certain educational standards.

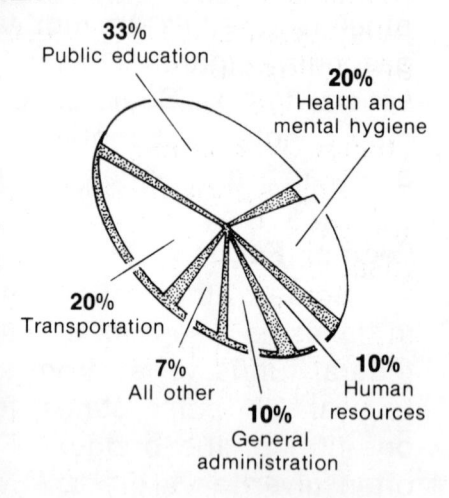

33% Public education
20% Health and mental hygiene
20% Transportation
7% All other
10% Human resources
10% General administration

How One State's Money Is Spent

Transportation and Highways

Many states spend fifteen to twenty percent of their yearly budgets on building and maintaining highways, roads, and bridges.

Health

Many states have state hospitals that offer special kinds of treatment. States also help pay the costs of certain patients in nursing homes. States often have guidelines for hospitals and doctors to follow. There are also guidelines for the sale of medicine. Restaurants must follow certain health regulations in the handling of food. School children are required to have health exams. The state pays to see that its guidelines are followed.

Human Resources
States may provide money to train the unemployed for new jobs. They offer assistance to needy and disabled people.

Other Expenses
The states have many other expenses.
1. *General administration.* This expense includes salaries and benefits for state employees and the maintenance of office buildings and equipment.
2. *State police force.* This group provides protection and law enforcement. It assists other organizations in crime prevention.
3. *Courts and prisons.* A series of courts handles civil and criminal cases. States usually have several correctional institutions and prisons.
4. *National Guard.* This citizens' militia provides local military protection in emergencies. It gives assistance during disasters.
5. *Regulatory agencies.* These groups provide rules for banks, insurance companies, and public utilities, such as telephone, gas, and electric companies. The state also watches over the safety standards and working conditions in factories, stores, and mines.
6. *Parkland.* States buy land to be used for parks. They spend money to improve existing parks.

State government requires billions of dollars each year and employs thousands of citizens. Strong state governments with careful planning provide programs that their citizens need.

9.5 ORGANIZATION OF STATE GOVERNMENT

Words to Know:

Legislators — Members of a state lawmaking body, whether they serve in the Senate or the House of Representatives.

Voting district — An area where a certain number of people live and vote for their government leaders.

President *pro tempore* — The elected leader in some state senates.

Speaker of the House — The leader of the House of Representatives.

The Legislative Branch

The legislative branch of each state has a lawmaking body that works nearly the same as the Congress, the lawmaking body of the federal government. The main duty of this lawmaking body is to pass laws. In most states the name for this group is the Legislature. Some states use names such as General Assembly or Legislative Assembly. The name General Court is used by the states of Massachusetts and New Hampshire.

Two Houses. Just like the Congress, state legislatures have two houses—the Senate and the House of Representatives. The state of Nebraska is the exception. It has only one house in its legislature. While no state has a legislature as large as Congress, they all differ in size. The state House of Representatives is always larger than the state Senate.

Members of the state Senate and House are elected by the voters in each state. The states are divided into voting districts. There are smaller districts for the House and larger districts for the Senate. In most states, the senators serve a four-year term, and the representatives serve for two years.

Organization of State Government — 173

Organization of One State Government

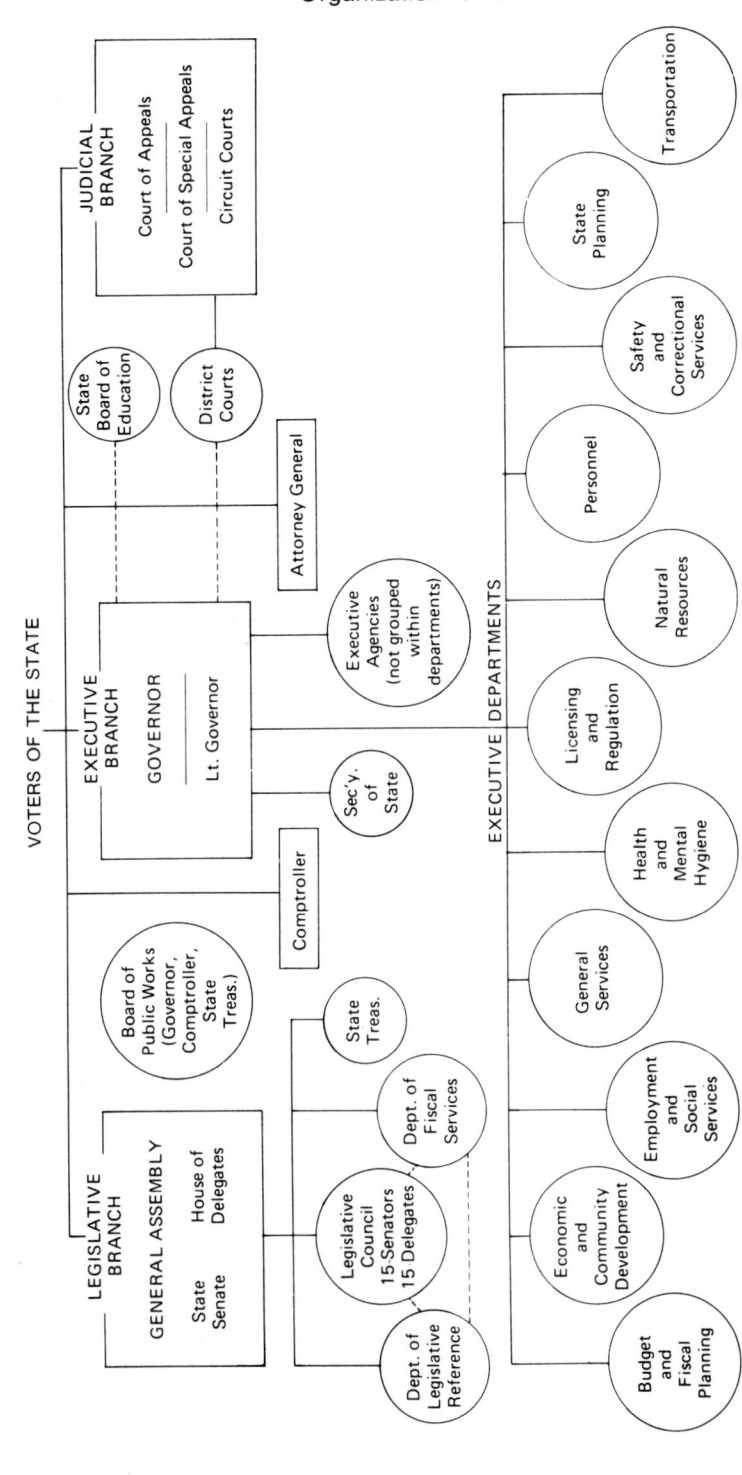

VOTERS OF THE STATE

JUDICIAL BRANCH
- Court of Appeals
- Court of Special Appeals
- Circuit Courts

EXECUTIVE BRANCH
- GOVERNOR
- Lt. Governor
- State Board of Education
- District Courts
- Attorney General
- Executive Agencies (not grouped within departments)
- Sec'y. of State
- Comptroller
- Board of Public Works (Governor, Comptroller, State Treas.)

LEGISLATIVE BRANCH
GENERAL ASSEMBLY
- State Senate
- House of Delegates
- State Treas.
- Dept. of Fiscal Services
- Legislative Council (15 Senators, 15 Delegates)
- Dept. of Legislative Reference

EXECUTIVE DEPARTMENTS
- Budget and Fiscal Planning
- Economic and Community Development
- Employment and Social Services
- General Services
- Health and Mental Hygiene
- Licensing and Regulation
- Natural Resources
- Personnel
- Safety and Correctional Services
- State Planning
- Transportation

Key ☐ – Elective   ○ – Non-elective

State Legislators Meet Once a Year. Most state legislatures meet once a year for sixty to ninety days. These meetings of the state lawmaking body are called *sessions*. If there is an emergency or a special need, the governor or the legislators themselves may call a special session.

When the legislature's regular session begins, the members form *committees*. Each of these small groups has a special task or job to do. There are committees to handle matters such as education, highways, courts, and local government needs. *Bills* which are ideas or suggestions for new laws, are first discussed in committees. These bills are sometimes rewritten or completely rejected (thrown out) by a committee. When bills are ready, they are presented to the entire legislature for approval.

Each house of the state legislature has a presiding leader or official. He appoints committees and their leaders. He conducts meetings or sessions in his part of the legislature. In most of the states, the lieutenant governor is the leader for the Senate. In the other states, a president *pro tempore* (temporary president) is elected by the members. In every state, the House of Representatives elects its leader, who is called the *Speaker of the House*.

How a Bill Becomes a State Law. In order for a bill to become a law, it first must be introduced by a member of the state legislature in either house. A committee then receives the bill and begins working on it. Amendments may be made, and parts of the bill may be rewritten. When the committee thinks the bill is in proper form, it is presented to all the members of the house where it was first introduced.

For approval, most states require a majority vote in favor of a bill. If the bill is approved by that house, then it is sent to the other house of the legislature for consideration. The same steps for making amendments or changes are followed in the other house. If the bill is also approved by the second house of the legislature, it is sent to the governor for his approval or veto.

If the governor approves the bill, it becomes law. If he *vetoes* (rejects) it, the bill may return to the legislature for more work. If the legislature still thinks the bill is a good one, members of the lawmaking body can override the governor's veto and the bill will still become law. In most states, this requires a two-thirds vote in favor of the bill. This is the same power that Congress has when the President vetoes a bill.

★*Activity 4.* Number your paper from 1 to 9. Write the answer for each question below.

1. What is the most common name for a state lawmaking body?
2. How many houses make up the legislature in most of the states?
3. Which state has only a one-house legislature?
4. How are all the members of the legislature chosen?
5. How often do most of the legislators meet?
6. What is the name of a small group of legislators who work on a special issue?
7. What are ideas for new laws called?
8. In most states, the lieutenant governor is the leader of the Senate. Who is the leader in the other state senates?
9. Who is the leader in the House of Representatives?

The Executive Branch

Words to Know:

Superintendent — A person who is in charge or who carries out a task or program.

Pardon — To release or excuse someone from paying a penalty; to free a person from jail or prison.

Mansion — A large home; the home of a governor or other important official.

Rehabilitation — To put back in good condition; to assist an individual in recovering his health or physical condition.

The executive branch of state government is made up of departments and agencies, and is headed by a governor. There are other government officials who assist with operating the state. As the chief executive, or leader, the governor has considerable power. His duties are much like the duties of the President of the United States. The governor can appoint heads of departments. He is in charge of drawing up the budget, which sets the amount of spending the state can do. The governor is commander-in-chief of the National Guard. He may call up the Guard in time of emergencies such as floods, hurricanes, or riots.

As the chief executive, the governor also has power in the legislative and judicial areas of state government. He may suggest certain bills to the legislature at any time. However, the governor usually does this when he meets with the legislature at the start of each session.

The governor has the power to appoint certain judges who serve in state courts. He may also shorten prison sentences, release prisoners, or even pardon a prisoner if special circumstances exist.

How a Governor Is Elected. A statewide election is held to select a governor. The state constitution lists the qualifications for a person seeking the office, including the minimum age. Forty-six states elect a governor for a four-year term. Only Arkansas, New Hampshire, Rhode Island, and Vermont limit their governor's term to two years.

In most states, the governor is provided with a place to live. This is often called the "executive mansion." Part of the state's chief executive's living expenses may also be paid.

Because of their importance and power, many state governors have later become presidential candidates. Governors who have later been elected President include William McKinley, Theodore Roosevelt, Woodrow Wilson, Calvin Coolidge, Franklin Roosevelt, Jimmy Carter, and Ronald Reagan.

Other State Officials. There are a number of other key officials in the state executive branch. In most states they are elected at the same time as the governor. In a few states, they may be appointed by the governor. Among some of the more important state officials are the following:

1. *Lieutenant governor.* The second most important official in a state. This person is elected in forty-one states. He or she serves as the leader of the state Senate in twenty-nine of the states.
2. *Attorney general.* The chief legal officer in the state. He advises the governor on matters dealing with the law.
3. *Secretary of state.* This official is usually elected. He keeps all official records, publishes laws passed by the state, and oversees much of the state's official business.

4. *Comptroller or state auditor.* This individual controls the spending of state money. He is also in charge of keeping financial records for the state.
5. *State treasurer.* He collects taxes due the state and pays bills owed by the state after they have been approved by the state auditor.
6. *Superintendent of public instruction.* The top educational official of the state. He works with the board of education to carry out the laws and requirements for teaching and learning in the state.

State Agencies. Many departments and agencies exist within the executive branch of each state government. States have grown rapidly in population, and therefore departments have grown in size and number. Most states have a department of human resources, which takes care of such things as public assistance and welfare. It also handles health services and vocational rehabilitation (finding employment for the mentally and physically handicapped).

Agencies to protect the environment and to control transportation are part of state governments. Every state has a board of education, with a superintendent or commissioner in charge. A labor board takes care of the problems of labor. A banking commission regulates the banks. Certain professionals and workers in the trades must obtain a license to work in a state. The state has special boards to give examinations to these people and to issue the licenses.

A physician needs to have a state license.

★**Activity 5.** Number your paper from 1 to 7. Choose the correct ending in Part B for each sentence in Part A. Write the correct letter next to the number.

Part A
1. The executive branch of a state government is...
2. The governor may...
3. A budget...
4. The governor can suggest bills...
5. A mansion is usually...
6. The lieutenant governor...
7. The attorney general...

Part B
a. appoint heads of most state departments and agencies.
b. is leader of the senate in about 29 states.
c. headed by a governor.
d. is the legal adviser to the governor.
e. provided for the governor and his family to live in while in office.
f. to the state legislature at any time.
g. sets the amount of spending a state can do.

Powers and Duties of a Governor
- Chief executive of the state.
- Nominates people to fill important state jobs.
- Determines how money is to be raised and spent.
- Commander-in-chief of military forces in the state.
- Sends state police and National Guard into areas where they are needed.
- Pardons prisoners in certain areas.
- Proposes laws to the legislature.
- Leader of his or her political party in the state.
- Presides at important ceremonies.

The Judicial Branch

Words to Know:

Boundary — The edge or dividing line marking the place where a state or other region ends.

Disorderly — Disturbing or upsetting the public peace.

Justice of the Peace — A local law official having the power to act on minor offenses and to perform marriages.

Municipal — Of or relating to a city or its government.

Magistrate — A minor law official similar to a justice of the peace.

Domestic — Having to do with home and family life.

Each state constitution grants the state government the power to keep law and order within the boundaries of the state. The legislative branch passes the laws, while the executive branch sees that the laws are carried out. The judicial branch, through a system of state courts, explains the laws and has power to punish those who break them.

State courts follow the same principles as federal courts. Cases are divided into civil cases and criminal cases. Civil cases deal with disputes between two or more parties. Criminal cases deal with violations of the state laws.

Types of State Courts. The organization of courts is almost the same in each state. There are lower courts, trial courts, and a higher court, usually called the state Supreme Court. Each of these types of courts is explained below.

1. **Lower state courts:** In some small, rural towns, there are justices of the peace. This court official tries civil cases involving small sums of money, performs marriages, and settles minor offenses,

such as disorderly conduct. In larger, more populated areas, the role of the justice of the peace is taken over by magistrate courts or municipal courts.

These lower courts are often separated into special courts that handle only one type of case. Some examples of such special courts are as follows:

- **Juvenile court.** Hears cases of juveniles (youths under eighteen) accused of breaking the law.
- **Domestic relations court.** Handles disputes or disagreements between husbands and wives and other family problems.
- **Small claims court.** Settles disputes over small sums of money, usually without a lawyer. This lets people seek justice without spending a great deal of money.
- **Municipal court.** This court deals with civil suits, minor criminal offenses, and probate. *Probate* refers to hearings to settle questions about who should receive the property of someone who died.

2. **General trial court.** Serious criminal and civil cases are handled in trial courts. Most cases are heard by a judge and jury. The cases may vary from dishonesty to robbery or murder.

3. **Higher state courts.** The highest court in the state is usually called the state Supreme Court. If an accused person thinks his case was not tried fairly in a lower court, he may appeal to the higher court. When hearing or considering an appeal, the state Supreme Court does not hold a new trial. Instead, the judges study the records and all of the evidence. Then they vote as to whether or not the accused person received a fair trial.

182 — The Judicial Branch

★*Activity 6.* Number your paper from 1 to 8. Decide where the actions described below would take place. Write the correct type of court next to each number.

Lower Court   General Trial Court   State Supreme Court

1. An accused person appeals his case to this court because he believes that his trial was not fair.
2. A serious criminal case involving murder is heard by a judge and a jury.
3. The judges study the evidence to decide if a case was tried fairly.
4. A justice of the peace performs a marriage.
5. A girl of sixteen has broken the law. A hearing is scheduled.
6. A dispute between two people led to a serious injury of one person. The case is brought to trial.
7. The judge decides how the property of a person who died should be handled.
8. A worker is charged with stealing tools worth sixty dollars. His case is being heard.

SUMMARY OF CHAPTER 9

State Constitutions

Since 1788, when the Constitution was approved, the country has grown from the original thirteen states to fifty states, each operating under its own constitution. These state constitutions are similar in that the power of the states is divided among three separate branches—legislative, executive, and judicial. Each state has rules and regulations to take care of individual needs. In the United States Constitution, some powers are kept for the states (reserved powers) and some are shared with the federal government (shared powers), such as the power to tax citizens.

A great deal of money is needed to run state governments. The state income tax is the greatest source of income for most states. States use the money to run their schools, build roads, provide health and welfare programs, and provide other services, such as police protection, recreation, cultural activities, National Guard, and courts of law.

Three Branches of State Government
The legislative branch of the state government has a lawmaking body called, in most states, the legislature. It is divided into two houses—the Senate and the House of Representatives. The members are elected by the voters in each state. Their main job is to pass laws.

The governor is the elected leader of the executive branch. He appoints heads of departments and can suggest bills to the legislature. He can appoint certain judges and has some control over prisoners (granting pardons). The state has other elected officials, such as a treasurer, a clerk, and an attorney general. Departments and agencies are run by the state to take care of services and the business of the state.

The judicial branch, with its system of courts, applies the laws and punishes criminals. There are three types of state courts: lower courts, to handle lesser civil and criminal cases; general trial courts with a judge and jury for more serious cases; and state Supreme Courts to handle appeals from the other courts.

• CHAPTER REVIEW ACTIVITY •

Number your paper from 1 to 10. Next to each number write the word that is missing. Use answers from the boxes below.

Each state in our country operates under its own 1) _____. The power of the states is divided among three 2) _____ of government. These state governments need a great deal of money to run properly. The state 3) _____ tax brings in the greatest amount of money. States use most of their money to run the 4) _____. They also provide health and 5) _____ programs.

```
income          welfare         schools
constitution    branches
```

Most state lawmaking bodies are called the 6) _____. The head of the executive branch of a state is called the 7) _____. Another elected official of the state who takes care of legal matters is the 8) _____. A state also has a judicial branch with a system of courts. The trial courts handle 9) _____ cases, both civil and criminal. In most states the state Supreme Court handles 10) _____ from the other courts.

```
governor      appeals        attorney general
serious       legislature
```

Chapter **10**

Local Government

Local governments were our nation's first governments. When the colonists settled in America, they quickly elected leaders and made laws to keep peace and order. Today, local government is still our most basic level of government. It protects our lives, our homes, and provides us with safe environments, schools, libraries, and other important services.

State governments decide what type of local government will exist in the state. Some local governments, such as school districts, take care of a single service. Others, such as counties and cities, have several responsibilities. The activities of one or more local governments affect people's lives every day.

Local governments receive charters, or plans of government, from state legislatures. These charters give local governments certain powers, such as the right to tax their citizens, to keep law and order, to own property, to sue and be sued, and to have the same rights as individuals in courts.

Local governments keep law and order.

10.1 COUNTY GOVERNMENTS

Words to Know:

Zones — Areas within a city or region that are reserved for different purposes, such as businesses or homes.

Prosecute — To take legal action against another for the purpose of punishment or settlement.

In forty-six of the states, the local governments are county governments. Connecticut and Rhode Island are divided into counties, but these are only divisions of the court systems in those states. Louisiana calls its local units *parishes*, while Alaska uses the term *district*.

During the early history of our country, counties existed to take care of the rural areas. For some people in remote sections the county government was the only government they had.

The number of counties varies from state to state. In each county, a city or town serves as the county seat. Like a state capital, the county seat is where county officials have their offices. These offices are often in a county courthouse or county-owned building.

Who Runs the County?

The county government is usually run by a county board, which is a group of elected officials. Some states use other names for this board, such as board of commissioners, board of supervisors, or commissioners court. This board may pass laws regulating public health and welfare matters. The county board may also set the amount of taxes, and may oversee road construction within its area. This group of ruling officials usually also makes *zoning* decisions. Zoning regulations are rules about how and where homes and businesses may be built. The county board also supervises the use of all county buildings, such as libraries, jails, and court buildings.

★Activity 1. Number your paper from 1 to 6. Choose a word to complete each sentence below. Write the word next to the number.

seat	local	districts
road	county	charters

1. Today, _____ governments are our most basic level of government. They protect our lives and provide services.
2. Some local governments, such as school _____, take care of a special service.
3. Local governments receive _____ from state legislatures.
4. In forty-six states, the local government is the _____ government.
5. Each county has a county _____ where the officials have their offices.
6. The county board manages _____ construction and zoning regulations.

Other County Officials

The people who live in the county elect other officials to carry out special duties. The following are officials found in most counties:

1. *Sheriff.* The chief county law enforcement officer. He carries out orders made by the court. He can arrest people who break the law. Most sheriffs are in charge of the county jail.

2. *County Clerk*. Keeps records of births, deaths, and marriages in the county. He or she also keeps copies of deeds, which are records of the sale of land or buildings.
3. *County Treasurer*. Supervises the taking in and spending of money by the county.
4. *County Auditor*. Examines the county's records concerning money and sees that they are kept properly and legally.
5. *Prosecuting Attorney* or *District Attorney*. Represents the county in court cases. He prosecutes people who have violated county or state laws.

Some larger counties have more officials, including a purchasing agent, public defender, park commissioner, public health nurses, and a coroner. A coroner is a person who investigates deaths that are violent and deaths that are not attended by a physician.

A judge hears a case in a county court.

★**Activity 2.** Number your paper from 1 to 6. Match each official in Column A with a duty in Column B. Write the correct letter next to each number.

Column A	Column B
1. Sheriff	a. Manages county money
2. Prosecuting Attorney	b. Works in court
	c. Supervises the county jail
3. Auditor	d. Keeps deeds and records
4. Clerk	e. Investigates deaths
5. Treasurer	f. Checks financial records
6. Coroner	

10.2 CITY GOVERNMENTS

City governments have become more important as our country has developed. The population of our country has shifted from rural to urban areas. City governments have the duty of managing large numbers of city residents. Some areas of a city may be very crowded. Then it is more difficult for a city government to maintain the safety, health, and education of those citizens.

Some of the everyday responsibilities of a city government are providing police and fire protection; keeping streets repaired; providing clean water, providing public transportation; and providing trash collection.

A city government also provides cultural and recreational activities that are an important part of city life. Libraries, museums, parks, gardens, art galleries, and theaters may be supported with city funds.

City Governments Get Charters from the State

State legislatures issue city charters to communities that want to become cities. A charter is a plan of government, which outlines the powers given to a city. This charter permits a city to have a governing group separate from the areas around it.

Cities are usually governed by one of three forms of government. The *mayor-council* is the most common type of city government. The two other most widely used forms of government are the *commission* and the *council-manager* type. Each of these types is explained below:

1. *Mayor-Council.* The chief executive or leader of this type of government is the mayor. Both he and the council are elected by the voters. Each member of the council represents a small area or section of the city, called a *ward*. Either the mayor or the council appoints the heads of the departments, which operate the city.

2. *Commission.* In this form of city government, usually there is no elected mayor. The city is run by a group of commissioners. There are usually five commissioners. Sometimes one of them will be selected by the others to act as mayor. He will be in charge of meetings and will represent the commission at official ceremonies.

   The voters often elect one commissioner to head each of the city's departments. That person supervises his department's activities and services, which may include garbage collection, police and fire protection, health care, or recreation. These commissioners then work together as a group to manage the city's government.

3. *Council-Manager.* This form, also called the city manager plan, has an elected council who acts as the city's lawmaking body. That council hires a city manager who carries out the city's business as the council directs. The city manager appoints heads of departments who are directly responsible to him. The city manager does not belong to any political party and does not have to run for office. Many people think that this allows the city manager to do the best job possible without having to please the voters. Under this system, the city is run like any big business firm.

10.3 OTHER TYPES OF LOCAL GOVERNMENT

There are other forms of local government besides the county and city. Small communities may be called towns, townships, villages, or boroughs. Many of these towns and villages have received a charter from the state to operate. Because these communities are much smaller than cities, their government is much simpler. There are fewer departments because fewer services need to be provided. Many of the mayors and council members are not paid. The mayor-council form is most often used in these communities.

New England Towns

Although the New England states are divided into counties, the towns are the basic unit of government. The town has a form of government called *direct democracy*, which means that all qualified voters meet together to conduct the town's business. Such meetings are held once a year or even more often, if necessary. The town's officers, called selectmen, are elected at the yearly meeting.

This New England type of government dates from the colonial times. In those days, the meetings were popular events, and almost everyone attended. Today, these gatherings are poorly attended even though the towns have grown. Some towns now elect representatives to attend rather than count on large numbers of the population to be present.

Townships

About sixteen states in the Middle Atlantic and Midwestern regions of our country have townships that provide government for some people. In general, townships are found in the rural parts of counties. People of the township usually elect officials to serve on a board of commissioners or trustees. This board makes rules and regulations for the township. The board may include a tax collector, a clerk, and a justice of the peace.

Villages and Boroughs

Some states in our country allow communities of 200 to 300 families to become villages or boroughs. They are in charge of running their own government. They are allowed to collect taxes, provide for street maintenance, set up a fire company, and provide for other services as needed. Most officials of a village or borough serve on a part-time basis because there is not enough business for a full-time position. When villages become too large, they may ask the state legislature to grant them a city charter.

Local Governments — 193

★**Activity 3.** Number your paper from 1 to 12. Choose a word to complete each sentence. Write the correct word next to each number.

state	commissioners	property
often	departments	rural
boroughs	democracy	more
mayor	zoning	mayor-council

1. City governments have become _____ important as our country grows.
2. There are _____ overcrowded areas in some cities.
3. A city government has _____ that are responsible for providing services to the people of that city.
4. A city charter is issued by the _____ legislature.
5. The most common form of city government is the _____ type.
6. If a city has a _____, he may be elected by the voters.
7. In a commission form of government, the city is run by a group of _____.
8. New England towns use a direct _____ form of government where all qualified voters meet to elect their leaders.
9. Villages and _____ may operate their own governments.
10. Townships are usually found in _____ parts of some counties.
11. A local government may own _____.
12. Regulations about where homes and businesses may be built are called _____ regulations.

SUMMARY OF CHAPTER 10

Local governments are our closest governments. They protect our homes, lives, and environment. They provide us with schools, libraries, and other services. County governments, with their elected county boards, take care of rural areas. City governments are growing in importance as the population shifts from the rural to urban areas. City governments have special problems because of overcrowding. Cities may be run by any one of three types of government — mayor-council, commission, or council-manager.

Towns and township governments are found in sections of the country. They also provide services to the communities they serve. Small growing areas, such as villages and boroughs, may decide to set up their own government. School districts are found in every state. A superintendent or commissioner is in charge of the school district.

• CHAPTER REVIEW ACTIVITY •

Number your paper from 1 to 5. Write the correct words to complete the paragraph.

Local governments are our nearest governments. They protect our 1)_____, lives, and our property. 2)_____ governments take care of rural areas. 3)_____ governments are growing in importance because the population is shifting from the rural to 4)_____ areas. Small growing areas, such as villages and 5)_____, may also set up their own government.

| City | homes | urban | County | boroughs |

Chapter **11**

Politics and Voting

11.1 POLITICAL PARTIES

Political parties are made up of groups of people who share common ideas or ways of thinking about government. These groups try to get their candidates into public offices where they will promote or use the group's ideas. Since the late 1700's, political parties have named most of the candidates for Congress, the vice-presidency, and the presidency.

Why People Join Political Parties

People have always tended to seek the company of others who have similar interests, beliefs, and needs. People go to places of worship that best express their religious beliefs. They join clubs and organizations which support the interests they value. People form groups to gain more power to protect their property or ideas. It is for this reason that political parties developed.

Throughout history, people have had different ideas about how to govern well. They have talked about and used various methods to achieve democracy and individual freedom. It was therefore logical that groups representing different approaches to government would appear. Political parties are not mentioned in the Constitution. They exist by custom, not by law.

11.2 HOW POLITICAL PARTIES DEVELOPED

Words to Know:
Coastal — Along the land beside the sea.
Accomplishments — Tasks or achievements completed.
Controversy — An argument or debate; a public debate.

Early forms of political parties existed in this country during the colonial times. There were two main groups with different ideas about government. One group, the *Whigs*, was opposed to the king and the Parliament, the governing body of England. The other group, the *Tories*, was loyal to the government of England. These Tories became known as *Loyalists* after the colonies broke with England. This is because they remained loyal to the king and to England.

The Federalists and the Anti-Federalists

After the colonists won the Revolutionary War, two groups formed which had different political and economic beliefs. The Federalist Party was made up mainly of coastal planters and merchants. This party supported a more powerful central government.

Opposing the Federalists were the Anti-Federalists, who believed that a less powerful central government with strong, independent states would make a better nation. In 1787, the Federalists were responsible for calling the Constitutional Convention which took place in Philadelphia. At this meeting the Constitution was written.

The Constitution was ratified by the convention and then sent to the states for their approval. Many of the states whose interests were supported by the Anti-Federalists feared that the Constitution gave the central government too much power. They would not ratify it until the Federalists said a Bill of Rights would be added once the new government was established.

The accomplishments of George Washington, the first President of the new government, were supported by the Federalists. Although Washington would have liked a government without political parties, it was our first President who put a Federalist (Alexander Hamilton) and an Anti-Federalist (Thomas Jefferson) in his first Cabinet. This was his attempt to share government responsibility with two parties. This proved unsuccessful. Later on, Washington carried out his duties with the help of only the Federalists.

★**Activity 1.** Number your paper from 1 to 8. Match each term in Column A with its description in Column B. Write the correct letter next to each number.

Column A

1. Political party
2. Constitution
3. Whigs
4. Tories
5. Federalists
6. Anti-Federalists
7. Bill of Rights
8. Controversy

Column B

a. Favored a strong central government.
b. Later known as Loyalists.
c. A group of people with the same ideas about government.
d. Opposed the Parliament and the king.
e. Dispute between two or more parties.
f. Makes no provision for political parties.
g. Added to the Constitution.
h. Believed in strong, independent states.

The Democratic Party Begins

The Federalist Party controlled the government until 1801. It helped create solid beginnings for the new country's government. In 1801, Thomas Jefferson was elected President. Jefferson led the Anti-Federalists, who changed their name to the Democratic-Republican Party. Later, this party would be known simply as the Democratic Party. This Democratic Party was in power during most of the time between 1801 and 1861. For short times the Whigs were in power. The Whigs were the successors of the Federalists.

Thomas Jefferson

First Sixteen Presidents of the United States:

	Party:	Began Term:
1. George Washington	Federalist	1789
2. John Adams	Federalist	1797
3. Thomas Jefferson	Democratic-Republican	1801
4. James Madison	Democratic-Republican	1809
5. James Monroe	Democratic-Republican	1817
6. John Quincy Adams	Democratic-Republican	1825
7. Andrew Jackson	Democratic	1829
8. Martin Van Buren	Democratic	1837
9. Wm. Henry Harrison	Whig	1841
10. John Tyler	Whig	1841
11. James Knox Polk	Democratic	1845
12. Zachary Taylor	Whig	1849
13. Millard Fillmore	Whig	1850
14. Franklin Pierce	Democratic	1853
15. James Buchanan	Democratic	1857
16. Abraham Lincoln	Republican	1861

The Issue of Slavery Influenced Political Parties

The question of slavery threatened the unity of the political parties. Both the Democratic and the Whig Parties were divided, with some members of each group favoring slavery, while others opposed it. It was this issue of slavery that led to a final split of the Whigs. Those persons against slavery organized a new political body, the Republican Party. In 1860, after almost sixty years of mostly Democratic power, the Republicans supported a man who was to become one of America's most famous leaders. That man was Abraham Lincoln.

11.3 TWO MAJOR POLITICAL PARTIES

Words to Know:

Western democracy — Democratic form of government that is found in most countries of the western half of the world.

Progressive — In favor of changing the government.

Although the Constitution did not mention parties, there are two major political parties in our country. Each party offers candidates for offices from the presidency to local government.

Many countries in Western democracy have a two-party system. The United States is one. Great Britain is another. A multi-party system makes it possible for the government to represent the majority of the people. This system is also fair to the political party out of power. Usually one of these parties promotes central government control. The other party, however, is usually more progressive, and believes in less government control. The two major parties that have held most of the power in this country are the Democratic and the Republican Parties.

The Democratic Party

The real beginning of the Democratic party was in 1827, when Andrew Jackson left the party that Thomas Jefferson started. Jackson felt that the party was being used for the good of the wealthy. He was dedicated to the idea that the federal government should represent the common man. Jackson became President in 1828.

Andrew Jackson and the Democratic Party

"Let the people rule."

Andrew Jackson, the son of poor immigrants, became an orphan at age 14. He later studied law and became a lawyer. He also became an Indian fighter, and was a general in the War of 1812. Because of his successful victory at the Battle of New Orleans, Jackson became a national hero.

Jackson's popularity as a war hero helped him defeat John Adams for the presidency in 1828. He became the seventh President of the United States. He was admired by the farmers and the working men, especially those in the new states in the west. He was one of the founders of the Democratic Party. He fought with Congress and the Supreme Court for the rights of the common people. He demanded a ten-hour working day for laborers. He encouraged the formation of labor unions. He called for banks to be inspected and set down strict rules for the running of banks to protect people's money.

Jackson was President for eight years, but his influence was felt for twenty years. This period was called the "Age of Jackson."

Andrew Jackson

The Republican Party

The Republican Party is the other powerful political party in our country. It had its beginnings in 1854. It began as a combination of several groups who were against many of the beliefs of the Democratic Party. It was formed primarily in opposition to slavery. Abraham Lincoln, long known for his firm stand against slavery, was nominated by this new Republican Party. In 1860, Lincoln was elected President of the United States.

Abraham Lincoln

Political Parties in Power Since 1861

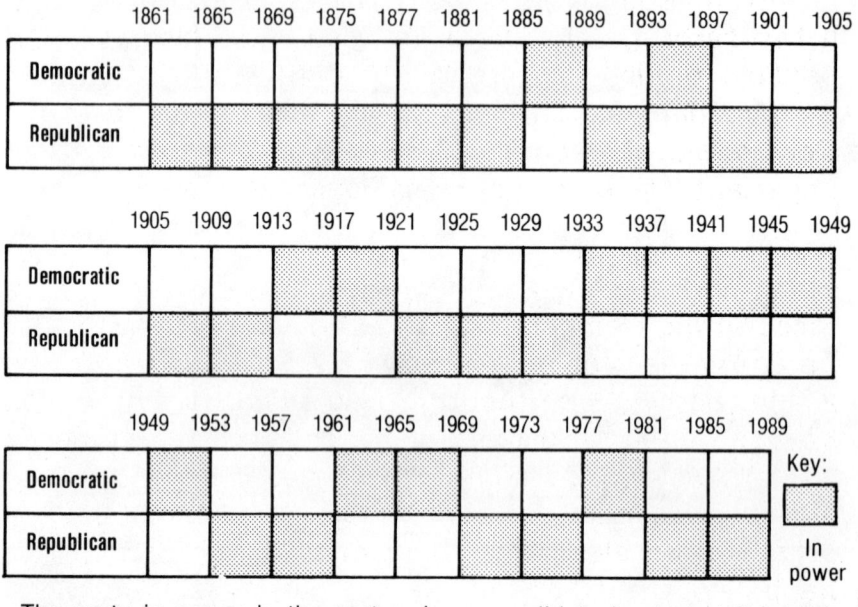

	1861	1865	1869	1875	1877	1881	1885	1889	1893	1897	1901	1905
Democratic							■		■			
Republican	■	■	■	■	■	■		■		■	■	■

	1905	1909	1913	1917	1921	1925	1929	1933	1937	1941	1945	1949
Democratic			■	■				■	■	■	■	■
Republican	■	■			■	■	■					

	1949	1953	1957	1961	1965	1969	1973	1977	1981	1985	1989
Democratic	■			■	■			■			
Republican		■	■			■	■		■	■	■

Key: ■ In power

The party in power is the party whose candidate is elected President.

★**Activity 2.** Number your paper from 1 to 6. Complete each sentence below with a word from the box.

| two-party | slavery | Democratic |
| Jackson | Federalist | Republican |

1. Thomas Jefferson began building a new party, which became known as the _____ Party.
2. The election of Thomas Jefferson marked the end of the _____ Party's control.
3. The Whig Party was split into two groups over _____.
4. The _____ Party stood solidly against slavery.
5. The United States is one of a number of countries that have a _____ political system.
6. _____ was dedicated to the idea that government should represent the common person.

11.4 MINOR PARTIES

Even though the United States is a country with a two-party system, there are also some less powerful political parties. These minor parties are referred to as *third* parties. They do not have the strength of the Democratic or Republican Party, but they have had an important place in American political history.

From time to time, people who want to run for office find that their political beliefs are different from those of the Democrats and Republicans. Therefore, to be considered for office, they have to be nominated by a third party. Even though these candidates have little chance of being elected, they do have an influence on the election outcome. It is possible for them to attract votes from one of the major candidates, thereby swinging the election in favor of the other party. This happened in 1912, when a third party, the Progressive Party, ran Theodore Roosevelt for President. Roosevelt did not win, but he drew votes away from William Taft, the Republican candidate. Because of this, the election was won by Woodrow Wilson, the Democratic nominee.

Third Party Ideas Have Influence

Some of the ideas of third parties may become part of the beliefs of the major parties, who may not have agreed with them at first. Third parties have dealt with issues such as the abolition (ending) of slavery, states rights, prohibition, women's suffrage (right to vote), and the abolition of child labor.

Minor Parties Have Limited Success

Minor parties have many obstacles standing in the way of their success. They usually do not have the financial support they need to promote their candidates and programs. Newspapers, television, and radio usually do not give minor party candidates much atten-

204 — Minor Parties

tion. In most cases, a minor party stands for only one issue. It may depend on the name of one person who is known for some popular issue, such as states rights or religious concerns.

In 1968, Governor George Wallace of Alabama formed the American Independent Party and was its candidate for President of the United States. Even though he was not elected, Wallace won a large number of votes. His campaign had a major effect on the outcome of the presidential election. Many Democrats voted for Wallace, thus allowing Republican candidate Richard Nixon to be elected with less than fifty percent of the nation's popular vote.

★*Activity 3.* Number your paper from 1 to 5. Complete each sentence in Part A with the correct ending in Part B. Write the correct letter next to each number.

Part A

1. Minor parties are referred to as...
2. In 1912, the Progressive Party...
3. Third parties have dealt with issues like...
4. Some obstacles standing in the way of third parties are...
5. In 1968, Governor George Wallace of Alabama...

Part B

a. states rights, prohibition, women's suffrage, and abolition of child labor.
b. the lack of financial support and little attention from the newspapers and television.
c. third parties.
d. formed the American Independent Party.
e. ran Theodore Roosevelt for President.

11.5 THE PARTIES IN ACTION

Words to Know:

Conservative — Tending to oppose or resist change.

Liberal — Tending to have political views that favor reforms and changes to recognize the rights of people.

Traditionally — Following the usual way of doing things.

Platform — A statement of ideas, policies, and beliefs of a political party.

Political parties exist for many reasons. They have certain policies that they believe in. They try to present candidates who will uphold these beliefs. Of the two major parties, the Republicans traditionally have been politically conservative. The Democrats have been more liberal. However, within the parties are groups with special interests that differ in some ways from the party's main stand. An example of this is the Southern Democrats, who have always been more conservative than the Democrats in other parts of the country.

Every four years party members come together for a convention. Here they nominate candidates for President and Vice-President. They prepare statements about what these candidates plan to do if elected. These statements of policy and promises are known as a *platform*.

A platform committee is made up of delegates from each state and territory of the country. They listen to suggestions and ideas for the platform even before the convention begins. They put these ideas together, and during the convention, they present a report on the platform. Sometimes the platform is accepted as presented. Sometimes certain parts of it are debated and even changed before the entire convention will accept the platform. The high point of the convention, of course, is when the President and Vice-President are nominated.

Other Functions of Political Parties

Besides nominating candidates and writing party platforms, political parties also have a number of other functions. They keep the public informed about what is going on in government at all levels (federal, state, local). They point out issues they feel are helpful or harmful to the people so the public can understand how they are affected. When a party's candidate is in office, the party helps govern by seeking support for the official as he or she tries to put party policy into action. When a party is not in power, it is called the *opposition party*. Members of the opposition party watch the party in power very closely. They point out changes in government they would like to see made, and suggest how this might be done. They always hope this will help their party in future elections.

Republican Party

Democratic Party

★**Activity 4.** Number your paper from 1 to 11. Complete each sentence below. Write the correct word next to each number.

> state territory differing
> platform issues four
> power presidential conservative
> debated ideas parties

1. Republicans traditionally have been more _____ than Democrats.
2. Sometimes members of the same party have _____ beliefs about good government.
3. National party conventions take place every _____ years.
4. A _____ is made up of statements of beliefs, policies, and candidates' promises.
5. The high point of a convention comes when the _____ candidate is nominated.
6. The platform committee is made up of delegates from each _____ and _____ of the country.
7. Political parties often point out _____ they think are helpful or harmful to people.
8. The opposition party closely watches the actions of the party in _____.
9. Political _____ have certain policies that they believe in.
10. The platform committee listens to _____ for the platform before the convention begins.
11. If certain parts of the platform are not _____, it is accepted as presented.

11.6 STATE PRIMARY ELECTIONS

Words to Know:

Ballot — The act or method of voting, or the piece of paper on which a vote is marked.

Campaign — All the activities that a candidate takes part in, hoping to be elected; includes public appearances, speeches, and ads.

The word *primary* means "first in order." So, the term *primary election* means the election that is held first, before the general election.

Political parties use the primary election method to choose members of their party to run for public office in a general election. A narrowing-down process takes place in the primary. Any number of possible candidates might run for a nomination in a primary. However, only one candidate from each party is chosen to run for an office in a general election. Then, in the general election, voters select the winning candidate.

Direct Primary

There are several types of primaries. The form most often used is the direct primary. In this type, party members who wish to run for office may request that their names be put on the ballot. Then they are voted on directly by the voters. There are two kinds of direct primaries: open, and closed.

Open Primary. An open primary has ballots for all the candidates. Voters may choose both the party and the candidate of their choice when they are in the privacy of the voting booth.

Closed Primary. A closed primary requires voters to declare in advance which party they want to vote for. They can vote only for candidates of that party.

Indirect Primary

In an indirect primary, delegates to party conventions are selected by members of that party rather than by the voters. Then at the party convention, these delegates choose candidates who will represent that party in the election.

Non-Partisan Primary

Non-partisan primaries are connected to no special political party. This type of primary is generally used for smaller local elections. Only a candidate's qualifications are considered by the people who vote.

Presidential Primary

One other type of primary is the *presidential primary*. Some states use this method to select delegates for the national convention. These delegates have promised to support a certain candidate. The candidate presents his or her delegates at the convention, and a vote for those delegates is the same as a vote for the candidate who presented them. A similar method is the *presidential preference primary*. In this primary voters choose delegates in the same way, but the delegates do not have to support certain candidates.

★*Activity 5.* Number your paper from 1 to 4. Write the kind of primary that each statement refers to.

Direct, open primary	Indirect primary
Direct, closed primary	Non-partisan primary

1. The voters choose the party and the candidate.
2. Only delegates to a party convention are chosen.
3. No political party is involved. This type of primary is used for small, local elections.
4. A voter declares which party he is voting for and then votes for the candidates of that party.

11.7 NATIONAL POLITICAL CONVENTIONS

Every four years, political parties hold national conventions to select their candidates for President and Vice-President, and to develop a party platform. These conventions take place before the November presidential elections. Citizens have the opportunity to follow the proceedings of the convention by television, radio, and printed news media.

Each major party has a national committee which selects the site for the convention. It also tells each state and territory how many delegate votes it will have. Sometimes a state or territory chooses to send more delegates than it has votes. When this happens, some delegates can cast only part of a vote.

Convention delegates are chosen in different ways: some in primary elections, some by state or district conventions, and some in presidential primaries. A delegate and an alternate are selected for each vote that a state or territory has. If for any reason the delegate is unable to vote, the alternate votes.

Before the national conventions meet, candidates campaign across the country to win support of delegates at the national meeting. At the convention, these candidates work to win *unpledged* delegate votes until the moment votes are cast. The successful candidate becomes the party's nominee for the national election.

The Keynote Address

After the national committee chairman calls the convention to order, the keynote address is given. This speech is made by an important party member who usually praises the national party, asks for cooperation among its members, and predicts party victory in the coming national election.

Committees Run the Convention

Four committees organize and run each national convention. Each state and territory is allowed one member on each committee. These committees are:

1. *Organization.* Nominates the permanent chairman and other officers of the convention.
2. *Rules.* Sets the rules and procedures for running the convention.
3. *Credentials.* Settles any dispute about which delegates from a state or territory may vote.
4. *Platform.* Develops and writes the principles and policies for the party. In writing the platform, the committee members usually try to include the ideas and views of the person who is most likely to be named the party's presidential candidate.

The Convention Proceeds

When the committees have completed their tasks and the party platform is approved by the delegates, the convention begins nominating people to be the party's presidential candidate.

Many speeches are given explaining why each person should be the nominee. The supporters of each major candidate often stage noisy demonstrations of enthusiasm. These demonstrations are meant to make other delegates think about voting for that candidate. After the first roll call, when every state and territory has been asked, in alphabetical order, if it wants to nominate anyone, the nominating is complete. Although most states do not offer a candidate, some states present the names of *favorite sons*—individuals who usually do not have a chance of being elected but who are highly respected by that state's delegates.

Once again the party chairman calls the roll. He asks each state and territory whom that state wants to support with its votes. Sometimes a candidate will win the party's nomination on the first roll call. This is often the case when a popular President has been nominated for a second term. However, when there are several popular candidates, the roll calls can go on for several days. Often a favorite son candidate will ask his supporters to change their votes to another candidate. This can help that person to be nominated.

Once the presidential candidate is named, he quickly meets with his advisers and decides on his choice for the vice-presidential nomination. Traditionally, the party nominates the individual the presidential candidate suggests.

The convention ends with the acceptance speeches of the newly-named candidates. After the convention, these candidates and their supporters face several months of campaigning. Presidential candidates usually try to bring together all the candidates who opposed each other during the primary campaigns. This shows unity to the nation's voters and improves the party's chances of winning the November election.

★*Activity 6.* Write the answer for each question.

1. What is the main duty of a delegate to a political convention?
2. What does the credentials committee do?
3. What is one way supporters show that they favor a candidate?
4. What does the term *favorite son* mean?
5. Why is it sometimes necessary to have several roll calls when voting at a convention?
6. Who chooses a party's candidate for Vice-President?

11.8 POLITICAL CAMPAIGNS

A political campaign is made up of those things which are done in an effort to get a candidate elected to a political office. A political campaign is the busiest between the time a candidate is nominated by his or her party and the time of the general election. However, some people who hope to be nominated may campaign for many months, or even years, to win first the party nomination and then the election. They use a great deal of energy convincing their party and the voters that they are best for a certain position.

A political campaign can be simple or complicated, depending on the importance of the office. The amount of competition for the office also affects the type of campaign. A person running for governor, a state congressman or senator, or mayor of a large city must have a well-organized campaign. These campaigns will also require a large amount of money. The most expensive and best organized campaigns are those carried on by candidates for national offices, such as the presidency.

A big, national campaign takes not only a great deal of money, but also many volunteers who work without being paid. Candidates are limited as to how much money they may accept as donations and how much they may spend on their campaigns. This is to make it difficult for any group to "buy," or unfairly influence a candidate to take care of their interests.

Raising Money to Run a Political Campaign

Many committees are involved in political campaigns, and a fund-raising committee is one of the most important. This group may seek money by appealing to supporters by mail. They may plan functions like dinners or barbecues, and sell tickets to people who wish to attend. Special interest groups who feel the candidate will support their ideas, help out financially. A candidate's own political party contributes some of the money to the campaign. Most candidates put up much of their own money. Therefore, it is difficult for many people to run for public office because of the great expense.

Why Money Is Needed

Money is needed for many different activities in a campaign. A campaign for a national election needs offices and staffs all over the country. The expense of paying the staffs and running the offices is large. That is why candidates depend so heavily on volunteers who donate their time to the candidate. Advertising on radio and television, in newspapers, and on posters, costs a great deal of money. Mailing letters requesting the support of voters is another expense. Candidates who travel from place to place to meet voters have to pay for the cost of travel. Often, candidates have planes, trains, or buses that take them and their workers all over the country. This expense is one of the biggest of a campaign.

A Campaign Staff

A campaign staff is usually made up of men and women who have worked with the candidate for a long while. They may even be personal friends.

Organization of a Typical Campaign Staff

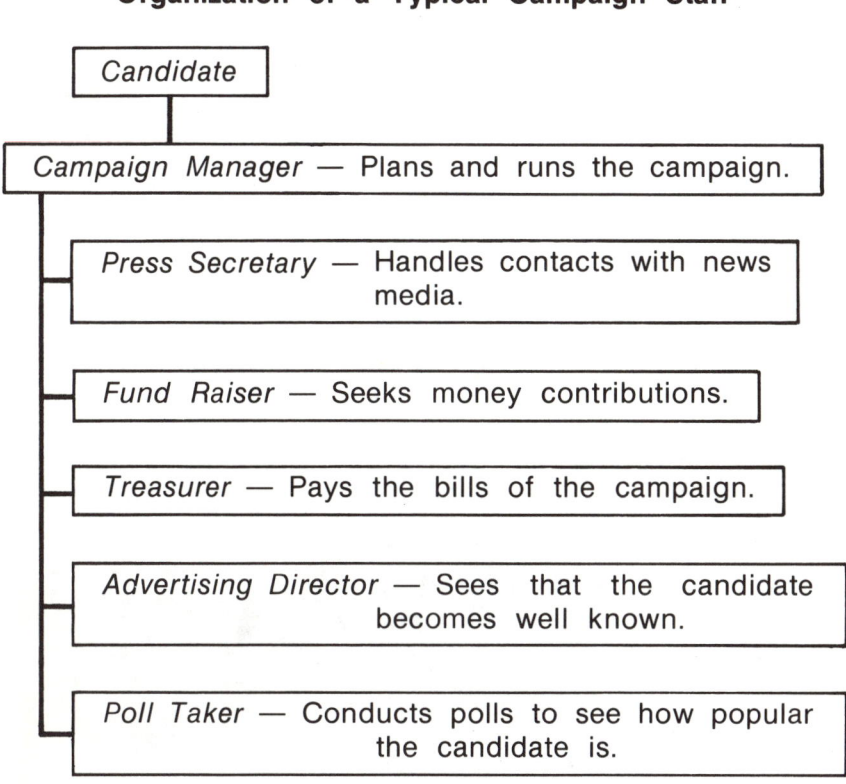

| Candidate |

| Campaign Manager — Plans and runs the campaign. |

- Press Secretary — Handles contacts with news media.
- Fund Raiser — Seeks money contributions.
- Treasurer — Pays the bills of the campaign.
- Advertising Director — Sees that the candidate becomes well known.
- Poll Taker — Conducts polls to see how popular the candidate is.

★*Activity 7.* Number your paper from 1 to 7. Answer these questions about the chart above.

1. Who makes sure that a candidate becomes well known?
2. Who decides on the plan for running the campaign?
3. Who pays the bills of the campaign?
4. Who handles contacts with the press?
5. For whom does the campaign staff work?
6. Who looks for ways to raise money?
7. Who conducts polls to find out how popular the candidate is?

11.9 THE RIGHT TO VOTE

Words to Know:

Unconstitutional — Not following the rule of the United States Constitution; unlawful.

Civil rights — Rights that belong to every American citizen. These rights are listed in the Constitution.

The right to vote is given and protected by the Constitution. This freedom to have a voice in choosing leaders is considered a privilege by many United States citizens. Unfortunately, all citizens do not take advantage of their right to vote. They may lack interest. They may feel that their vote would not make any difference. They may not know how to register to vote. Some non-voters may feel that their government is running well and no change is needed. Other non-voters may not have the qualifications to vote.

Citizens Are Encouraged to Vote

The qualifications to be a voter are few and simple. When the Constitution was written, it left to the states the right to make certain requirements of voters. Through the years, a number of state requirements have been questioned. In many cases, these requirements have been judged unconstitutional. No one may be denied the right to vote because of race, color, sex, or religion. The Civil Rights Acts of the 1950's, 1960's, and 1970's struck down many barriers that stood in the way of voting rights. Some people were kept from voting by threats of violence or loss of job if they went to the polls. The civil rights laws did away with things that interfered with citizens' freedom to vote.

Who May Register to Vote

In all the states except North Dakota, a voter must register in his or her own county. At age 18, a United States citizen must be allowed to vote if he or she has all the other qualifications. A person must have lived in a state for a certain period of time. Although the length of time varies from state to state, it is generally thirty days. Most states will not let a person vote if he or she is mentally ill and committed to a hospital. Persons who have been convicted of certain serious crimes may not be permitted to vote. Some states will not permit anyone to vote who has received a dishonorable discharge from the armed forces.

Federal, state, and local government employees may vote, but must follow certain rules when taking part in political activities. The Hatch Acts, passed by Congress in 1939 and 1940, say that a government worker may not hold political office, serve as a delegate to a political convention, or serve as a candidate's campaign manager.

At one time many states required that a voter should be a property owner. This requirement is now unlawful. Also, poll taxes are no longer permitted. Some voters had to pay a tax for the privilege of voting. These two requirements were difficult for low-income citizens and kept many people from voting.

Two other government voting requirements had to do with language. At one time certain states demanded that voters pass a literacy test to demonstrate their ability to read and write before they could vote. Since 1975, it has been against the law to keep certain groups from voting because they do not speak English. In some cases, where certain numbers of voters in a community do not speak English, voting material is provided in their native language.

218 — Who May Vote

★Activity 8. Number your paper from 1 to 6. Choose the word that completes each sentence from the ones given. Write the correct word next to each number.

1. The _____ to have a voice in choosing leaders is considered a privilege by American citizens.
   (duty, freedom, job)
2. Some people do not vote because they feel that their vote will not make a _____.
   (majority, difference, party)
3. The Constitution let the _____ set requirements for voters.   (people, states, parties)
4. The Civil Rights Acts struck down many barriers that stood in the way of _____ rights.
   (voting, all, religious)
5. A person cannot be kept from voting because of _____, color, sex, or religion.
   (age, residence, race)
6. Some citizens were kept from voting by people who _____ them.   (greeted, threatened, worked for)

★Activity 9. Only four of the phrases below will correctly complete the following statement. Write the numbers of the correct phrases on your paper.

> "A person of age 18 years may vote unless he or she..."

1. is mentally ill and committed to a hospital.
2. is a member of the armed forces.
3. has been dishonorably discharged from the armed forces.
4. is a resident of the state for less than thirty days.
5. does not have a job.
6. has been convicted of a serious crime.

Susan B. Anthony, A Fighter for Women's Rights

American women have had to fight for their right to vote. A few states gave women this privilege in the 1800's. However, it was not until 1920 that the Nineteenth Amendment to the Constitution was ratified. This amendment gave women throughout the country the right to vote.

Susan B. Anthony (1820-1906) was a heroine of the woman suffrage movement. She worked hard to help women win the right to vote. At one time she was the editor of *Revolution* magazine, which published articles about rights. Once she was even arrested for voting! Her trial called attention to the cause for which she was working. During her lifetime she saw a number of states allow women to vote, but she died fourteen years before all American women were given the right to vote by the Nineteenth Amendment. She is remembered for her contribution to the welfare of women.

Women marched to show that they wanted the right to vote.

Registration

Qualified persons who wish to become voters must register in the voting district of their residence. A person may register at the courthouse of the voting district. Sometimes other places of registration will be set up. The names of persons who register will be recorded on the district's list of qualified voters. These lists of voters are important. Otherwise, people could vote more than once in different places and cause elections to be dishonest. Another reason for registration is to have a record of which voters live in certain places and who may legally vote on local matters.

Many feel that a permanent registration system is the easiest method for keeping a record of active voters. This means that it is necessary to register only once. Any voter who votes regularly is considered an active voter. If a voter fails to vote in a certain number of elections, his or her name will be taken off the list of active voters. To vote again, the person would have to re-register.

Some states, few in number, require voters to re-register from time to time, even if they do vote. Officials feel that they can keep more accurate records of active voters this way. They can then drop from their lists the names of inactive voters who fail to register.

Casting a Ballot

Special places set up where people can vote are called *polls*. Often schools or church halls are used for this purpose. Officials working at the polls check their records for a voter's name before they allow him or her to vote.

Voting may be done by a **paper ballot** or by a machine that shows the ballot. A ballot is a list of all candidates, the parties they represent, and sometimes suggested bills or amendments. The ballot usually organizes the information in one of two ways. About half of the states group the names of candidates according to the office they are seeking. This means that the names of candidates of all parties are all mixed together under the title of the office. The other states group candidates first by party, and then by office.

Today voting is done in the privacy of a voting booth. This is the case whether the ballot is marked by hand or recorded on a voting machine. Having the freedom to vote privately is an important part of the election process. Early in the country's history, people were required to vote by voice or by raising their hands. Later, when ballots were first used, different sizes of and colors of ballots were made for each candidate, so others were able to see whom a person voted for in many situations. Today, care is given to using paper ballots of the same size and color. This helps the voting process be as honest as possible.

Voting Districts

Each vote that is cast should count just as much as another vote. Since state and federal representatives are selected on the basis of population, redistricting is often necessary to make voting fair. This means that the boundaries of voting districts are set according to the number of people living within them. As populations change, these boundaries may have to be redrawn. In the United States, the population has been moving from rural areas to the city, so urban areas need more representatives, and rural areas need fewer representatives. This redistricting has not always been done fairly. Certain court cases of the past few decades have pointed to this problem. Great effort has been made by honest officials to form the districts so that each citizen will be fairly represented in federal and state government.

Absentee Ballots

If a citizen is not going to be in his own voting district for a primary or general election, he may request an absentee ballot, in person or by mail. This is a ballot available a certain length of time before the actual election day. The ballot may be marked and turned in ahead of time.

★*Activity 10.* Number your paper from 1 to 9. Complete the sentences below with words from the box. Write the correct word next to each number.

privacy	machine	record
population	courthouse	polls
ballot	absentee	permanent

1. Usually people register to vote at the _____ in their voting district.
2. One reason for registration is to have a _____ of which people may legally vote.
3. A _____ registration system means that it is necessary to register only once.
4. Special places set up for people to vote are called _____.
5. A _____ contains the names of all candidates to be voted on.
6. Today voting is done in the _____ of a voting booth.
7. Some ballots are marked by hand, while others are recorded by _____.
8. Redistricting is necessary when _____ changes occur.
9. An _____ ballot is used by people who are not going to be in their own voting district at election time.

11.10 HOW PEOPLE CAN HAVE A PART IN MAKING LAWS

In addition to voting for candidates for public office, voters may also vote on how they feel about certain issues. Their votes can bring about new laws.

The Referendum

Certain bills are presented to voters at the polls for them to accept or reject. This process is called a *referendum*. This takes place only at the state level. There are different kinds of referendums.

Petition Referendum. After a law is passed by the state legislature, citizens may circulate, or pass around, a petition for signatures objecting to the law. If enough people show their objection by signing this document, the *petition referendum* will be placed on the ballot. Voters may then cast a vote for or against the law at the polls. Enough opposing votes will kill the law.

Optional Referendum. In some states the legislature may choose to refer a proposed law to the public for acceptance or rejection. This is called an *optional referendum*. In this case, the legislature is not forced by law to refer the law to the voters, but it does so willingly. Usually the issues referred to the public are those which have caused a great deal of controversy.

Mandatory Referendum. There are times when state laws *require* that certain issues be sent to the voters for their approval or rejection. For such cases, a *mandatory referendum* is used. For example, a state may use a mandatory referendum to change its state constitution. Delaware is the only state that may change its constitution without public approval.

Initiative

In some states, citizens can suggest a new law to be presented to voters. The suggested law is called an *initiative*, or a *proposition*. A petition must be signed by a certain number of people before the initiative can be placed on the ballot. If a majority of voters are in favor of the law, the law goes into effect.

Recall

If citizens believe that an elected official needs to be removed from office before his or her term has expired, they may use the *recall* process. They must draw up a petition, get a great number of signatures, and meet certain legal requirements. Then the recall issue is placed on the ballot. If a majority of the voters are in favor of the recall, the elected person must leave office.

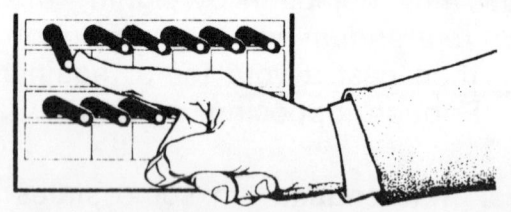

★*Activity 11.* Number your paper from 1 to 8. Write *Yes* or *No* for each question below.

1. Must you be a property owner in order to vote?
2. Do citizens pay a poll tax before they can vote?
3. Must you pass a test of reading and writing before you can vote?
4. Must a citizen speak English to be allowed to vote?
5. Are referendums used at the state level?
6. Do voters ever have a chance to approve or reject suggested laws?
7. May states change their constitutions?
8. Can an elected official be voted out of office?

SUMMARY OF CHAPTER 11

Political Parties

Political parties are groups of citizens who share many of the same beliefs about good government. These groups present candidates for office who will support their ideas. Although political parties are not provided for in the Constitution, they have existed in this country since colonial times. The original political groups—the Whigs, Tories, Federalists, and Anti-Federalists—developed into two present-day parties. These are the Democratic Party, led in the early period of the country's history by Thomas Jefferson and Andrew Jackson, and the Republican Party, which grew out of an anti-slavery movement and the presidency of Abraham Lincoln.

Minor, or third, parties appear from time to time. Although no third party candidate has ever been elected President, minor party nominees do affect election outcomes. They take votes from major parties, and they call attention to certain issues.

Primaries, Conventions, and Campaigns

Most states hold primary elections, where voters choose both candidates for the general election and delegates to political conventions. The delegates usually support a certain candidate. These conventions are followed by the general election, where the voters actually choose the office holder.

Every four years, political parties hold national conventions where delegates decide on candidates and party policies for the coming election. The conventions are followed by political campaigns. The candidates spend several months trying to convince voters that they should be elected to office. These campaigns are expensive and require a great deal of money to pay for staff, advertising, and travel. Volunteers are necessary so that campaign costs may be kept as low as possible. Laws regulate where campaign money can come from and how much a candidate may accept.

Voting

The Constitution guarantees citizens the right to vote. Still, many groups, such as women and minorities, have had to struggle for this right. Citizens consider voting a privilege, but some do not vote.

States decide who may vote by requiring certain qualifications. However, the federal government sees that voting requirements and practices are fair for all groups.

A person must register before he or she can vote. Each voter's name must be recorded on a list of qualified voters a certain number of days before the election. This record helps keep track of properly-qualified voters and reduces dishonesty in voting.

Most voting today is done on a voting machine, although some areas use handmarked ballots. All voting is done in the privacy of a voting booth.

Voting districts are set up according to population so that each citizen's vote will count the same as any other person's. As population changes take place, redistricting is necessary.

In addition to voting for candidates, people may also vote on ideas for new laws or changes in existing laws. The processes of presenting the laws directly to the voters are called the referendum and the initiative. Voters may also use the recall process to remove an elected official from office should it be necessary to do so.

• CHAPTER REVIEW ACTIVITY •

Number your paper from 1 to 10. Write the answer to each question below.

1. What are the two major political parties?
2. Why are third parties important?
3. Which election takes place first — the primary election or the general election?
4. How often are national political conventions held?
5. What is the purpose of a national political convention?
6. Why are political campaigns expensive?
7. Do all voters have to register first?
8. Do voters in all the states have to meet the same requirements?
9. Why do Americans value their right to vote?
10. Citizens can vote for the candidate of their choice. What else might be on a ballot for a voter to consider?

Chapter **12**

A Look At Other Governments

12.1 GOVERNMENTS DIFFER

In this chapter you will learn about different forms of government and how they operate. Many governments, including the United States, are democracies. You will see how the democratic government of Great Britain compares with our country.

You will learn about countries that are not democracies. One of these countries is the Union of Soviet Socialist Republics (USSR). This country is commonly called the Soviet Union, or Russia. Its government is run by the Communist Party. You will find out some of the differences between democracy and communism. You will learn how the lives of citizens are involved with the governments in these different countries.

12.2 THE UNITED STATES GOVERNMENT IS A DEMOCRACY

Word to Know:
Adopt — To take and make as one's own.

Governments, in some form, have existed for as long as people have lived together in groups. The government of the United States of America developed over the years into the form we know today. It is a constitutional government. The government is run by rules and laws written into our Constitution.

The authors of the Constitution had learned from the past. They adopted the best ideas from other systems of government. Our constitution calls for a group of states to be joined together by the laws of a national, central government. The United States government is a democracy because it is based on the principle that people are important. It is run by the people and serves the people.

Many other countries have similar democracies based on a constitution. These are known as constitutional democracies. They are also based on the principle that the people are the most important part of the nation. Rules and laws in these democracies are made to benefit individuals and to protect their rights and freedoms.

On the other hand, there are systems of government in the world based on the principle that the country itself is more important than the people who make up the country. They believe that people have a strong responsibility to serve the country. This is the basis of communist governments in some nations. Most decisions are made by the government. The people have little say in running the government or in making the laws that control their lives.

12.3 DEMOCRATIC FORMS OF GOVERNMENT

Words to Know:

Parliamentary leadership — Form of democracy which has a prime minister who is also a member of the lawmaking body.

Presidential leadership — Form of democracy which places executive authority in one elected official. The power to make laws is placed in another branch or body.

Popular vote — Vote of the people; each voter has an equal voice.

British — Having to do with the country of Great Britain.

There are many countries with democratic governments in the world today. The people of these countries depend on their elected representatives in government to make the laws and rules that keep their freedoms safe. Two important forms of democracy are those that have parliamentary leadership and those that have presidential leadership.

Parliamentary Leadership

Many forms of government give all of the power to one central group of people. Often this group of elected officials is called a *parliament*. The government of Great Britain is a good example of this. Although the British government is really a constitutional monarchy, the Parliament holds the power. It makes the laws and names the prime minister, who is the chief executive. The Parliament, then, holds all of the legislative power and all of the executive power. Local governments exist, but only to help Parliament with some of its duties. This type of government is democratic because the people elect the leaders that represent them. Many other countries have parliamentary leadership, including France, Japan, Israel, and Spain.

Presidential Leadership

A government with presidential leadership divides the power between a central group and several local groups. Sometimes this is done by the power of an even higher authority, such as a constitution, as in the United States. The constitution describes how the power of government is to be divided.

In the United States certain powers are held by the national, or central, government; and other powers are given to the states, or local governments. The chief executive, or President, is head of the executive branch. He is elected by popular vote. The legislative power is given to another branch. The state governments also have executive and legislative branches. Some countries that follow this form of presidential leadership are the United States, Mexico, and Switzerland.

Comparing Government Systems

	United States	Great Britain
Form of Government	Presidential leadership Federal system, with three branches of government Two-party system	Parliamentary leadership One government body, the Parliament Multiple parties
Leader	President elected by by the people	Prime Minister elected by Parliament
Personal Freedom	Guaranteed by the Constitution	Guaranteed by common law and carefully observed tradition.

Forms of Democracy

★*Activity 1.* Number your paper from 1 to 6. Each sentence beginning in Part A has its ending in Part B. Choose the letter of the correct ending. Write that letter next to each number.

Part A

1. In a democracy,...
2. In democratic countries with parliamentary leadership,...
3. In democratic countries with presidential leadership,...
4. All of the power in the British government...
5. In the United States and other countries with presidential leadership, local governments...
6. In countries with presidential leadership, the chief executive...

Part B

a. the executive and legislative power is held by one central group.
b. is elected by popular vote.
c. the central, or national, group separates the legislative and executive powers.
d. the people rule.
e. is held by the Parliament.
f. also have the power to make laws and elect officials.

The United Kingdom is made up of England, Scotland, Wales, and Northern Ireland.

The term *Great Britain* is commonly used in place of *United Kingdom*.

12.4 COMPARING THE GOVERNMENTS OF GREAT BRITAIN AND THE UNITED STATES

Two large islands in northwestern Europe form the nation of Great Britain. The largest island includes England, Scotland, and Wales. The upper part of the second island is Northern Ireland. The southern portion of this island is the independent country of Ireland, which is not part of Great Britain. The people who live within Great Britain are called English, Scottish, Welsh, or Irish, depending on where they live. Often people from these countries are simply called British.

In looking at Great Britain's government as an example of a parliamentary form, we can compare it to our own presidential form. Although the forms may be different, both countries are democracies and have been for a long time. The United States has had its form for more than two hundred years, while Great Britain has had its present form of rule for more than one hundred years. Both governments are based on a constitution, but they are quite different.

The United States Constitution is a carefully-worded document. Everything is written down, even the amendments that have been made through the years. Only part of Great Britain's Constitution is in writing. This is made up from the laws passed by Parliament, from old documents such as the Magna Carta, and from common law. Common law is a group of laws based on customs of the people. The unwritten part of the Constitution includes many traditions, especially the way the Cabinet and the monarch work together.

The chief executive of Great Britain is the prime minister. The prime minister is selected by the controlling party in Parliament, and is formally appointed by the monarch. He or she is not elected as directly by the people as the President of the United States is.

234 — Great Britain's Government

A second difference between the parliamentary and presidential forms of government is that the British Parliament has one strong, central branch of government, which both makes the laws and sees that they are enforced. The United States government has three branches, to balance and separate the power.

A third difference between the two systems is the use of the veto, the power to reject or refuse new legislation. While the President has the power to veto a bill, and uses it from time to time, the prime minister does not have such a power. Although the monarch of Great Britain does have veto authority, it has not been used since the early 1700's.

★**Activity 2.** Number your paper from 1 to 7. Complete the sentences below with words from the box.

parliamentary	Wales	three	one
Constitution	elected	England	
Northern Ireland	veto	Scotland	

1. The countries that make up Great Britain are _____, _____, _____, and _____.
2. Great Britain's government is an example of a _____ form of government.
3. Great Britain's government is run by _____ strong legislative branch.
4. The United States government has _____ separate branches.
5. Both the United States and Great Britain have a _____, but Great Britain's is mostly unwritten.
6. The prime minister of Great Britain is not _____ directly by the people as our President is.
7. In Great Britain, the prime minister has no power to _____ a bill.

A Monarchy That Is Run Like a Democracy

Words to Know:

Generation — The stages or steps in a family's history. For example, a grandfather, a father, and a son are three *generations*

Ceremony — A formal act or celebration in honor of a special event.

Figurehead — A person who is the leader because of his or her name or rank. That person has no real power to make decisions for the group.

Great Britain is officially a monarchy because the head of the government is a king or queen. This title and position is hereditary, which means that it has been handed down from generation to generation. Great Britain has been ruled by Queen Elizabeth since 1952. The Queen is a figurehead, or a symbol to the British people. She approves laws passed by Parliament, although they can become laws without her approval. She signs all important documents and makes speeches to Parliament from time to time. The people look forward to her appearances at ceremonies and special events. The Queen and members of the royal family are highly respected and honored by the British citizens. However, the country's government is run by the prime minister and elected officials, making it a democracy.

★*Activity 3.* Number your paper from 1 to 5. Write the answer to each question below.

1. What is a monarch?
2. How did Queen Elizabeth become a monarch?
3. What is a figurehead?
4. What are some of the duties of the monarch in Great Britain?
5. Who runs the government in Great Britain?

The British Parliament Has Two Houses

Words to Know:

Inherit — To receive something from another after he or she leaves or dies.

Conservative Party — One of the two major political parties in Great Britain. It usually tries to keep the old ways and is against change.

Labour Party — The other major political party in Great Britain. It is usually supported by the workers.

"The Government" — The name given to the political party that is in control in Parliament. It includes the prime minister and his or her Cabinet.

"The Opposition" — The name given to the party that does not have control in Parliament. It always has fewer members than the "Government" party.

The government of Great Britain is run by a law-making body called the Parliament. Parliament works much like the United States Congress. Parliament is made up of two houses, the House of Lords and the House of Commons. Only the members of the House of Commons are elected. A member of the House of Lords receives his or her membership by inheriting it or as an honor granted by the government. Unlike the United States Congress, where both houses are elected, Parliament has only one elected house.

The House of Lords. There are about one thousand members in the House of Lords. This group examines all bills proposed by the House of Commons. Although the House of Lords cannot reject a bill, they can delay its passage. The House of Commons can make a bill a law by voting to approve it two years in a row. The House of Lords also serves as the highest court in Great Britain. It hears cases on appeal from the lower courts, just as the United States Supreme Court does.

The House of Commons. The real power of Parliament is held by the House of Commons. Its 635 members make the laws. One of its members from the majority party becomes prime minister. The prime minister, in turn, selects the heads of government departments. The members of the House of Commons come mainly from the two major political parties in Great Britain, the Conservative Party and the Labour Party.

The Role of Political Parties in the House of Commons. As in the United States, there are two major political parties in Great Britain. These are the Conservative Party and the Labour Party. During a general election, members of the House of Commons are chosen. When the election is over, one of these two parties will have more seats than the other. This party is the majority party and is known as the "Government." The other party is known as the "Opposition." This term comes from the word *oppose*, which means "to be against something." One party is opposed to the other.

Both the "Government" and the "Opposition" have important roles. The leader of the "Government" is the prime minister. The prime minister chooses the Cabinet and department heads from members of the "Government" party. The policies and ideas of the "Government" are put into practice when this winning party takes over. The "Opposition" party keeps check on the party in power by questioning. Four days a week a question period is held in the House of Commons for this purpose. The "Opposition" uses this time to present their views. The "Opposition" is always trying to win the support of the members and return to power.

★**Activity 4.** Number your paper from 1 to 5. To which country does each sentence refer? Write *United States* or *Great Britain* next to each number.

1. The lawmaking body is called Parliament.
2. All members of the Congress are elected.
3. The House of Lords serves as the highest court.
4. The House of Commons has elected members.
5. The Supreme Court hears cases on appeal from the lower courts.

★**Activity 5.** Number your paper from 1 to 5. Which house does each phrase describe? Write *House of Lords* or *House of Commons* next to each number.

1. Approves bills proposed by the House of Commons.
2. Some receive memberships by inheriting them.
3. Makes the laws and names the prime minister.
4. Serves as the highest court in Great Britain.
5. Members mainly come from the Conservative and the Labour Parties.

★**Activity 6.** Number your paper from 1 to 5. Match the terms in Column A with their descriptions in Column B. Write the correct letter next to each number.

Column A
1. Labour
2. Conservative
3. "Government"
4. "Opposition"
5. Prime minister

Column B
a. Majority party in House of Commons is called this.
b. The leader of the "Government," and of the country.
c. The party that is opposed to the majority party.
d. The party that favors doing things in the old way.
e. Party that is usually supported by the workers.

12.5 SOME GOVERNMENTS ARE NOT DEMOCRACIES

One type of government that is not a democracy is a dictatorship. This is probably the oldest form of government. In a dictatorship, all power is held by one person or a small group of people. The people serve the government with little voice in how the government is run. Two examples of complete dictatorships in the twentieth century have been Fascist Italy (1922-1943), and Nazi Germany (1933-1945). The rulers in both these nations did away with those individuals who tried to oppose them. Even more recently, in Uganda, Africa, Idi Amin Dada took over the country and named himself President-for-Life. His eight-year rule was cruel, and thousands died until his government was overthrown in 1979.

Another form of government that is not democratic is communism. The Soviet Union is the oldest communist government. Other communist nations are the People's Republic of China, Vietnam, Cuba, and Yugoslavia.

12.6 COMMUNIST GOVERNMENT OF THE SOVIET UNION

Words to Know:

Communism — A system in which the community owns all the property and individuals share goods. There is no private ownership.

Collective farms — Farms that are owned by the group of people who work on them. The workers share the goods.

The Communist government of the Soviet Union came into power in 1917. At that time the ruler, called the Czar, was overthrown, and the Communists took over. Under this new rule, the government ran all the industries such as iron, steel, oil, coal, and railroads. The large homes and property of wealthy people were divided up among the peasants, or poor people of the country. There were also small farms that joined together to form larger farms, called *collective* farms. Factory workers and farmers were urged to give up personal comforts to build up the country's industry. In modern times, people live under many restrictions. The government controls everything, from industry to the newspapers people read. Private ownership of business or property is not allowed. This is very different from the United States, where private ownership is encouraged.

How the Soviet Government Is Organized

The Soviet Union is made up of fifteen smaller union republics. Each has a lawmaking body or council called a *soviet*. Actually, these councils have very litte power. They do no more than carry out the laws made by a group called the Supreme Soviet. This Supreme Soviet is made up of representatives from the fifteen republics. It makes laws for the whole nation. It also runs the departments of the government that handle such things as finance, defense, foreign affairs, industry, and agriculture. The republics make few of their own laws. In the United States, although Congress makes laws for the whole country, the states do make many of their own laws.

The head of the government is called the Premier. He is the chairman of a group called the Council of Ministers, who are appointed by the Supreme Soviet. The Council of Ministers has a great deal of power. It has more power than the President of the United States or a prime minister has. All of Russia's leaders are members of the Communist Party, the only political party in the Soviet Union.

★Activity 7. Number your paper from 1 to 5. Complete each sentence in Part A by choosing its ending in Part B. Write the correct letter next to each number.

Part A
1. The Soviet Union does not run...
2. In the Soviet Union the government controls...
3. Private ownership of business and property in the United States is...
4. The Supreme Soviet, made up of representatives from the republics,...
5. The head of the government in the Soviet Union...

Part B
a. not only allowed, but is encouraged.
b. is called the Premier.
c. everything from industry to the newspapers.
d. makes laws for the whole nation.
e. its government as democratic countries do.

Government of the Soviet Union

Premier
Chief Administrator

Council of Ministers
About 95 members. Controls the economic and cultural life. Controls foreign relations.

Supreme Soviet of the U.S.S.R.
Two-house legislature. About 1500 members. Passes laws proposed by Communist Party leaders. Appoints members of the Council of Ministers.

The Only Party Is the Communist Party

In the United States and other democracies, at least two major political parties with different ideas are always trying to gain control of the government. This is not true in the Soviet Union. There is one political party — the Communist Party. The government simply accepts all the decisions of the party and makes them into laws. All the members of the government are also members of the Communist Party.

In contrast, the United States government is made up of members who belong to different political parties, with sometimes very different views. Even within one party, members have different ideas about running the government. The final decision about how the government is to be run is made by the voters — the American people.

When a Russian citizen votes, there is only one candidate for an office. If the voter does not favor that candidate, he can simply cross out the name. Sometimes voters are afraid to vote against someone by crossing out the name because they do not have complete privacy in voting. Unless one-half of the voters cross out a name, the candidate is elected. Few candidates ever lose an election. Failure to vote in the Soviet Union is a serious matter and may be reported to the police.

Not Everyone Can Join the Communist Party

A person wishing to join the Communist Party in the Soviet Union must apply and go through an investigation before he or she is accepted. Young people between the ages of 18 and 23 must have been members of the Young Communist League. This is a youth group that teaches and trains children in party ideals. All people who apply also spend a year working for the party to show that they are loyal. After this year of probation is passed, a person then becomes a member of the party. Every workplace in the Soviet Union — factory, government office, school, store, village, collective farm, or armed forces station — has a small Communist Party group of loyal members.

Organization of the Communist Party

There are hundreds of thousands of small Communist Party groups throughout the country. One of the duties of members is to act as "watchdog" for the party. For example, members observe how their fellow factory workers do their jobs. They check to see if factory managers meet their quotas, or amounts of goods they are required to produce. Workers can lose their jobs if they do not please the party group in their place of work. Most of the important positions in the workplace are filled by Communist Party members. It is difficult for Russians to get ahead in the Soviet Union if they do not belong to the Communist Party. All these small groups and other larger groups are joined together by the Politburo. This powerful group of fifteen members makes most of the important decisions for the party.

"Worker and Woman Collective Farmer"

This 80-foot high statue stands at the entrance to the Exhibition of Economic Achievements in Moscow, capital of the Soviet Union.

244 — Government of the Soviet Union

Political Parties in Democratic Countries

In the United States and other democratic countries, people may join any political party they choose. This could be one of the major parties or a third, or minor, party. They may choose not to join any party at all. This freedom of expression is one feature of democratic forms of government. Because most industry in the United States, for example, is privately owned and operated, political parties are not concerned with work quotas. This is the concern of the owner of the business and his desire to make a profit. Workers, in most democratic countries, are not hired, promoted, or fired because of the political party they belong to.

★*Activity 8.* Number your paper from 1 to 6. Select a word from the box below that completes each sentence. Write the correct word beside each number.

1. There is _____ political party to join in the Soviet Union.
2. When a Russian citizen votes, he may _____ out the name of a candidate he does not support.
3. Membership in the Communist Party is _____ to some Soviet citizens.
4. The Young Communist League is a youth group that teaches Communist _____.
5. Communist Party members in a place of work observe how _____ do their jobs.
6. In _____ countries, people may join any political party they choose.

open	one	ideals
workers	some	cross

The Soviet Constitution

The Soviet Union has a written Constitution just as the United States and other countries do. It has been rewritten three times in the last sixty years. One important part of the Constitution points out that the Communist Party is the guiding force behind the government. This article of the Constitution states in part:

> "**The leading and guiding force of Soviet society and the nucleus of its political system . . . is the Communist Party of the Soviet Union.**"

In contrast, the United States Constitution makes no mention of political parties. The parties were free to develop over the years.

Constitutional Rights, Freedoms, and Duties

The Soviet Constitution mentions "rights, freedoms, and duties," as the United States Constitution does. Rights such as freedom of speech, press, and assembly are allowed in the Soviet Union. The Constitution grants these rights but only "with the aims of building communism." There have been many reports in the press of Soviet citizens being arrested for speaking out against the government. Newspapers may print the news after it is approved by a government agency. The Communist Party has an official news agency called Tass, which selects the news to be released to the public.

In the United States there is no government agency telling the newspapers what to print. Newspapers are not owned by the government as they are in the Soviet Union. The owners of the newspapers in the United States decide what to print.

Everyday Life in Democratic Countries and in Communist Countries

The opportunities people have to make choices and to control their own lives depend on where they live. People have different interests, religions, and ideas about how government should be run. Only in democratic countries do citizens have a choice of political parties.

There are other choices available in democratic countries. People may join private groups, clubs, or societies. These may include church groups, political groups, youth groups, small business associations, or sports organizations. The organizations make rules and laws to govern themselves and keep order. These groups may have to follow guidelines set by federal or local governments, but after these guidelines are met, the group is free to operate as the members decide. If members do not agree with the rules, they may work to change them. If they are still unhappy, they can give up their membership by leaving the group. They may even start their own group, whether it be a church, political party, or small club, and try to persuade others to join.

The Flag of Russia

Government of the Soviet Union — 247

In countries ruled by the Communist Party, such as the Soviet Union, opportunities for people to form small, private organizations is limited or even forbidden. However, it has been impossible for governments to limit all private groups, although many countries have tried. Churches and church groups, for instance, continue to exist in most countries, and are privately run.

★*Activity 9.* Number your paper from 1 to 7. Choose the correct word to complete each sentence from the words given. Write your answer next to each number.

1. The Constitution of the _____ (Soviet Union, United States) states that the Communist Party is the guiding force behind the government.
2. The United States Constitution makes no mention of political _____ (elections, parties).
3. The Soviet Constitution mentions freedom of speech, but there are press reports of citizens being _____ (arrested, concerned) for speaking against the government.
4. Tass is the news agency that selects the news to print in the _____ (Soviet Union, United States).
5. In the United States, the owners of the _____ (government, newspapers) decide what to print.
6. In _____ (communist, democratic) countries there are many choices to be made, such as joining small private groups, clubs, and societies.
7. Communist governments find it impossible to limit all private groups; _____ (churches, parties) still exist in most communist countries.

SUMMARY OF CHAPTER 12

All countries are ruled by some form of government. Many are democracies. Other countries have systems of government run according to the ideals of the Communist Party.

Democratic countries usually follow the parliamentary or presidential forms of government. In the parliamentary form all power to make laws (legislative power) and to carry out the laws (executive power) is given to a single group, often called a Parliament. An example of this is the government of Great Britain. In the presidential form, the legislative and executive powers are given to separate groups. This type of government is found in the United States.

Great Britain and the United States

Although Great Britain and the United States are both democracies, their governments operate in different ways. The British prime minister is not elected by direct popular vote as our President is. He or she is the leader of the majority party in the House of Commons, one of the two houses of Parliament. The other house is the House of Lords. Only members of the House of Commons are elected; the Lords receive their titles by inheriting them, or as an honor. Great Britain also has a monarch, who serves as a figurehead.

Both the United States and Great Britain have two major political parties. One party or the other is usually in control of the government in these countries.

Communism and Democracy

In countries run by the Communist Party, such as the Soviet Union, the government controls everything. There is only one political party for voters to choose candidates from — the Communist Party. In the United States, Great Britain, and other democratic countries, candidates come from two or more political parties. Citizens may vote for any candidate and join any political party. In the Soviet Union citizens can join the Communist Party only if they are accepted. They must prove themselves by working hard for the party for a year before they can become members. Small groups of these members are found in all places of work. These loyal members act as "watchdogs" for the party, making sure all workers are doing their jobs. To get a good job in the Soviet Union, a person must be a Communist Party member.

The Soviet Constitution does include rights and freedoms for its citizens, but everything must be done for the benefit of the Communist Party. Freedom of press and speech are limited. If a person speaks out against the government, he may be arrested. The government also limits what news the public may know. In the United States, citizens may speak out against the government and its leaders.

Another difference between democratic and communist countries is the opportunity for citizens to form private groups, clubs, and organizations. In communist countries, the formation of these private groups is not allowed. Democratic countries allow and even encourage citizens to take part in private groups.

• CHAPTER REVIEW ACTIVITY •

Number your paper from 1 to 10. Choose the correct word or words to complete each sentence. Write your answer next to the number.

1. _____ countries usually follow either the parliamentary or presidential form of government. (Democratic, Communist)
2. An example of a country with the parliamentary form of government is _____. (Great Britain, the United States, the Soviet Union)
3. An example of a country with a presidential form of government is _____. (Great Britain, the United States, the Soviet Union)
4. The _____ is not elected directly by popular vote. (President, prime minister)
5. The members of the House of _____ receive their titles by inheriting them. (Commons, Lords)
6. The United States and Great Britain each have _____ major political parties. (one, two, three)
7. In countries run by the _____ Party, the government controls almost everything. (political, Communist)
8. Loyal Communist Party members act as _____ for the party in all places of work. (leaders, watchdogs, members)
9. In the United States, citizens _____ speak out against the government. (may, may not)
10. In _____ countries, citizens are allowed to take part in private groups. (democratic, communist)

Chapter 13

Citizenship

13.1 UNITED STATES CITIZENS

The United States is sometimes called a "melting pot." This is because people of many different races and nationalities have come from other countries to live here. An American citizen may have a great-grandfather who was German and a great-grandmother who was Irish. Through intermarriage, these nationalities become mixed. The citizen is not German or Irish, but American. Even though a great deal of "melting" like this has taken place in America, many people keep some of the culture, the traditions and customs, of their family members who first settled in this country. The United States is a country of many cultures.

Ukrainians in America continue their custom of decorating eggs with intricate designs.

A person may be an American citizen by birth. A person who was born in another country may become an American citizen through a process called "naturalization." No matter how they become citizens, Americans enjoy many rights. There are responsibilities of citizenship, as well. A responsible citizen respects the rights of others.

13.2 MANY PEOPLE HAVE SETTLED IN THE UNITED STATES

Words to Know:

Immigrant — A person who enters a new country in order to settle there.

Revolution — A sudden political overthrow of a government. Some citizens' lives could be endangered.

Famine — A serious shortage of food, causing people to starve.

Refuge — Protection; shelter.

Refugee — A person who flees from his country to find refuge from harm.

Asian — A person who lives in Asia, the world's largest continent.

Latin American — A person who lives in one of the countries of Latin America. These countries are south of the United States. Their languages, such as Spanish or Portuguese, have come from the Latin language.

Why People Came

The first settlers came to this country to gain the freedom they did not have in the countries of their birth. Through the years, immigrants have come to the United States in great numbers. Many were escaping unfair treatment or seeking the freedoms guaranteed by the United States Constitution.

Certain groups immigrated to this country at different times for different reasons. For example, revolutions and famines drove people from their own lands. These people chose the United States as the land of refuge and opportunity. Large numbers of immigrants came as laborers.

Limits on Immigration

One period of time when few immigrants came to this country was during the Great Depression in the 1930's. There were so few jobs available then that many Americans were out of work.

Immigrants crowded on a ship in 1871.

Between 1900 and 1930 most immigrants to the United States came from Europe. Our country had put limits on the number of people from other parts of the world who could enter. The immigration law of 1965 changed those limits. Now about eighty percent of new immigrants are Asian or Latin American.

As the law stands now, there is a set number of immigrants who may be admitted to the United States each year. The number of immigrants from any one country has a limit. In certain situations refugees from political or religious persecution are also allowed. Examples of this are the Vietnamese and Cambodians who came to the United States after the Vietnam War.

Often more people wish to come to the United States than the yearly limit allows. Then each case is judged by itself. People who are relatives of United States citizens have a better chance of being admitted than those who are not. People who have special talents or job skills may qualify over those who do not.

★**Activity 1.** Number your paper from 1 to 6. Complete each sentence in Part A with its ending in Part B. Write the correct letter next to each number.

Part A

1. The United States is sometimes called a "melting pot" because...
2. A person born in the United States...
3. Immigrants may become naturalized citizens by...
4. Many immigrants have come to the United States to...
5. During the Great Depression of the 1930's,...
6. After the war in Vietnam, many Vietnamese and Cambodians...

Part B

a. doing certain things required by law.
b. escape mistreatment, famines, and revolutions in the countries of their birth.
c. people of many different races and nationalities live here.
d. becomes a United States citizen at birth.
e. came to this country as political refugees.
f. there were few jobs available in the United States.

Immigrants Contribute to the United States

Immigrants and their offspring have enriched the American way of life. Two examples are Andrew Carnegie and Cesar Chavez.

Andrew Carnegie. Andrew Carnegie and his family arrived in America from Scotland in 1848. He was thirteen years old. His family was quite poor. Every member tried to work hard and to be honest. Andrew had a number of low-paying jobs during his youth. His hard work helped him advance in the companies where he worked. Carnegie finally went into the steel business. He made a fortune by the time he reached middle age. Carnegie believed in sharing his wealth. He gave millions of dollars to education, libraries, and the cause of peace.

Cesar Chavez. Cesar Chavez was born in Arizona in 1927. His parents were of Mexican birth and had come to the United States from Mexico. When he was a boy, he and his family became migrant farmworkers in California. Migrant farmworkers harvest crops, and move from place to place as the crops ripen and need to be picked. Chavez dedicated his life to help farmworkers. He organized the poor and underpaid workers. By using peaceful means, he helped them get better pay and working conditions. Change did not always come easily. Under Chavez's leadership, the grape pickers refused to work for almost five years. Finally, the farm owners agreed to give the pickers work contracts and higher pay.

Cesar Chavez

13.3 TYPES OF CITIZENSHIP

Words to Know:

Diplomat — A person appointed or named to represent his country in another country.

Native country — The country a person belongs to by birth.

Deport — To send away or to expel from a country.

Naturalization — The act of giving full citizenship to a person of foreign birth.

United States Citizens by Birth

Most Americans are native-born. This means they are citizens simply because they were born in the United States or in one of its territories. A person born to American parents in a foreign country is also a United States citizen. In most cases a child born to foreign parents in the United States is considered a United States citizen. These parents must be living according to the laws of the United States at the time of the child's birth. This is not true for people representing other governments in this country, such as diplomats. They are subject to the laws of their own country; therefore, their children become citizens of their parents' native country. When there is any question about whether or not a person is legally a United States citizen, the matter must be settled by the Department of Justice.

United States Citizens by Naturalization

Aliens are persons who are citizens of another country but are in the United States for any of a number of reasons. They must abide by the laws of this country. They enjoy most of the rights of an American citizen. They may be visitors. They may have jobs here and plan at some time to return to their own countries. Many aliens hope to become citizens of the

United States. It is possible for them to do so by means of a legal process called *naturalization*. For whatever reasons they are in this country, aliens must register once a year in January with the United States Immigration and Naturalization Service.

The Immigration and Naturalization Service, an agency which is part of the Department of Justice, is in charge of laws having to do with aliens. The agency says who may enter this country, who may be naturalized, and who is to be deported. An alien who is deported must leave this country and return to the country of his or her birth. Congress has made a number of regulations concerning reasons why an alien might be deported. It may be because the person has committed a serious crime. Perhaps the person is loyal to some government that is unfriendly to the United States.

Rules for Naturalization. Congress has made rules for aliens to follow in order to become naturalized citizens. These rules say that aliens must:
1. Be at least eighteen years of age.
2. Have lived in the United States for
    a. five years, or
    b. three years, if married to a United States citizen, or
    c. less time, if the person has served a year in some branch of the armed services.
3. Make an application, or a request, for naturalization to the Immigration authorities.
4. Be able to speak, read, and write English reasonably well.
5. Have two witnesses testify that they are good, honest people.
6. Know about the history of the United States and its government.

7. Take an examination about United States history and government.
8. Promise not to support any government or belief that would overthrow the government of the United States.
9. Make an oath of loyalty to the United States in court before a judge.

After aliens have successfully done these things, they become citizens of the United States, with all the rights and privileges of citizens by birth. There is an exception to this. No former alien may become President of the United States. The children of naturalized citizens automatically become citizens when their parents do. These children must be under the age of 16 and living in the United States at the time.

It is possible for naturalized citizens to lose citizenship. This can happen for a number of reasons. However, usually it is because the aliens were dishonest and untruthful about themselves when they became naturalized citizens. Taking away citizenship has to be done by court order. The proper process of law must be followed.

Political Asylum. This country also offers to aliens a protection called political asylum. The word *asylum* refers to a place of safety. *Political asylum* means a place where a person is safe from the dangerous actions or beliefs of his or her own country or government. From time to time, there will be news reports about persons who defect from their native countries and are seeking political asylum in the United States. They may be visitors, athletes, artists, sailors, or workers for another government, who feel mistreated by their own countries. The United States offers protection to such people until it is clear why they wish to

Naturalized Citizens — 259

leave their native lands. If reasons for their actions are strong enough, the aliens are allowed to stay. They may apply for United States citizenship just like any other aliens.

★**Activity 2.** Number your paper from 1 to 10. Complete each sentence with a word from the box. Write that word next to the number.

aliens	January	deported	Immigration
citizen	Justice	birth	naturalization
asylum	country		

1. Most Americans are citizens by _____.
2. A person born to American parents in a foreign country is a United States _____.
3. Children born in the United States to parents who represent another government become citizens of their parents' _____.
4. Questions about who is legally a United States citizen are settled by the _____ and Naturalization Service.
5. Citizens of other countries who are in the United States are called _____.
6. Aliens must register with the Immigration and Naturalization Service each _____.
7. The Immigration and Naturalization Service is an agency of the _____ Department.
8. An alien who is _____ is forced to leave this country and return to his or her own country.
9. The legal process a person must go through to become a United States citizen is called _____.
10. A person seeking _____ is looking for a safe place to live.

13.4 RIGHTS OF CITIZENSHIP

Words to Know:

Grand jury — Investigates the charges against a person accused of a crime; decides if a trial should be held.

Acquitted — Cleared from charges made.

Impartial — Fair; not taking sides

Responsible people realize that they must give as well as take if they want to get along with other people. This is the way that family members, classmates, friends, and even governments can get along. No one group or person can have things his way completely. To have agreement, sometimes a compromise is necessary.

A compromise was made at the First Congress that met in New York in 1789 after the Constitution was approved. Some Anti-Federalist members of the Congress, including Thomas Jefferson, felt that the Constitution gave too much power to the federal government. They were afraid this might mean that American citizens could lose some of the rights they had struggled so hard to get. These men agreed to accept the Constitution only if it contained a Bill of Rights. They thought the Constitution should clearly state the rights individuals were entitled to. This Bill of Rights, the first ten amendments of the Constitution, was added by the First Congress. The rights the Anti-Federalists asked for and the Federalists agreed to are listed below:

1. Citizens should have freedom of religion, speech, press, assembly (to gather together in groups), and petition (to make requests concerning government and laws).

2. Citizens should have the right to bear arms (have guns for protection).

3. Government should not station troops (soldiers) in people's homes without their permission.

4. No unreasonable searches or seizures of homes or businesses can be made without a warrant.

5. Before a person can be tried, he or she must be indicted (accused after evidence has been studied) by a grand jury. There must be a good reason for a trial. No one may be tried for the same crime twice. A person who is acquitted is free of the charge forever.

6. Persons accused of crimes have the right to a speedy trial before a fair jury that is impartial.

7. A jury must be used if more than twenty dollars is involved in a lawsuit.

8. No one can be made to pay extremely high bail or fines, and must not be given punishment that is cruel and unusual.

9. Individuals have rights other than those listed in the Bill of Rights. Any right not written down is known as a reserved right.

10. If certain powers are not given to the federal government, or denied to the states, then these powers belong to the states.

★**Activity 3.** Number your paper from 1 to 11. Read each right listed below. Write the number of the amendment that guarantees that right next to each of your numbers.

1. Right to bear arms.
2. Right to a speedy trial before a fair jury.
3. Rights other than those listed in the Bill of Rights.
4. No unreasonable searches or seizures without a warrant.
5. Freedom of religion.
6. No cruel or unusual punishment.
7. Freedom of speech.
8. Freedom of the press.
9. No trial without indictment (a list of charges).
10. Freedom of assembly (to gather in groups).
11. Freedom of petition (requests concerning government laws or regulations).

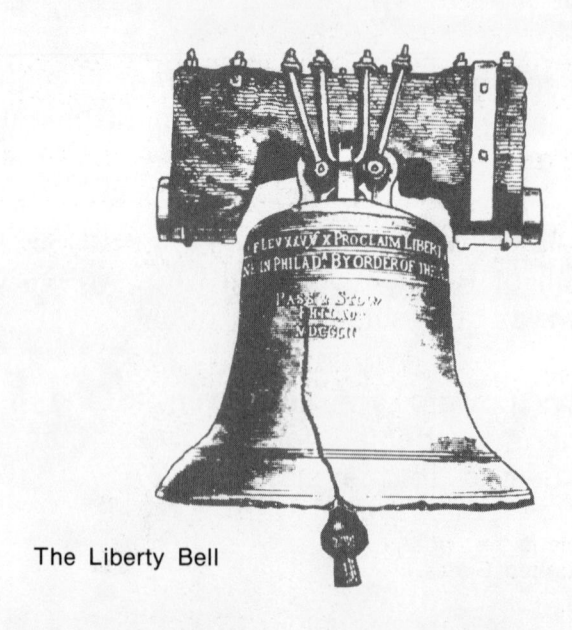

The Liberty Bell

Using the Rights of Citizenship

Certain rights are guaranteed to all American citizens. No two human beings are exactly alike. Each person is born with different talents and abilities. No two people look exactly alike or act just the same. In school everyone does not make the same grades. Not everyone has the same academic or athletic ability, or the same artistic or musical talent. In the business world everyone is not capable of doing the same job. Some people become rich and famous, while others lead simple, quiet lives. So what does the Declaration of Independence mean when it says, "...All men are created equal..."? Equality among citizens is based on opportunities and rights. How rights are used is up to the individual. American citizens are born with the rights named in the Constitution and its Amendments. Naturalized citizens receive them with their citizenship. Even though these rights do not have to be earned, they do have to be protected. Citizens do this by using their rights wisely and respecting the rights of others.

The bald eagle is the national bird of the United States.

How Some Rights May or May Not Be Used

What are some of the responsibilities citizens have in using and protecting their rights? What is the proper use of a right? What is not a proper use? Some of the rights contained in the first ten amendments are listed below, along with examples of how they may be used.

Right: Freedom of Religion

Citizens May: Worship as they please and join any church they wish.

Citizens May Not: Interfere with anyone else's religious freedom.

Right: Freedom of Speech

Citizens May: Speak their feelings, even about government, without fear of punishment.

Citizens May Not: Harm others with their speech or prevent others from speaking freely.

Right: Freedom of Assembly

Citizens May: Gather in groups to discuss issues or to demonstrate peaceably.

Citizens May Not: Assemble to cause a riot or to damage people or property.

Right: To Bear Arms

Citizens May: Own approved firearms for purposes of recreation and protection.

Citizens May Not: Use firearms in unlawful ways.

Right: Reserved

Citizens May: Enjoy certain rights not listed in the Bill of Rights, such as to travel freely anywhere in the country.

Citizens May Not: Use these reserved rights to do anything unlawful.

Right: Freedom of the Press

Citizens May: Publish opinions and criticisms of issues without fear of punishment.

Citizens May Not: Publish false statements or pictures that would harm an individual or group.

★*Activity 4.* Number your paper from 1 to 10. Answer the questions. Write *Yes* or *No* next to each number.

1. May citizens worship as they please?
2. May citizens assemble to start a riot?
3. May citizens say how they feel about the government without fear of punishment?
4. May citizens own approved firearms to use for hunting?
5. May citizens publish lies in order to hurt a certain group?
6. May citizens gather for peaceful demonstrations?
7. May citizens publish their opinions and criticisms of current affairs without fear of punishment?
8. May citizens use their reserved rights to break a law?
9. May citizens use firearms in unlawful ways?
10. May citizens enjoy rights that are not listed in the Bill of Rights?

13.5 DUTIES OF CITIZENS

Rights and protections could not survive unless citizens took their duties seriously. These include civic duties—support of the government, observance of laws, and defense of the country. There are also political duties—taking part in government by helping elect government representatives who will best serve the people.

Even before citizens are old enough to vote, they can still serve their country and communities by studying in school about their government. They can learn about good citizenship by participating in school and community projects that require cooperation and a democratic attitude. In school, these projects might include playing in the school band, taking part in student government, and respecting school rules, teachers, and fellow classmates. In the community, young citizens can hold membership in clubs that promote patriotism. They can also volunteer time to one of many community groups that help other people achieve a better quality of life.

An important duty for all citizens is to gain a knowledge of laws that affect them and their communities. They are expected to obey the laws. They are encouraged to express their opinions about which laws they feel are serving the people well and which laws they feel are not. Young people can prepare for the day when they will be voters by keeping up with current events in local, state, national, and international communities.

★**Activity 5.** Number your paper from 1 to 6. The sentences in Part A are not complete. Find their endings in Part B. Write the correct letter next to each number.

Part A

1. Three civic duties are...
2. An important political duty of a voter is to help...
3. Students who are too young to vote may serve their country by...
4. In the community, young citizens can join...
5. An important duty for all citizens is to gain a knowledge...
6. Young people can prepare for the day they will be voters by keeping up with...

Part B

a. clubs that promote patriotism.
b. elect government representatives who will best serve the people.
c. of laws that affect them and their communities.
d. support of the government, observance of laws, and defense of the country.
e. current events in their country and the world.
f. studying in school about their government.

Pledge of Allegiance to the Flag
I pledge allegiance to the flag of the United States of America and to the Republic for which it stands, one Nation under God, indivisible, with liberty and justice for all.

STATUE OF LIBERTY

The Statue of Liberty stands on Liberty Island in New York Harbor. Made of copper hammered on iron, it stands 151 feet tall. A newly restored "Miss Liberty" was given a hundredth birthday celebration during the Fourth of July week in 1986. This symbol of freedom was a gift to the United States from France and dedicated by President Grover Cleveland in October, 1886. Throughout the past hundred years, the sight of the statue has greeted great numbers of immigrants as they have sailed into New York Harbor.

Close by Liberty Island is Ellis Island. It was an immigrant station until 1954. Many immigrants to the United States were required to stay there for a period of time to determine whether they were eligible to enter the country.

How fitting it is that a bronze plaque on the Statue of Liberty seems to give an invitation to all who would seek freedom in the United States. It contains the words from the poem, "The New Colossus," by Emma Lazarus, who befriended immigrants. It reads:

> Give me your tired, your poor,
> Your huddled masses, yearning to breathe free,
> The wretched refuse of your teeming shore.
> Send these, the homeless, tempest tossed, to me;
> I lift my lamp beside the golden door.

SUMMARY OF CHAPTER 13

The United States is known as a "melting pot" because its citizens represent so many nationalities. Throughout the history of the United States, immigrants from many lands have flocked to its shores. The first settlers were escaping what they felt was unfair treatment in the countries of their birth. Other settlers came to escape famine and revolutions, or to have an opportunity to improve their lives.

Between 1900 and 1930, a large number of immigrants came to the United States from European countries. More recently, the largest number of immigrants have come from Asian and Latin American countries. There are limits on how many immigrants are admitted from different countries. Our country offers a home to refugees. It also grants political asylum to people who defect from their countries for strong reasons.

Anyone born in the United States or in its territories becomes a United States citizen. Anyone born of American parents anywhere in the world also becomes a United States citizen. However, children born to people representing their governments in the United States are not United States citizens. An alien is someone who was born in another country, but who is in the United States as a visitor, a worker, or a student. An alien may become a naturalized United States citizen by meeting certain requirements.

United States citizens are guaranteed rights by the Bill of Rights. Citizens also have duties. Some of these duties are required by law. Responsible citizens do more than what is required by law. They take an interest in government. They take part in community activities, and they vote regularly. When citizens carry out their duties and respect the rights of others, the quality of life is made better for everyone.

• CHAPTER REVIEW ACTIVITY •

Number your paper from 1 to 17. Choose words from the box to complete the paragraphs below. Write the correct word next to each number.

The first settlers came to America to escape 1)_____ treatment. Later, other people came to escape 2)_____ or 3)_____. Some came to better their lives. Before 1930, most of these immigrants came from 4)_____ countries. Now most immigrants come from 5)_____ and Latin American countries. America also offers a home to religious or 6)_____ refugees.

An 7)_____ is someone born in another country and who is in the United States as a visitor, worker, or 8)_____. An alien is required to do certain things by 9)_____ in order to become a United States citizen. People born in the United States or born of American citizens anywhere in the 10)_____ are United States citizens.

A foreigner who feels that he is mistreated may seek a place of safety, or political 11)_____, in the United States. This person is 12)_____. If his reasons are accepted, he may remain and apply for citizenship.

United States citizens have certain 13)_____ given by the Bill of Rights. Citizens also have 14)_____ that are required by law. Responsible citizens also learn about their 15)_____. They 16)_____ regularly. They use their rights 17)_____.

revolution	Asian	unfair	European
famine	rights	asylum	student
investigated	law	alien	world
political	vote	duties	wisely
government			

APPENDIX

THE DECLARATION OF INDEPENDENCE
(Adopted in Congress July 4, 1776)

The Unanimous Declaration of the Thirteen United States of America

When, in the course of human events, it becomes necessary for one people to dissolve the political bands which have connected them with another, and to assume among the powers of the earth, the separate and equal station to which the laws of nature and of nature's God entitle them, a decent respect to the opinions of mankind requires that they should declare the causes which impel them to the separation.

(A Declaration of Independence)

We hold these truths to be self-evident, that all men are created equal, that they are endowed by their Creator with certain unalienable rights, that among these are life, liberty, and the pursuit of happiness. That to secure these rights, governments are instituted among men, deriving their just powers from the consent of the governed. That whenever any form of government becomes destructive of these ends, it is the right of the people to alter or to abolish it, and to institute new government, laying its foundation on such principles and organizing its powers in such form, as to them shall seem most likely to effect their safety and happiness. Prudence, indeed, will dictate that governments long established should not be changed for light and transient causes; and accordingly all experience hath shown that mankind are more disposed to suffer, while evils are sufferable, than to right themselves by abolishing the forms to which they are accustomed. But when a long train of abuses and usurpations, pursuing invariably the same object evinces a design to reduce them under absolute despotism, it is their right, it is their duty, to throw off such government, and to provide new guards for their future security.

(A Bill of Indictment)

Such has been the patient sufferance of these colonies; and such is now the necessity which constrains them to alter their former systems of government. The history of the present King of Great Britain is a history of repeated injuries and usurpations, all having in direct object the establishment of an absolute tyranny over these states. To prove this, let facts be submitted to a candid world.

He has refused his assent to laws, the most wholesome and necessary for the public good.

He has forbidden his governors to pass laws of immediate and pressing importance, unless suspended in their operation till his assent should be obtained; and when so suspended, he has utterly neglected to attend to them.

He has refused to pass other laws for the accommodation of large districts of people, unless those people would relinquish the right of representation in the legislature, a right inestimable to them and formidable to tyrants only.

He has called together legislative bodies at places unusual, uncomfortable, and distant from the depository of their public records, for the sole purpose of fatiguing them into compliance with his measures.

He has dissolved representative houses and repeatedly, for opposing with manly firmness his invasions on the rights of the people.

He has refused for a long time, after such dissolutions, to cause others to be elected; whereby the legislative powers, incapable of annihilation, have returned to the people at large for their exercise; the state remaining in the meantime exposed to all the dangers of invasion from without, and convulsions within.

He has endeavored to prevent the population of these states; for that purpose obstructing the laws for naturalization of foreigners, refusing to pass others to encourage their migrations hither, and raising the conditions of new appropriations of lands.

He has obstructed the administration of justice, by refusing his assent to laws for establishing judiciary powers.

He has made judges dependent on his will alone, for the tenure of their offices, and the amount and payment of their salaries.

He has erected a multitude of new offices, and sent hither swarms of officers to harass our people, and eat out their substance.

He has kept among us, in times of peace, standing armies without the consent of our legislatures.

He has affected to render the military independent of and superior to the civil power.

He has combined with others to subject us to a jurisdiction foreign to our constitution, and unacknowledged by our laws; giving his assent to their acts of pretended legislation:

For quartering large bodies of armed troops among us;

For protecting them, by a mock trial, from punishment for any murders which they should commit on the inhabitants of these states;

For cutting off our trade with all parts of the world;

For imposing taxes on us without our consent;

For depriving us in many cases, of the benefits of trial by jury;

For transporting us beyond seas to be tried for pretended offenses;

For abolishing the free system of English laws in a neighboring province, establishing therein an arbitrary government, and enlarging its boundaries so as to render it at once an example and fit instrument for introducing the same absolute rule into these colonies;

For taking away our charters, abolishing our most valuable laws, and altering fundamentally the forms of our governments;

For suspending our own legislatures, and declaring themselves invested with power to legislate for us in all cases whatsoever.

He has abdicated government here, by declaring us out of his protection and waging war against us.

He has plundered our seas, ravaged our coasts, burned our towns, and destroyed the lives of our people.

He is at this time transporting large armies of foreign mercenaries to complete the works of death, desolation and tyranny, already begun with circumstances of cruelty and perfidy scarcely paralleled in the most barbarous ages, and totally unworthy the head of a civilized nation.

He has constrained our fellow citizens taken captive on the high seas to bear arms against their country, to become the executioners of their friends and brethren, or to fall themselves by their hands.

He has excited domestic insurrections amongst us, and has endeavored to bring on the inhabitants of our frontiers, the merciless Indian savages, whose known rule of warfare, is an undistinguished destruction of all ages, sexes, and conditions.

(A Statement of Independence)

In every stage of these oppressions we have petitioned for redress in the most humble terms: our repeated petitions have been answered only by repeated injury. A prince whose character is thus marked by every act which may define a tyrant is unfit to be the ruler of a free people.

Nor have we been wanting in attentions to our British brethren. We have warned them from time to time of attempts by their legislature to extend an unwarrantable jurisdiction over us. We have reminded them of the circumstances of our emigration and settlement here. We have appealed to their native justice and magnanimity, and we have conjured them by the ties of our common kindred to disavow these usurpations, which would inevitably interrupt our connections and correspondence. They too have been deaf to the voice of justice and of consanguinity. We must, therefore, acquiesce in the necessity, which denounces our separation, and hold them, as we hold the rest of mankind, enemies in war, in peace, friends.

We, therefore, the representatives of the United States of America, in General Congress, assembled, appealing to the Supreme Judge of the world for the rectitude of our intentions, do, in the name, and by the authority of the good people of these colonies, solemnly publish and declare, that these united colonies are, and of right ought to be free and independent states; that they are absolved from all allegiance to the British Crown, and that all political connection between them and the state of Great Britain, is and ought to be totally dissolved; and that as free and independent states, they have full power to levy war, conclude peace, contract alliances, establish commerce, and to do all other acts and things which independent states may of right do. And for the support of this declaration, with a firm reliance on the protection of Divine Providence, we mutually pledge to each other our lives, our fortunes, and our sacred honor.

Signed by John Hancock of Massachusetts as President of the Congress and by the fifty-five other Representatives of the thirteen United States of America.

THE CONSTITUTION OF THE UNITED STATES

PREAMBLE

We the people of the United States, in order to form a more perfect Union, establish justice, insure domestic tranquility, provide for the common defense, promote the general welfare, and secure the blessings of liberty to ourselves and our posterity, do ordain and establish this Constitution for the United States of America.

ARTICLE I

The Legislative Branch

Section 1. All legislative powers herein granted shall be vested in a Congress of the United States, which shall consist of a Senate and House of Representatives.

The House of Representatives

Section 2. (1) The House of Representatives shall be composed of members chosen every second year by the people of the several states, and the electors in each state shall have the qualifications requisite for electors of the most numerous branch of the state legislature.

(2) No person shall be a representative who shall not have attained to the age of twenty-five years, and been seven years a citizen of the United States, and who shall not, when elected, be an inhabitant of that state in which he shall be chosen.

(3) Representatives and direct taxes shall be apportioned among the several states which may be included within this Union, according to their respective numbers, *[which shall be determined by adding to the whole number of free persons, including those bound to service for a term of years, and excluding Indians not taxed, three-fifths of all other persons]. The actual enumeration shall be made within three years after the first meeting of the Congress of the United States, and within every subsequent term of ten years, in such manner as they shall by law direct. The number of representatives shall not exceed one for every thirty thousand, but each state shall have at least one representative; [and until such enumeration shall be made, the state of New Hampshire shall be entitled to choose 3,

---

*Brackets [ ] indicate parts that have been changed or set aside by amendments.

Massachusetts 8, Rhode Island and Providence Plantations 1, Connecticut 5, New York 6, New Jersey 4, Pennsylvania 8, Delaware 1, Maryland 6, Virginia 10, North Carolina 5, South Carolina 5, and Georgia 3].

(4) When vacancies happen in the representation from any state, the executive authority thereof shall issue writs of election to fill such vacancies.

(5) The House of Representatives shall choose their speaker and other officers; and shall have the sole power of impeachment.

The Senate

Section 3. (1) The Senate of the United States shall be composed of two senators from each state, [chosen by the legislature thereof,] for six years; and each senator shall have one vote.

(2) Immediately after they shall be assembled in consequence of the first election, they shall be divided as equally as may be into three classes. The seats of the senators of the first class shall be vacated at the expiration of the second year, of the second class at the expiration of the fourth year, and of the third class at the expiration of the sixth year, so that one-third may be chosen every second year; [and if vacancies happen by resignation, or otherwise, during the recess of the legislature of any state, the executive thereof may make temporary appointments until the next meeting of the legislature, which shall then fill such vacancies].

(3) No person shall be a senator who shall not have attained to the age of thirty years, and been nine years a citizen of the United States, and who shall not, when elected, be an inhabitant of that state for which he shall be chosen.

(4) The Vice-President of the United States shall be president of the Senate, but shall have no vote, unless they be equally divided.

(5) The Senate shall choose their other officers, and also a president *pro tempore,* in the absence of the Vice-President, or when he shall exercise the office of President of the United States.

(6) The Senate shall have the sole power to try all impeachments. When sitting for that purpose, they shall be on

oath or affirmation. When the President of the United States is tried, the Chief Justice shall preside: and no person shall be convicted without the concurrence of two-thirds of the members present.

(7) Judgment in cases of impeachment shall not extend further than to removal from office, and disqualification to hold and enjoy any office of honor, trust, or profit under the United States: but the party convicted shall neverthelss be liable and subject to indictment, trial, judgment, and punishment, according to law.

Organization of Congress

Section 4. (1) The times, places, and manner of holding elections for senators and representatives, shall be prescribed in each state by the legislature thereof; but the Congress may at any time by law make or alter such regulations, [except as to the places of choosing senators].

(2) The Congress shall assemble at least once in every year, [and such meeting shall be on the first Monday in December,] unless they shall by law appoint a different day.

Section 5. (1) Each house shall be the judge of the elections, returns, and qualifications of its own members, and a majority of each shall constitute a quorum to do business; but a smaller number may adjourn from day to day, and may be authorized to compel the attendance of absent members, in such manner, and under such penalties as each house may provide.

(2) Each house may determine the rules of its proceedings, punish its members for disorderly behavior, and, with the concurrence of two-thirds, expel a member.

(3) Each house shall keep a journal of its proceedings, and from time to time publish the same, excepting such parts as may in their judgment require secrecy; and the yeas and nays of the members of either house on any question shall, at the desire of one-fifth of those present, be entered on the journal.

(4) Neither house, during the session of Congress, shall, without the consent of the other, adjourn for more than three days, nor to any other place than that in which the two houses shall be sitting.

Section 6. (1) The senators and representatives shall receive a compensation for their services, to be ascertained by law, and paid out of the treasury of the United States. They shall in all cases, except treason, felony, and breach of the peace, be privileged from arrest during their attendance at the session of their respective houses, and in going to and returning from the same; and for any speech or debate in either house, they shall not be questioned in any other place.

(2) No senator or representative shall, during the time for which he was elected, be appointed to any civil office under the authority of the United States, which shall have been created, or the emoluments whereof shall have been increased during such time; and no person holding any office under the United States, shall be a member of either house during his continuance in office.

Section 7. (1) All bills for raising revenue shall originate in the House of Representatives; but the Senate may propose or concur with amendments as on other bills.

(2) Every bill which shall have passed the House of Representatives and the Senate, shall, before it becomes a law, be presented to the President of the United States; if he approve he shall sign it, but if not he shall return it, with his objections to that house in which it shall have originated, who shall enter the objections at large on their journal, and proceed to reconsider it. If after such reconsideration two-thirds of that house shall agree to pass the bill, it shall be sent, together with the objections, to the other house, by which it shall likewise be reconsidered, and if approved by two-thirds of that house, it shall become a law. But in all such cases the votes of both houses shall be determined by yeas and nays, and the names of the persons voting for and against the bill shall be entered on the journal of each house respectively. If any bill shall not be returned by the President within ten days (Sundays excepted) after it shall have been presented to him, the same shall be a law, in like manner as if he had signed it, unless the Congress by their adjournment prevent its return, in which case it shall not be a law.

(3) Every order, resolution, or vote to which the concurrence of the Senate and House of Representatives may be necessary (except on a question of adjournment) shall be presented to the President of the United States; and before the same shall take

effect, shall be approved by him, or being disapproved by him, shall be repassed by two-thirds of the Senate and House of Representatives, according to the rules and limitations prescribed in the case of a bill.

Powers Granted to Congress

Section 8. The Congress shall have power:

(1) To lay and collect taxes, duties, imposts, and excises, to pay the debts and provide for the common defense and general welfare of the United States; but all duties, imposts, and excises shall be uniform throughout the United States;

(2) To borrow money on the credit of the United States;

(3) To regulate commerce with foreign nations, and among the several states, and with the Indian tribes;

(4) To establish an uniform rule of naturalization, and uniform laws on the subject of bankruptcies throughout the United States;

(5) To coin money, regulate the value thereof, and of foreign coin, and fix the standard of weights and measures;

(6) To provide for the punishment of counterfeiting the securities and current coin of the United States;

(7) To establish post offices and post roads;

(8) To promote the progress of science and useful arts, by securing for limited times to authors and inventors the exclusive right to their respective writings and discoveries;

(9) To constitute tribunals inferior to the Supreme Court;

(10) To define and punish piracies and felonies committed on the high seas, and offenses against the law of nations;

(11) To declare war, grant letters of marque and reprisal, and make rules concerning captures on land and water;

(12) To raise and support armies, but no appropriation of money to that use shall be for a longer term than two years;

(13) To provide and maintain a navy;

(14) To make rules for the government and regulation of the land and naval forces;

(15) To provide for calling forth the militia to execute the laws of the Union, suppress insurrections and repel invasions;

(16) To provide for organizing, arming, and disciplining, the militia, and for governing such part of them as may be employed

in the service of the United States, reserving to the states respectively, the appointment of the officers, and the authority of training the militia according to the discipline prescribed by Congress;

(17) To exercise exclusive legislation in all cases whatsoever, over such district (not exceeding ten miles square) as may, by cession of particular states, and the acceptance of Congress, become the seat of the government of the United States, and to exercise like authority over all places purchased by the consent of the legislature of the state in which the same shall be for the erection of forts, magazines, arsenals, dockyards, and other needful buildings; —And

(18) To make all laws which shall be necessary and proper for carrying into execution the foregoing powers, and all other powers vested by this Constitution in the government of the United States, or in any department or officer thereof.

Powers Forbidden to Congress

Section 9. (1) The migration or importation of such persons as any of the states now existing shall think proper to admit, shall not be prohibited by the Congress prior to the year one thousand eight hundred and eight, but a tax or duty may be imposed on such importation, not exceeding ten dollars for each person.

(2) The privilege of the writ of *habeas corpus* shall not be suspended, unless when in cases of rebellion or invasion the public safety may require it.

(3) No bill of attainder or *ex post facto* law shall be passed.

(4) No capitation, [or other direct,] tax shall be laid, unless in proportion to the census or enumeration herein before directed to be taken.

(5) No tax or duty shall be laid on articles exported from any state.

(6) No preference shall be given by any regulation of commerce or revenue to the ports of one state over those of another: nor shall vessels bound to, or from, one state, be obliged to enter, clear, or pay duties in another.

(7) No money shall be drawn from the treasury, but in consequence of appropriations made by law; and a regular statement and account of the receipts and expenditures of all public money shall be published from time to time.

(8) No title of nobility shall be granted by the United States: And no person holding any office of profit or trust under them, shall, without the consent of the Congress, accept of any present, emolument, office, or title, of any kind whatever, from any king, prince, or foreign state.

Powers Forbidden to the States

Section 10. (1) No state shall enter into any treaty, alliance, or confederation; grant letters of marque and reprisal; coin money; emit bills of credit; make anything but gold and silver coin a tender in payment of debts; pass any bill of attainder, *ex post facto* law, or law impairing the obligation of contracts, or grant any title of nobility.

(2) No state shall, without the consent of the Congress, lay any imposts or duties on imports or exports, except what may be absolutely necessary for executing its inspection laws: and the net produce of all duties and imposts, laid by any state on imports or exports, shall be for the use of the treasury of the United States; and all such laws shall be subject to the revision and control of the Congress.

(3) No state shall, without the consent of Congress, lay any duty of tonnage, keep troops, or ships of war in time of peace, enter into any agreement or compact with another state, or with a foreign power, or engage in war, unless actually invaded, or in such imminent danger as will not admit of delay.

ARTICLE II

The Executive Branch

Section 1. (1) The executive power shall be vested in a President of the United States of America. He shall hold his office during the term of four years, and, together with the Vice-President, chosen for the same term, be elected, as follows:

(2) Each state shall appoint, in such manner as the legislature thereof may direct, a number of electors, equal to the whole number of senators and representatives to which the state may be entitled in the Congress: but no senator or representative, or person holding an office of trust or profit under the United States, shall be appointed an elector.

(3) [The electors shall meet in their respective states, and vote by ballot for two persons, of whom one at least shall not be an

inhabitant of the same state with themselves. And they shall make a list of all the persons voted for, and of the number of votes for each; which list they shall sign and certify, and transmit sealed to the seat of the government of the United States, directed to the president of the Senate. The president of the Senate shall, in the presence of the Senate and House of Representatives, open all the certificates, and the votes shall then be counted. The person having the greatest number of votes shall be the President, if such number be a majority of the whole number of electors appointed; and there be more than one who have such majority, and have an equal number of votes, then the House of Representatives shall immediately choose by ballot one of them for President; and if no person have a majority, then from the five highest on the list the said House shall in like manner choose the President. But in choosing the President, the votes shall be taken by states, the representation from each state having one vote; a quorum for this purpose shall consist of a member or members from two-thirds of the states, and a majority of all the states shall be necessary to a choice. In every case, after the choice of the President, the person having the greatest number of votes of the electors shall be the Vice-President. But if there should remain two or more who have equal votes, the Senate shall choose from them by ballot the Vice-President.]

(4) The Congress may determine the time of choosing the electors, and the day on which they shall give their votes; which day shall be the same thoughout the United States.

(5) No person except a natural-born citizen, or a citizen of the United States at the time of the adoption of this Constitution, shall be eligible to the office of President; neither shall any person be eligible to that office who shall not have attained to the age of thirty-five years, and been fourteen years a resident within the United States.

(6) In case of the removal of the President from office, or of his death, resignation, or inability to discharge the powers and duties of the said office, the same shall devolve on the Vice-President, and the Congress may by law provide for the case of removal, death, or resignation or inability, both of the President and Vice-President, declaring what officer shall then act as President, and such officer shall act accordingly, until the disability be removed, or a President shall be elected.

(7) The President shall, at stated times, receive for his services, a compensation, which shall neither be increased or diminished during the period for which he shall have been elected, and he shall not receive within that period any other emolument from the United States, or any of them.

(8) Before he enter on the execution of his office, he shall take the following oath or affirmation: —"I do solemnly swear (or affirm) that I will faithfully execute the Office of President of the United States, and will to the best of my Ability, preserve, protect, and defend the Constitution of the United States."

Section 2. (1) The President shall be commander in chief of the Army and Navy of the United States, and of the militia of the several states, when called into the actual service of the United States; he may require the opinion, in writing, of the principal officer in each of the executive departments, upon any subject relating to the duties of their respective offices, and he shall have power to grant reprieves and pardons for offenses against the United States, except in cases of impeachment.

(2) He shall have power, by and with the advice and consent of the Senate, to make treaties, provided two-thirds of the senators present concur; and he shall nominate, and by and with the advice and consent of the Senate, shall appoint ambassadors, other public ministers and consuls, judges of the Supreme Court, and all other officers of the United States, whose appointments are not herein otherwise provided for, and which shall be established by law: but the Congress may by law vest the appointment of such inferior officers, as they think proper, in the President alone, in the courts of law, or in the heads of the departments.

(3) The President shall have power to fill up all vacancies that may happen during the recess of the Senate, by granting commissions which shall expire at the end of their next session.

Section 3. He shall from time to time give to the Congress information of the state of the Union, and recommend to their consideration such measures as he shall judge necessary and expedient; he may, on extraordinary occasions, convene both houses, or either of them, and in case of disagreement between them, with respect to the time of adjournment, he may adjourn them to such time as he shall think proper; he shall receive ambassadors and other public ministers; he shall take care that the laws be faithfully executed, and shall commission all the officers of the United States.

Section 4. The President, Vice-President, and all civil officers of the United States, shall be removed from office on impeachment for, and conviction of, treason, bribery, or other high crimes and misdemeanors.

ARTICLE III
The Judicial Branch

Section 1. The judicial power of the United States, shall be vested in one Supreme Court, and in such inferior courts as the Congress may from time to time ordain and establish. The judges, both of the Supreme and inferior courts, shall hold their offices during good behavior, and shall, at stated times, receive for their services, a compensation, which shall not be diminished during their continuance in office.

Section 2. (1) The judicial power shall extend to all cases, in law and equity, arising under this Constitution, the laws of the United States, and treaties made, or which shall be made, under their authority; — to all cases affecting ambassadors, other public ministers and consuls; — to all cases of admiralty and maritime jurisdiction; — to controversies to which the United States shall be party; — to controversies between two or more states; [between a state and citizens of another state;] between citizens of different states; — between citizens of the same state claiming lands under grants of different states, and between a state, or the citizens thereof, and foreign states, [citizens or subjects].

(2) In all cases affecting ambassadors, other public ministers and consuls, and those in which a state shall be party, the Supreme Court shall have original jurisdiction. In all other cases before mentioned, the Supreme Court shall have appellate jurisdiction, both as to law and fact, with such exceptions, and under such regulations as the Congress shall make.

(3) The trial of all crimes, except in cases of impeachment, shall be by jury; and such trial shall be held in the state where the said crimes shall have been committed; but when not committed within any state, the trial shall be at such place or places as the Congress may by law have directed.

Section 3. (1) Treason against the United States, shall consist only in levying war against them, or in adhering to their enemies, giving them aid and comfort. No person shall be convicted of treason unless on the testimony of two witnesses to the same overt act, or on confession in open court.

(2) The Congress shall have power to declare the punishment of treason, but no attainder of treason shall work corruption of blood, or forfeiture except during the life of the person attained.

ARTICLE IV
Relation of the States to Each Other

Section 1. Full faith and credit shall be given in each state to the public acts, records, and judicial proceedings of every other state. And the Congress may by general laws prescribe the manner in which such acts, records, and proceedings shall be proved, and the effect thereof.

Section 2. (1) The citizens of each state shall be entitled to all privileges and immunities of citizens in the several states.

(2) A person charged in any state with treason, felony, or other crime, who shall flee from justice, and be found in another state, shall on demand of the executive authority of the state from which he fled, be delivered up, to be removed to the state having jurisdiction of the crime.

(3) [No person held to service or labor in one state, under the laws thereof, escaping into another, shall, in consequence of any law or regulation therein, be discharged from such service or labor, but shall be delivered up on claim of the party to whom such service or labor may be due.]

Federal-State Relations

Section 3. (1) New states may be admitted by the Congress into this Union; but no new state shall be formed or erected within the jurisdiction of any other state; nor any state be formed by the junction of two or more states, or parts of states, without the consent of the legislatures of the states concerned as well as of the Congress.

(2) The Congress shall have power to dispose of and make all needful rules and regulations respecting the territory or other property belonging to the United States; and nothing in this Constitution shall be so construed as to prejudice any claims of the United States, or any particular state.

Section 4. The United States shall guarantee to every state in this Union a republican form of government, and shall protect each of them against invasion; and on application of the legislature, or of the executive (when the legislature cannot be convened) against domestic violence.

ARTICLE V
Amending the Constitution

The Congress, whenever two-thirds of both houses shall deem it necessary, shall propose amendments to this Constitution, or, on the application of the legislatures of two-thirds of the several states, shall call a convention for proposing amendments, which, in either case, shall be valid to all intents and purposes, as part of this Constitution, when ratified by the legislatures of three-fourths of the several states, or by conventions in three-fourths thereof, as the one or the other mode of ratification may be proposed by the Congress; provided [that no amendment which may be made prior to the year one thousand eight hundred and eight shall in any manner affect the first and fourth clauses in the ninth section of the first article; and] that no state, without its consent, shall be deprived of its equal suffrage in the Senate.

ARTICLE VI
National Debts

(1) All debts contracted and engagements entered into, before the adoption of this Constitution, shall be as valid against the United States under this Constitution, as under the Confederation.

Supremacy of the National Government

(2) This Constitution, and the laws of the United States which shall be made in pursuance thereof, and all treaties made, or which shall be made, under the authority of the United States, shall be the supreme law of the land; and the judges in every state shall be bound thereby, anything in the constitution or laws of any state to the contrary notwithstanding.

(3) The senators and representatives before mentioned, and the members of the several state legislatures, and all executive and judicial officers, both of the United States and of the several states, shall be bound by oath or affirmation, to support this

Constitution; but no religious test shall ever be required as a qualification to any office or public trust under the United States.

ARTICLE VII
Ratifying the Constitution

The ratification of the conventions of nine states, shall be sufficient for the establishment of this Constitution between the states so ratifying the same.

Done in convention by the unanimous consent of the states present the seventeenth day of September in the year of our Lord one thousand seven hundred and eighty-seven and of the independence of the United States of America the twelfth. In witness thereof we have hereunto subscribed our names,

George Washington — President and deputy from Virginia

Delaware
George Read
Gunning Bedford, Jr.
John Dickinson
Richrd Bassett
Jacob Broom

Maryland
James McHenry
Dan of St. Thomas Jenifer
Daniel Carroll

Virginia
John Blair
James Madison, Jr.

North Carolina
William Blount
Richard Dobbs Spaight
Hugh Williamson

South Carolina
John Rutledge
Charles Cotesworth Pinckney
Charles Pinckney
Pierce Butler

Georgia
William Few
Abraham Baldwin

New Hampshire
John Langdon
Nicholas Gilman

Massachusetts
Nathaniel Gorman
Rufus King

Connecticut
William Samuel Johnson
Roger Sherman

New York
Alexander Hamilton

New Jersey
William Livingston
David Brearley
William Paterson
Jonathan Dayton

Pennsylvania
Benjamin Franklin
Thomas Mifflin
Robert Morris
George Clymer
Thomas FitzSimmons
Jared Ingersoll
James Wilson
Gouverneur Morris

AMENDMENTS TO THE CONSTITUTION

(The first ten amendments are the Bill of Rights.)

AMENDMENT 1. **Freedom of Religion, Speech, and the Press; Rights of Assembly and Petition**

Congress shall make no law respecting an establishment of religion, or prohibiting the free exercise thereof; or abridging the freedom of speech, or of the press; or the right of the people peaceably to assemble, and to petition the government for a redress of grievances.

AMENDMENT 2. **Right to Bear Arms**

A well-regulated militia, being necessary to the security of a free state, the right of the people to keep and bear arms shall not be infringed.

AMENDMENT 3. **Housing of Soldiers**

No soldier shall, in time of peace be quartered in any house, without the consent of the owner, nor in time of war, but in a manner to be prescribed by law.

AMENDMENT 4. **Search and Arrest Warrants**

The right of the people to be secure in their persons, houses, papers, and effects, against unreasonable searches and seizures, shall not be violated, and no warrants shall issue, but upon probable cause, supported by oath or affirmation, and particularly describing the place to be searched, and the persons or things to be seized.

AMENDMENT 5. **Rights in Criminal Cases**

No person shall be held to answer for a capital, or otherwise infamous crime, unless on a presentment or indictment of a grand jury, except in cases arising in the land or naval forces, or in the militia, when in actual service in time of war or public danger; nor shall any person be subject for the same offense to be twice put in jeopardy of life or limb; nor shall be compelled in any criminal case to be a witness against himself, nor be deprived of life, liberty, or property, without due process of law; nor shall private property be taken for public use, without just compensation.

AMENDMENT 6. Rights to a Fair Trial

In all criminal prosecutions, the accused shall enjoy the right to a speedy and public trial, by an impartial jury of the state and district wherein the crime shall have been committed, which district shall have been previously ascertained by law, and to be informed of the nature and cause of the accusation; to be confronted with the witnesses against him; to have compulsory process for obtaining witnesses in his favor, and to have the assistance of counsel for his defense.

AMENDMENT 7. Rights in Civil Cases

In suits at common law, where the value in controversy shall exceed twenty dollars, the right of trial by jury shall be preserved, and no fact tried by a jury, shall be otherwise re-examined in any court of the United States, than according to the rules of the common law.

AMENDMENT 8. Bails, Fines, and Punishments

Excessive bail shall not be required, nor excessive fines imposed, nor cruel and unusual punishments inflicted.

AMENDMENT 9. Rights Retained by the People

The enumeration in the Constitution, of certain rights, shall not be construed to deny or disparage others retained by the people.

AMENDMENT 10. Powers Retained by the States and the People

The powers not delegated to the United States by the Constitution, nor prohibited by it to the states, are reserved to the states respectively, or to the people.

AMENDMENT 11. Lawsuits Against States

The judicial power of the United States shall not be construed to extend to any suit in law or equity, commenced or prosecuted against one of the United States by citizens of another state, or by citizens or subjects of any foreign state.

AMENDMENT 12. Election of the President and Vice-President

The electors shall meet in their respective states and vote by ballot for President and Vice-President, one of whom, at least, shall not be an inhabitant of the same state with themselves; they shall name in their ballots the person voted for as President, and in distinct ballots the person voted for as Vice-President, and they shall make distinct lists of all persons voted for as President, and of all persons voted for as Vice-President, and of the number of votes for each, which lists they shall sign and certify, and transmit sealed to the seat of the government of the United States, directed to the president of the Senate; — the president of the Senate shall, in the presence of the Senate and House of Representatives, open all the certificates and the votes shall then be counted; — the person having the greatest number of votes for President, shall be the President, if such number be a majority of the whole number of electors appointed; and if no person have such majority, then from the persons having the highest numbers not exceeding three on the list of those voted for as President, the House of Representatives shall choose immediately, by ballot, the President. But in choosing the President, the votes shall be taken by states, the representation from each state having one vote; a quorum for this purpose shall consist of a member or members from two-thirds of the states, and a majority of all the states shall be necessary to a choice. And if the House of Representatives shall not choose a President whenever the right of choice shall devolve upon them, [before the fourth day of March next following,] then the Vice-President shall act as President, as in the case of the death or other constitutional disability of the President. — The person having the greatest number of votes as Vice-President, shall be the Vice-President, if such number be a majority of the whole number of electors appointed, and if no person have a majority, then from the two highest numbers on the list, the Senate shall choose the Vice-President; a quorum for the purpose shall consist of two-thirds of the whole number of senators, and a majority of the whole number shall be necessary to a choice. But no person constitutionally ineligible to the office of President shall be eligible to that of Vice-President of the United States.

AMENDMENT 13. Abolition of Slavery

Section 1. Neither slavery nor involuntary servitude, except as a punishment for crime whereof the party shall have been duly convicted, shall exist within the United States, or any place subject to their jurisdiction.

Section 2. Congress shall have power to enforce this article by appropriate legislation.

AMENDMENT 14. Civil Rights

Section 1. All persons born or naturalized in the United States, and subject to the jurisdiction thereof, are citizens of the United States and of the state wherein they reside. No state shall make or enforce any law which shall abridge the privileges or immunities of citizens of the United States; nor shall any state deprive any person of life, liberty, or property, without due process of law; nor deny to any person within its jurisdiction the equal protection of the laws.

Section 2. Representatives shall be apportioned among the several states according to their respective numbers, counting the whole number of persons in each state, [excluding Indians not taxed]. But when the right to vote at any election for the choice of electors for President and Vice-President of the United States, representatives in Congress, the executive and judicial officers of a state, or the members of the legislature thereof, is denied to any of the male inhabitants of such state, being twenty-one years of age, and citizens of the United States, or in any way abridged, except for participation in rebellion, or other crime, the basis of representation therein shall be reduced in the proportion which the number of such male citizens shall bear to the whole number of male citizens twenty-one years of age in such state.

Section 3. No person shall be a senator or representative in Congress, or elector of President and Vice-President, or hold any office, civil or military, under the United States, or under any state, who, having previously taken an oath, as a member of Congress, or as an officer of the United States, or as a member of any state legislature, or as an executive or judicial officer of any state, to support the Constitution of the United States, shall have engaged in insurrection or rebellion against the same, or given aid or comfort to the enemies thereof. But Congress may by a vote of two-thirds of each House, remove such disability.

Section 4. The validity of the public debt of the United States, authorized by law, including debts incurred for payment of pensions and bounties for services in suppressing insurrection or rebellion, shall not be questioned. But neither the United States nor any state shall assume or pay any debt or obligation incurred in aid of insurrection or rebellion against the United States, or any claim for the loss or emancipation of any slave; but all such debts, obligations, and claims shall be held illegal and void.

Section 5. The Congress shall have power to enforce, by appropriate legislation, the provisions of this article.

AMENDMENT 15. Negro Suffrage

Section 1. The right of citizens of the United States to vote shall not be denied or abridged by the United States or by any state on account of race, color, or previous condition of servitude.

Section 2. The Congress shall have power to enforce this article by appropriate legislation.

AMENDMENT 16. Income Taxes

The Congress shall have power to lay and collect taxes on incomes, from whatever source derived, without apportionment among the several states, and without regard to any census or enumeration.

AMENDMENT 17. Direct Election of Senators

(1) The Senate of the United States shall be composed of two senators from each state, elected by the people thereof for six years; and each senator shall have one vote. The electors in each state shall have the qualifications requisite for electors of the most numerous branch of the state legislatures.

(2) When vacancies happen in the representation of any state in the Senate, the executive authority of such state shall issue writs of election to fill such vacancies: *Provided*, That the legislature of any state may empower the executive thereof to make temporary appointments until the people fill the vacancies by election as the legislature may direct.

(3) This amendment shall not be so construed as to affect the election or term of any senator chosen before it becomes valid as part of the Constitution.

AMENDMENT 18. Prohibition of Liquor

Section 1. After one year from the ratification of this article the manufacture, sale, or transportation of intoxicating liquors within, the importation thereof into, or the exportation thereof from the United States and all territory subject to the jurisdiction thereof for beverage purposes is hereby prohibited.

Section 2. The Congress and the several states shall have concurrent power to enforce this article by appropriate legislation.

Section 3. This article shall be inoperative unless it shall have been ratified as an amendment to the Constitution by the legislatures of the several states, as provided in the Constitution, within seven years from the date of the submission hereof to the states by the Congress.

AMENDMENT 19. Woman Suffrage

Section 1. The right of citizens of the United States to vote shall not be denied or abridged by the United States or by any state on account of sex.

Section 2. Congress shall have power to enforce this article by appropriate legislation.

AMENDMENT 20. Terms of the President and Congress

Section 1. The terms of the President and Vice-President shall end at noon on the 20th day of January, and the terms of senators and representatives at noon on the third day of January, of the year in which such terms would have ended if this article had not been ratified; and the terms of their successors shall then begin.

Section 2. The Congress shall assemble at least once in every year, and such meeting shall begin at noon on the third day of January, unless they shall by law appoint a different day.

Section 3. If, at the time fixed for the beginning of the term of the President, the President elect shall have died, the Vice-President elect shall become President. If a President shall not have been chosen before the time fixed for the beginning of his term, of if the President elect shall have failed to qualify, then the Vice-President elect shall act as President until a President shall have qualified; and the Congress may by law provide for the case wherein neither a President elect nor a Vice-President elect shall have qualified, declaring who shall then act as President, or the manner in which one who is to act shall be selected, and such person shall act accordingly until a President or Vice-President shall have qualified.

Section 4. The Congress may by law provide for the case of the death of any of the persons from whom the House of Representatives may choose a President whenever the right of choice shall have devolved upon them, and for the case of the death of any of the persons from whom the Senate may choose a Vice-President whenever the right of choice shall have devolved upon them.

Section 5. Sections 1 and 2 shall take effect on the 15th day of October following the ratification of this article.

Section 6. This article shall be inoperative unless it shall have been ratified as an amendment to the Constitution by the legislatures of three-fourths of the several states within seven years from the date of its submission.

AMENDMENT 21. Repeal of Prohibition

Section 1. The eighteenth article of amendment to the Constitution of the United States is hereby repealed.

Section 2. The transportation or importation into any state, territory, or possession of the United States for delivery or use therein of intoxicating liquors, in violation of the laws thereof, is hereby prohibited.

Section 3. This article shall be inoperative unless it shall have been ratified as an amendment to the Constitution by conventions in the several states, as provided in the Constitution, within seven years from the date of the submission hereof to the states by the Congress.

AMENDMENT 22. Limitation of Presidents to Two Terms

Section 1. No person shall be elected to the office of the President more than twice, and no person who has held the office of President, or acted as President, for more than two years of a term to which some other person was elected President shall be elected to the office of the President more than once. But this article shall not apply to any person holding the office of President when this article was proposed by the Congress, and shall not prevent any person who may be holding the office of President, or acting as President, during the term within which this article becomes operative from holding the office of President or acting as President during the remainder of such term.

Section 2. This article shall be inoperative unless it shall have been ratified as an amendment to the Constitution by the legislatures of three-fourths of the several states within seven years from the day of its submission to the states by the Congress.

AMENDMENT 23.   Suffrage in the District of Columbia

Section 1. The district constituting the seat of government of the United States shall appoint in such manner as the Congress may direct: A number of electors of President and Vice-President equal to the whole number of senators and representatives in Congress to which the district would be entitled if it were a state, but in no event more than the least populous state; they shall be in addition to those appointed by the states, but they shall be considered, for the purposes of the election of President and Vice-President, to be electors appointed by a state; and they shall meet in the district and perform such duties as provided by the twelfth article of amendment.

Section 2. The Congress shall have power to enforce this article by appropriate legislation.

AMENDMENT 24.   Poll Taxes

Section 1. The right of citizens of the United States to vote in any primary or other election for President or Vice-President, for electors for President or Vice-President, or for senator or representative in Congress, shall not be denied or abridged by the United States or any state by reason of failure to pay any poll tax or other tax.

Section 2. The Congress shall have power to enforce this article by appropriate legislation.

AMENDMENT 25.   Presidential Disability and Succession

Section 1. In case of the removal of the President from office or of his death or resignation, the Vice-President shall become President.

Section 2. Whenever there is a vacancy in the office of the Vice-President, the President shall nominate a Vice-President who shall take office upon confirmation by a majority vote of both houses of Congress.

Section 3. Whenever the President transmits to the president pro tempore of the Senate and the speaker of the House of Representatives his written declaration that he is unable to discharge the powers and duties of his office, and until he transmits to them a written declaration to the contrary, such powers and duties shall be discharged by the Vice-President as acting President.

Section 4. Whenever the Vice-President and a majority of either the principal officers of the executive departments or of such other body as Congress may by law provide, transmit to the president pro tempore of the Senate and the speaker of the House of Representatives their written declaration that the President is unable to discharge the powers and duties of his office, the Vice-President shall immediately assume the powers and duties of the office as acting President.

Thereafter, when the President transmits to the president pro tempore of the Senate and the speaker of the House of Representatives his written declaration that no inability exists, he shall resume the powers and duties of his office unless the Vice-President and a majority of either the principal officers of the executive department or of such other body as Congress may by law provide, transmit within four days to the president pro tempore of the Senate and the speaker of the House of Representatives their written declaration that the President is unable to discharge the powers and duties of his office. Thereupon Congress shall decide the issue, assembling within forty-eight hours for that purpose if not in session. If the Congress, within twenty-one days after receipt of the latter written declaration, or, if Congress is not in session, within twenty-one days after Congress is required to assemble, determines by two-thirds vote of both houses that the President is unable to discharge the powers and duties of his office, the Vice-President shall continue to discharge the same as acting President; otherwise, the President shall resume the powers and duties of his office.

AMENDMENT 26.   Suffrage for 18-Year-Olds

Section 1. The right of citizens of the United States, who are eighteen years of age or older, to vote shall not be denied or abridged by the United States or by any state on account of age.

Section 2. The Congress shall have power to enforce this article by appropriate legislation.

Index

Absentee ballots, 222
Accused persons, rights of, 141-146
ACTION, 134
Adams, John, 38
Aeronautics, 130
Age, and voting, 44, 217
Agencies,
 in Executive Office, 93, 104-106
 independent, 111, 124-139
Agnew, Spiro, 102
Agriculture, Department of, 115
Alaska, 159, 161
Aliens, 256
Ambassador, 98, 112
Amendments, 48, 50-63, 260-261
American Independent Party, 204
Anti-Federalists, 37, 196-198
Anthony, Susan B., 219
Appeals courts, 91, 141, 145-146, 156
Apportion, 147, 152
Armed forces, 117, 122
Arms, bearing, 43, 55, 261, 288
Arrests, 141, 245
Assemblies, colonial, 5, 16
Assembly, right of, 51, 52, 260, 288
Articles of Confederation, 26-28
Asian, 252-253
Attorney General, 103-104, 109

Ballots, 208, 220-224
Bankruptcy, 130-131
Bill of Rights, 13, 14, 37, 43, 50-59, 260
 definition of, 87
Bills, 77-83
Board of Commissioners, County, 186
Board of Supervisors, County, 186
Borough, 162, 192
Branches of government, 34-35, 45-48, 68-157
Budget, 98-99
 states', 168-171
Bugging, 56
Bureau of Indian Affairs, 115
Bureau of Labor Statistics, 117

Bureau of Prisons, 114
Bureaucracy, 136-137

Cabinet, 109-110
 definition of, 103
 members of, 103
Campaigns, 213-215
Candidate, 60
Capitol, 73
Carnegie, Andrew, 255
Carter, Jimmy, 100, 177
Census Bureau, 116
Central Intelligence Agency, 105
Charters, 185, 190-192
Chavez, Cesar, 255
Checks and balances, 34, 163
Chief Diplomat, 98
Chief Executive, 92
Chief Justice, 148-149
Church, 10, 15, 53, 220
Circuits (judicial), 145
Citizen, definition of, 74
Citizenship
 duties, 266
 responsibilities, 264-265
 rights, 260-263
City government
 officials, 189-190
 types of, 190-191
City manager, 191
City-states, 4-5
Civil, 55, 58
Civil rights, 154
Civil Rights Acts, 216
Civil servants, 130
Civil War, 61-62
Clerk of the House, 81
Cleveland, Grover, 268
Closed primaries, 208
Coast Guard, 118
Collective farms, 239-240
Colonists, 3, 13-20, 23-28
Commander-in-Chief, 98
Commerce
 definition of, 110
 department of, 93, 110, 116, 137
Commissioner, 190
Committee on credentials, 211

297

Committees
  of Congress, 78
  party, 211
Common law, 233
Communications, regulation of, 127
Communism, 239
Communist Party, 241-246
Community, 1-2
Compromises, 31-32, 260
Conference committee, 82-83
Congress, 68-90
  committees, 78
  duties, 76
  limits on, 87
  organization, 71
  origin, 26-27, 34
  powers, 85
Congressional Record, 80
Connecticut, 17, 186
Conservatives, 205
Conservative Party, 236-237
Constitution
  state, 162-166
  U.S., 17, 28, 32, 33-38, 275-287
Constitutional Convention, 27-30, 196
Constitutional democracy, 229
Consul, 112
Consulate, 112
Consumer protection, 127
Continental Congresses, 19-20
Contract, 15
Conventions
  constitutional, 27
  party, 210-212
Coolidge, Calvin, 177
Coroner, 188
Corps of Engineers, 117
Council of Economic Advisers, 105
Council of Environmental Quality, 105
Council of Ministers, 240
Counterfeit money, 113, 144
County officials, 186-188
Courts
  state, types of, 180-181
  U.S., types of, 140-157
Credentials, committee on, 211
Criminal cases, 9, 57
Custom, definition of, 2
Customs Service, 113
Czar, 239

Debate, 60
Declaration of Independence, 20, 23, 271-274
Defendant, 10, 143
Defense, Department of, 93, 117-118, 137
Delegates, 26-29
Democracy, 4-5, 191
Democratic Party, 198-200
Departments, Cabinet, 93, 109-123
Deport, 256
Depression, 130-131, 252-253
Desegregation, 154
Dictator, 4-5
Dictatorship, 8, 239
Direct democracy, 191-192
Discrimination, 169
District courts, 143-144
District of Columbia, 69-70
Districts
  congressional, 72
  school, 185
Divine right, 13
Double jeopardy, 57
Due process, 57

Education, Department of, 93, 121, 137
Elastic clause, 87-88
Election, definition of, 95
Elections, 95
  primaries, 208-209
Electors, 95
Electoral College, 95-96
England, 3, 9-15, 19-21, 230-238
Enabling act, 161
Endowment, 130
Energy, Department of, 93, 120, 137
Environmental Protection Agency, 128
Examinations, 258
Executive branch, 34-35, 91-108
Executive Office, 104

Fair and speedy trial, 57
Famine, 252
Farmers Home Administration, 115
Favorite sons, 211
Federal, definition of, 26
Federal bureaucracy, 136-137
Federal Bureau of Investigation, 114

Federal Communications Commission, 127
Federal courts, 142-143
Federal Deposit Insurance Corporation, 131
Federal system of government, 26, 28
Federal Trade Commission, 127
Federalists, 37, 40, 196-198
Figurehead, 235
Filibuster, 82
First Congress, 19, 260
First reading, 81
Fish and Wildlife Service, 115
Flags, 246, 248
Floor leaders, 76
Ford, Gerald, 102
Fourteenth Amendment, 61, 66
Freedom
   of assembly, 51, 52, 260, 288
   from cruel punishment, 58, 261, 289
   from double jeopardy, 57, 261
   of the press, 51, 52, 260, 288
   of religion, 51, 54, 260, 288
   of speech, 51, 54, 260, 288
Frequency, 126-127

Generation, 235
George III, 20
Ghetto, 130, 134
Government
   branches of, 34, 35, 45-46, 68-69
   city, 189-191
   county, 186-188
   early development, 2
   other local, 191-192
Governor
   duties, 176
   qualifications, 177
Grand jury, 55-57, 260
Grant, 169
Great Britain, 20, 228, 230, 233-237
Great Depression, 130-131, 252-253
Greece (ancient), 4-5

Hamilton, Alexander, 37, 197
Harding, Warren, 101
Hatch Acts, 217
Health and Human Services, Department of, 93, 110, 120, 137
Henry II, 9-10, 22
Highways, 118
Hooker, Thomas, 17
House of Burgesses, 15
House of Commons, 13, 236-237
House of Lords, 13, 236
House of Representatives, 45, 50, 71-72, 74, 76-78, 80-84, 89
Housing and Urban Development, Department of, 93, 118, 137
Humanities, 130-131
Human resources, 170-171

Immigrant, 252-255, 268
Immigration and Naturalization Service, 114, 257
Impartial, 260-261
Impeachment, 148
Income tax, 99, 168
Independent agencies, 124-139
Indict, 55, 261
Initiative, 224
Interior, definition of, 110
Interior, Department of, 93, 115, 137
Internal Revenue Service, 113
Interstate, definition of, 126
Interstate Commerce Commission, 124, 126

Jackson, Andrew, 198, 200
Jamestown, 15-16
Jefferson, Thomas, 20, 197-198
Joint committees, 78
Judges
   courts of appeals, 145-146
   district courts, 143-144
   Supreme Court, 148-149
Judicial branch, 31, 140-157
Juries, 10, 57-58, 143
Justice, 26, 146
Justice, Department of, 93, 114, 137
Justice of the peace, 180
Juvenile courts, 141

King John, 10-11

Labor, Department of, 93, 117, 137
Labor unions, 200
Labour Party, 236

Latin America, 252
Law enforcement, 114, 171, 185
Leadership, parliamentary and presidential, 230-231
Lawsuit, 9, 58
Legislative branch, 34, 45, 68-90
Legislators, 172, 174
Legislatures (state)
  early development of, 9
  laws, 174-175
  organization of, 172-173
  sessions, 174
Liberal, 205
Lieutenant governor, 173, 177
Limited government, 34, 163
Lincoln, Abraham, 61, 199, 201
Literacy tests, 217
Local governments, 185-194
Loyalists, 196

Madison, James, 50
Magistrate, 180
Magna Carta, 10-11, 23, 233
Majority opinion, 151
Majority party, 71-72, 237
Majority vote, 81
Marshall, John, 149
Mayflower Compact, 15, 23
Mayor, 190-191
McKinley, William, 101
Measurements, 85
Medicare, 121
Melting pot, 251
Migrant, 255
Military, 87, 117
Militia, 55, 179
Minister, 112
Minority parties, 237
Minutemen, 19
Monarchy, 8, 13, 235
Municipal, 180

National Aeronautics and Space Administration (NASA), 130, 137
National Association for the Advancement of Colored People (NAACP), 153
National Foundation on the Arts and the Humanities, 131, 137
National Guard, 171
National Park Service, 115

National political conventions
  committees, 210-211
  nominations, 211
National Security Council, 104-105
National Student Volunteer Program, 134
Native-born, 256
Naturalization, 251, 256-258
Navy, 85, 87, 117
New England, 191
New Jersey Plan, 29, 31
New York City, 38
Newspapers, 17, 54, 245
Nixon, Richard, 100-102, 204
Nobility, 84
Nuclear Regulatory Commission, 128, 137

Occupational Safety and Health Administration (OSHA), 117
Office of Management and Budget, 105
Oligarchy, 8
Open primaries, 208
Optional referendums, 223
"The Opposition," 236-237

Pardon, 100, 176
Parishes, 186
Parks, 171
Parliament, 13-14, 196, 230, 236-237
Parliamentary leadership, 230
Patents, 154-155
Patent Office, 116
Patricians, 6
Peace Corps, 134
Petition, 51-52, 224, 262
Petition of Right, 13-14, 22
Pilgrims, 15-16
Plaintiff, 10
Platform, 205-206
Plebeians, 6
Politburo, 243
Political asylum, 258-259
Political parties
  activities, 205-206
  campaigns, 213-215
  history of, 195-196
  major parties, 198-201
  minor parties, 203-204
Poll tax, 44, 217

Polls, 220
Pony Express, 133
Popular sovereignty, 33, 163
Postal Service, 132
Powers
  reserved, 166
  shared, 166
Preamble, 42, 45
Premier (Soviet), 240
President, 92
  duties, 98-100
  how selected, 95
  qualifications, 96
  term of office, 96-97
  succession, 101-102
President of the Senate, 72
President *pro tempore*, 172, 174
Presidential leadership, 230-231
Presidential primary, 209
Press, freedom of, 17, 23, 52, 54
Primaries, 208-209
Prime Minister, 230, 233-234
Principle, 31
Private ownership, 240
Prohibition, 44, 63
Progressive Party, 203
Proposition, 224
Prosecuting attorney, 188
Public schools, 17
Puritans, 17

Qualifications
  for citizenship, 256-259
  for members of Congress, 74
  for presidency, 96
Quartering of troops, 55
Queen Elizabeth II, 235

Railroads, 124
Ratification
  of Constitution, 37
  of Amendments, 43-44, 60-63
Reading of bills, 81
Reagan, Ronald, 100, 177
Recall, 224
Referendums
  definition of, 223
  types of, 223
Refugee, 252
Registration of voters, 220

Regulatory agency, 125
Rehabilitation, 176, 178
Religion, 18, 50-54
Representative, 71
  requirements for, 74
Republic, 6
Republican Party, 199, 201-203
Reserved powers, 59, 162
Residency requirements
  for citizenship, 257
  for office, 74, 96
  for voting, 217
Retired Senior Volunteer Program (RSVP), 134
Revolution, 252
Revolutionary War, 19
Rights
  of accused persons, 261
  of citizens, 260-265
  civil, 154, 216
Rockefeller, Nelson, 102
Roll-call vote, 211
Rome, 6-7
Roosevelt, Franklin, 96-97, 100-101
Roosevelt, Theodore, 203
Rules Committee, 211

Safeguards, 26, 28
Sales tax, 168-169
School districts, 185
Search and seizure, 56
Second Continental Congress, 19
Secret ballot, 221
Secret Service, 113
Secretaries of Executive Departments, 91, 103
Segregation, 147, 153-154
Selectmen, 191
Senate
  state, 172-175
  United States, 71-72
Senators, 7, 71
  requirements for, 74
Seniority, 75, 78
Separation of powers, 34, 163
Service agency, 125, 130-132, 134
Sessions, 75-76
Sheriff, 187
Slavery, 61-62
Social Security Administration, 120
Social work, 130

Soil Conservation Service, 115
Soviet Union, 239-249
Speaker of the House
  U.S., 72, 76
  states, 172, 174
Speech, freedom of, 51, 54, 260, 288
Stamp Act, 19
Standing committees, 78
State, Department of, 93, 112, 137
State of the Union Message, 80, 99
Statehood, 159
States
  agencies, 178
  expenditures, 170-171
  income, 168-169
  officials, 176-178
Statue of Liberty, 268
Sue, 60
Suffrage, 203, 219
Superintendent, 176
Supreme Court
  authority, 147
  decisions, 151-154
  justices, 148-149
  powers, 149
  sessions, 148
Supreme Soviet, 240

Taft, William, 203
Tass, 245
Tax court, 155
Taxation, 10, 19, 99, 168-169
Taxes, state, 168
Television, 127
Territorial courts, 154
Territories, 160-161
Tories (Loyalists), 196
Town meetings, 191
Townships, 191-192
Trade, 85
Transportation, Department of, 93, 118, 137
Treasury, Department of, 93, 113, 137
Treaty, 26, 159
Trial courts, 143

Unconstitutional, 147, 151, 216
Union of Soviet Socialist Republics (USSR), 228
  Constitution, 245-246
United States of America, 158
United States Postal Service, 132
United States Reports, 151
Unpledged delegates, 210
Unwritten constitution, 233
Urban, 110

Veteran, 75
Veto, 7, 80, 82, 234
Vice-President, 92, 96, 102, 210-212
Villages, 191-192
Virginia Plan, 29, 31
Volunteers in Service to America (VISTA), 134
Voting, 216-224
  process, 220-222
  qualifications, 217
  registration, 220
Voting district, 172

Wallace, George, 204
War Department, 109-110
Ward, 190
Warrant, 55
Washington, George, 19, 38, 40, 109, 197
Watergate, 100
Ways and Means Committee, 78
Weather Bureau, 116
Weights and measures, 85
Welfare, 110
Whigs, 196, 198-199
White House Office, 104
Wilson, Woodrow, 101, 203
Wiretapping, 56
Witness, 55
Women's rights, 219

Youth Challenge Program, 134

Zenger, John Peter, 17, 23
Zoning, 186